# ENGLISH POETRY
*A Critical Introduction*

*By the same Author*
Wordsworth: A Re-interpretation
A Guide to English Literature

# English Poetry

## A CRITICAL INTRODUCTION

### F. W. BATESON

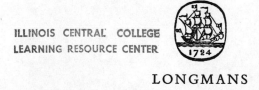

**LONGMANS**

LONGMANS GREEN AND CO LTD
48 Grosvenor Street, London W1
Associated companies, branches and representatives throughout the world

First published 1950
Second Edition © F. W. Bateson 1966

PRINTED IN GREAT BRITAIN BY
THE CAMELOT PRESS LTD., LONDON AND SOUTHAMPTON

*To Jan*

# THE ANTI-ROMANTICS

So we are the music-unmakers, it seems –
Against pastoral pipings disinfecting your dreams;
At La Belle Sauvage, sir, the sardonic 'irregulars',
Of skylarks, etc., the scarers, the nobblers of Pegasus . . .

Treeless in their towns that acquisitive age
Filched the last foxglove from the prefigured ledge.
Unhappy those hunters! their hybridization
Grew a Goliath for a neurotic nation.

I have heard them hallooing in the guilty wood,
Papa and Grandpapa by the poltergeist pursued;
Green were the grasses-O under the weeping ashes,
But combine, crawler and mole-drain have settled the hashes

Of the Shires and their squires, the peaches in the pleasance:
Lucy and Lycidas, you must re-learn your lessons.
See, Pope, 'tis Science holds the Muse's hand
'As laughing Ceres re-assumes the land.'

Man makes the country. And money made the town;
But devaluation will melt Sir Midas down.
In Whitehall meanwhile, much-waistcoated, wandering,
The poemless persons – what are *they* pondering?

# Preface to Second Edition

The first edition of *English Poetry* (1950) was without a Preface, its place being taken by the truculent stanzas on the opposite page (now reprinted with some minor textual changes). 'The Anti-Romantics' was an attempt to summarize in the idiom of Auden a scholar-critic's verdict on the England in which he had grown up. As a countryman who had been active throughout the 1930s in local politics and local education – and an enthusiastic officer of the Buckinghamshire War Agricultural Executive Committee for most of the last war – I saw the 'poemless persons' who constitute the upper tiers of the Civil Service, and indeed the managerial class in general, as the special enemy of my democratic brand of non-supernatural Christianity. And for me the proof of their inhumanity was their inability to read English poetry; if they read poetry at all it was only as a 'superior' escape from reality.

The book's immediate cause is implicit in the poem. In October 1945, while still a half-time official in the Ministry of Agriculture and the agricultural correspondent of *The Observer* and the *New Statesman*, I became for the first time an Oxford don. And before long I found myself teaching English literature there all the time. Oxford was full of hungry intellectual sheep in those days – many of them just demobilized after years in the Services – who looked up to the complacent and reactionary English Faculty and were not always fed. *English Poetry* is a by-product of the tutorials and weekly seminars I held with that idealistic first post-war generation. Between us we were determined to make the study of English literature an aid to the democratic way of life in twentieth-century England instead of the examination-grind it had degenerated into in Oxford – with the grotesque claims of Anglo-Saxon on the undergraduate's time making it necessary to terminate English literature there at the year 1830.

I was already in my forties then, but in spite of the differences in our ages I felt a far greater sense of identity with my Oxford pupils than with my Oxford colleagues, individually amiable though most of them were. With the shining exception of C. S. Lewis, English Literature as the dons promulgated it stood for nothing better in the last analysis than self-centred emotional indulgences by the individual reader. Against this debased Romanticism my pupils and I set our faces. Above all, we wished to humanize the great English classics through a sympathetic understanding of the original context, public and private, which had made them possible – neither cut off from their social roots and historical background (as the American 'New Critics' were then demanding), nor overloaded with moral 'values' (as the *Scrutiny* group tended to do).

I am afraid I wrote *English Poetry* in much too much of a hurry – six weeks to be precise (with the section on 'Tears, Idle Tears' added a little later). Re-reading it recently I could not help noticing gaps in the argument as well as a generally over-insistent tone, italics, for example, being used far too often to impose an emphasis that ought to have been left to the reader's good sense. But to re-write it today would make it a less coherent work and with the missionary zeal perhaps compromised. I have, however, made a number of drastic changes in Chapter 1, and I have substituted for the section on literary history in the 'Conclusion' an essay on the function of criticism that was originally printed in *Essays in Criticism* (vol. III, no. 1, January 1953). Readers who are interested in such things will find replies by William Empson and I. A. Richards in *Essays in Criticism* to the attacks I make on their critical irresponsibility on pp. 177–81 below. F. R. Leavis answered back in *Scrutiny*, Spring 1953. *Essays in Criticism* had been founded by me partly to provide a medium for the new Oxford criticism and partly to follow up the combination of scholarship and criticism I had tried to practise in *English Poetry*. The article now included in the 'Conclusion' is, I suppose, the nearest I ever got to defining in so many words the direction I was hoping English literary criticism would take in the more or less immediate future. I do not recant one word of it today, even if some of those hopes have been disappointed.

*Corpus Christi College,*                                    *F. W. B.*
*Oxford*

# *Contents*

## I

### THE DEFINITION OF POETRY

## II

### APPLICATIONS OF THE DEFINITION

### CONCLUSION

# ACKNOWLEDGEMENTS

For permission to use copyright material I am indebted to the following: The author and Messrs. Faber and Faber Ltd. for 'Oxford' from *Another Time* by W. H. Auden; Messrs. George Allen and Unwin Ltd. for 'Oxford' from *Collected Poems* by Lionel Johnson.

# I

## *THE DEFINITION OF POETRY*

THE DEFINITION OF LOVE

# I

# The Primacy of Meaning

WHAT is a poem *for*? The orthodox account seems to be that a poem justifies itself when it gives the proper reader a proper 'pleasure', this peculiarly poetic pleasure either being combined with 'instruction' (the Neo-Classic or moralistic formula) or else without any such didactic adulteration (the Romantic version). And stated like this in general terms the proposition sounds reasonable enough in either of its forms; it is only when one starts to spell out the pleasure principle as an ultimate poetic criterion that the difficulties arise. An introduction to English poetry that claims to be critical will have to begin with some of the more elementary of these difficulties – which are ethical and logical rather than aesthetic, and more theoretically formidable than is always recognized.

Consider, for example, this exposition of how poetry works by William Peterfield Trent, a scholar of considerable distinction in his day who was a Professor of English Literature for many years at Columbia University, New York:

A fine frenzy seizes the poet's heart and brain, transmits itself to his verse, passes through that medium into me, and, losing for the time being its creative quality, is transformed into that more or less passive state we call rapture. This is to me the supreme value of great poetry, that, more than anything else, with fewer draining demands upon my store of vitality, my time, my purse – in short, upon the essential me and my accessories – it lifts me higher toward heaven, opens my eyes more surely to the Beatific Vision, wraps me 'out of space, out of time', transmutes me and transforms me more completely and ecstatically than any other transmuting and transforming agent of which I have knowledge.[1]

The point about the undrained purse is an American gloss. Otherwise, however, this curious apology for poetry is an accurate enough exposition of what a good poem was supposed to be and do at the beginning of this century. The key phrase is 'that more or less passive state we call rapture'. Poetry according to this account – which is the complement from the reader's point of view of the Romantic doctrine of inspiration – occurs in a psychologically passive condition. The poet's spontaneous emotional overflow parallels the reader's spontaneous emotional ecstasy. In order to achieve this modern equivalent of the medieval mystic's Beatific Vision

[1] *Greatness in Literature* (1905), p. 228.

of God, the reader of poetry does not have to *do* anything – except allow the words of the poem to impinge briefly on his consciousness exactly as if he was reading a newspaper.

The discrepancy between the peculiarly exalted pleasure offered the reader by the Romantic critics and the trifle required from him – a 'more or less passive state' – is acute to the point of embarrassment. The literary conscience rebels. Like any other human satisfaction poetry must surely somehow be 'earned'. The fact that in suitable circumstances the reading of a poem does give many of us great pleasure is not to be denied, but something crucial has clearly been left out of the definition. It is the something-for-nothing implication of this theory of poetry that makes it so difficult to accept. And the difficulty, it is clear, is a moral difficulty.

The Romantic theory of poetry survived the 1914–18 war – indeed, the theory is still flourishing in certain quarters today – but a certain deflation, an air almost of desperation, begins to accompany its re-statement. Here, for example, is Francis Chellifer, Aldous Huxley's hero and *alter ego*, meditating upon the mystery of poetry in *Those Barren Leaves* (1925):

What is it that makes the two words 'defunctive music' as moving as the Dead March out of the *Eroïca* and the close of *Coriolan*? Why should it be somehow more profoundly comic to 'call Tullia's ape a marmosite' than to write a whole play of Congreve? And the line, 'Thoughts that do often lie too deep for tears' – why should its effect lie where it does? Mystery. This game of art strongly resembles conjuring. The quickness of the tongue deceives the brain. It has happened, after all, often enough. Old Shakespeare, for example. How many critical brains have been deceived by the quickness of *his* tongue? Because he can say: 'Shoughs, water-rugs and demi-wolves' and 'defunctive music', and 'the expense of spirit in a waste of shame' and all the rest of it, we credit him with philosophy, a moral purpose and the most penetrating psychology.

The Romantic explanation of the poetic process is not abandoned, but it has been devalued. Old Shakespeare does not provide the Beatific Vision; he is only a conjurer, his art is only a game. Nevertheless poetic rapture of a sort was still available for Huxley's passive recipient.

The devaluation, the air almost of moral disgust, is repeated and heightened in the novels of Evelyn Waugh. Dennis Barlow, the hero of *The Loved One* (1948), may be taken as a representative intellectual of our more recent culture:

Dennis sat in one of the arm-chairs, put his feet on the trolley and settled himself to read. Life in the Air Force had converted him from an amateur to a mere addict. There were certain trite passages of poetry which from a diverse multitude of associations never failed to yield the sensation he craved; he never experimented;

these were the branded drug, the sure specific, big magic. He opened the anthology as a woman opens her familiar pack of cigarettes . . . 'I wither slowly in thine arms,' he read. 'Here at the quiet limit of the world,' and repeated to himself: 'Here at the quiet limit of the world. Here at the quiet limit of the world' . . . as a monk will repeat a single pregnant text over and over again in prayer.

The woman opens her packet of cigarettes as Dennis opens his anthology – which proves to have been the second edition of *The Oxford Book of English Verse* (1939). But, though poetry is now a drug and not merely a conjuring trick, the theoretical assumptions are still the same. Old Tennyson – whose 'Tithonus' provides the phrases that Dennis was intoning – is not simply a master of prestidigitation like Old Shakespeare; the poet is now a peddler of narcotics. But again the poetic drug works. Taken in small doses the Romantic prescription can still be guaranteed apparently to act on the poetry-addict with overwhelming psycho-physical effect. Poetry has become, if only in the wry terms of Waugh's comedy, one of the more *recherché* perversions, like sexual flagellation: deplorable no doubt, but secretly delicious in its irrational way.

Waugh's hero used a standard anthology, whereas in *Those Barren Leaves* the hero was in effect his own anthologist. (Huxley's excellent *Texts and Pretexts* did not follow until 1932.) The connection between the Romantic way of reading poetry and anthologies has in fact always been a close one. Even Dennis's preference for 'trite passages of poetry' – a preference well catered for in almost every recent anthology of English verse – has its theoretical counterpart, as will be seen shortly.

It is a significant fact that the first English anthology in the modern sense – in other words, the first representative collection of English poems of all periods – did not appear until 1737; that is, on the eve of the pre-Romantic era of Gray, Collins, Akenside, Shenstone, Smart and the Wartons. A *sine qua non* of rapture is 'intensity', one of the most hard-worked terms in the critical vocabulary of the nineteenth century, and poetic intensity inevitably implies the short poem. According to Poe's 'The Poetic Principle', the absolute temporal maximum that can be expected from any reader at one time is half an hour. It was for this reason, as he explains in 'The Philosophy of Composition', that he had had to keep 'The Raven' down to about a hundred lines (actually 108). Poe even provides a formula:

The extent of a poem may be made to bear mathematical relation to its merit, – in other words, to the excitement or elevation, – again in other words, to the degree of the true poetical effect which it is capable of inducing; for it is clear that the brevity must be in direct ratio of the intensity of the intended effect: this, with one proviso, – that a certain degree of duration is absolutely requisite for the production of any effect at all.

The accuracy of Poe's arithmetic can be confirmed from later anthologies. Thus Palgrave's *Golden Treasury* (1861), the most successful anthology ever compiled, includes only two poems that decisively exceed this limit – 'Lycidas' (193 lines) and 'Intimations of Immortality' (203 lines). Gray's 'Elegy' only runs to 128 lines. On the other hand, there are few very short poems in it.

The popularity of anthologies has been at the expense of the poets' own collections of their poems. Some sobering statistics were recently assembled by J. W. Saunders,[1] which showed that T. S. Eliot and W. H. Auden were the only contemporary poets making more than a pittance from their writings. On the other hand, *The Oxford Book of English Verse* had sold more than half a million copies by 1950.[2] But the wrong critical moral can easily be drawn from such facts and figures. It is not true that there is no market for contemporary poetry today; the fact is that the common reader prefers to buy his poetry through that dubious middleman the anthologist. On the premises of Romantic poetic theory he is right to do so. The doctrine of rapture was never specific about the relationship of one rapturous moment with another, their internal interconnections or their common background. A more realistic attitude to poetry recognises that a poet's poems tend to hang together, the not-so-good with the good, the early poems with the later poems. In an anthology, however a poem floats in the air, detached from its native roots, its foliage confused with that of very different poems by very different poets, whose juxtaposition may well be entirely accidental. The typical anthology of contemporary verse in English is often arranged alphabetically, three or four poems by Conrad Aiken preceding one or two poems by Kingsley Amis and so on down to Wain and Yeats. The natural effect of such associations on any but the most sophisticated or well-informed reader is to assimilate the separate poets as well as the various poems by each poet. All the poets the particular editor has decided to include seem to be writing the same sort of poetry or even variations upon a single poem. The more critical reader, on the other hand, once he has emerged from the thirty or so minutes of emotional excitement recommended by Poe, is likely to feel justifiably irritated. His historical sense, he will feel, has been affronted and contradicted. The historical truth is that what a popular anthologist lumps together as modern poetry will almost always include two or three generations of poets who are not writing even approximately similar

---

[1] *Essays in Criticism*, iv (1954), 243-81.      [2] Information supplied by the publishers.

poems. *The Oxford Book of Modern Verse* (1936), which was edited by no less a person than Yeats himself, runs from Walter Pater, who was born in 1839, to George Barker who was born in 1913. It is true Yeats did arrange his poets by their order of birth (though that too can be mis-leading), but the logical corollary of such an arrangement – that each poet's poems should be in the order of their composition or publication – is constantly flouted, and particularly crassly, as it happens, in the case of his own poems.[1]

Robert Graves and Laura Riding once collaborated in a lively *Pamphlet against Anthologies* (1928), which came to the drastic conclusion that all anthologies are bad, if some are perhaps worse than others. The specialist selection, one that is limited to a single poetic genre in a restricted period, has its obvious uses for students, and the miscellany – in which a number of writers deliberately associate themselves for a common purpose (Dryden's various collections, *The Yellow Book*, *Wheels*, Michael Roberts's Faber anthology of the Auden group) – is a legitimate form of group demonstration. Of anthologies proper the best is that in which the editor resists the natural tendency of the form to blur distinctions of style and content by providing his own differentiations in the notes. A biographical and bibliographical head-note is a useful device, and difficult expressions and allusions ought always to be elucidated in short tactful footnotes. The progress of the Romantic theory of the reader's rôle in poetry can in fact be measured – by an extension of Poe's formula – by the presence or absence of such editorial notes in the anthologies. In the eighteenth century such things were almost the rule, not only in such omnibus collections as *The Works of the English Poets*, to which Johnson's *Lives of the Poets* was originally prefixed, but also in the more modest compilations such as Goldsmith's *Beauties of English Poetry* (1767) and Henry Headley's sensible *Select Beauties of Ancient English Poetry* (1787). The tradition was still being observed in a sort of way in *The Golden Treasury* as well in Palgrave's immediate successor and rival – Archbishop Trench's *Household Book of English Poetry* (1868). But by this time the anti-intellectualist implications of the doctrine of intensity had begun to spread downwards, and more recent selections of the Palgrave type have been much less informative. *The Oxford Book of English Verse* (1900) is entirely without notes. Instead of the critical comments and explanations found in earlier selections, Quiller-Couch confined himself to a few marginal glosses of the obsolete words – a practice continued in the otherwise excellent *Poets of the English*

---

[1] The first five poems of the fourteen Yeats allotted himself are all from *The Winding Stair* (1933). These are followed by poems from the collections of 1928, 1921, 1933, 1914, 1919 and 1933 in that order.

*Language* recently edited by W. H. Auden and Norman Holmes Pearson
(5 vols., 1950). And other reputable anthologists have been equally
uninformative. Even the more or less scholarly affairs, like the 'period'
*Oxford Books*, Robert Bridges's *Spirit of Man* and Norman Ault's pioneer-
ing collections, rarely provide more than references to the sources of the
texts printed.

Nor is this state of affairs confined to the anthologies. The same editorial
reticence is to be found in most modern reprints of the English poets. The
'Cambridge English Classics' and many of the 'Oxford Poets', to cite only
two standard series issued by their respective University Presses, contain
no explanatory notes at all, though as a sop to the academic conscience
elaborate textual collations are included (which only one reader in a
thousand ever looks at). This is in striking contrast with the eighteenth-
and nineteenth-century editions of the English poetical classics; almost all
of those which have any pretensions to scholarship provide either notes or
a biographical-critical introduction, often both. I am not referring here to
the *magna opera* like Zachary Grey's *Hudibras* (1744), or the Elwin-
Courthope edition of Pope (1871-89), but to such more or less hack
productions as Fenton's Waller (1729), Langhorne's Collins (1765),
George Gilfillan's 'British Poets' (1853-60), or the 'Muses' Library'
series issued by A. H. Bullen in the early 1890s. Apparently up to about
1900 or so readers of English poetry *expected* to have the obscure expressions and the literary and topical allusions explained to them. And then,
apparently quite suddenly, the expectation ceased. Plain-text reprints and
anthologies without notes, instead of being the cheap and nasty exception,
became the rule over the whole published price-range from the private
presses to 'The World's Classics' and 'Everyman's Library'. With minor
exceptions this is still the situation today.

I. A. Richards has given it as his opinion that 'the capacity to read
intelligently seems undoubtedly to have been greater among educated
men in Coleridge's time than it is today'. He adds that it was 'maintained –
for modes of meaning close in structure to those in Wordsworth, Shelley
or Keats – until towards the end of the nineteenth century. Then came a
sudden decline in performance.'[1] The verdict confirms the evidence
already summarized. The inability to read poetry intelligently was largely
due to the absence of aids to intelligent reading in the standard anthologies
and reprints. What had poetry to do with the intelligence? In the more or
less passive state called rapture the poem was expected to read itself. The
fact that it took a whole century for the implications of Romantic poetic

[1] *Coleridge on Imagination* (1934), p. 193.

theory to seep down to the ordinary reader of poetry can no doubt be ascribed to the persistence of Neo-Classic assumptions and practices in the schools and the universities. Latin and Greek poetry, it was sufficiently obvious, do not read themselves.

The immediate casualty in all this was 'meaning'. If there has been some improvement recently in the general capacity to read poetry intelligently, the credit is largely due to I. A. Richards himself, whose critical career began with the collaboration with C. K. Ogden provocatively entitled *The Meaning of Meaning* (1923). What *does* 'meaning' mean? For the moment we may be content with Leonard Bloomfield's preliminary definition: 'the *meaning* of a linguistic form' is 'the situation in which the speaker utters it and the response which it calls forth in the hearer'.[1] Since a poem is a continuum of linguistic forms, poetic meaning must be presumed to be the situation in which the poet writes combined with the reader's response to it. In simpler terms, poetic meaning subsists in a poet-reader relationship. Now it is precisely this relationship that the individualism of the nineteenth century always tended to undercut. According to John Stuart Mill – who succeeded in combining a rational attitude to non-poetry with an emotional view of poetry – whereas prose is heard poetry is overheard.[2] In other words, the poet for Mill must be unaware – or at least pretend to be unaware – of the poet-reader relationship, though it continued to be implicit, of course, in the use of language by the poet. What are overheard are, after all, *words*.

And a similar unawareness of the poet, except as the accidental source of emotional stimulus, was assumed in the reader. It is true the Victorian public could not have too many biographies of its poets; it was precisely the difference between poetry and non-poetry that made the poets such fascinating reading. But the relevant point of connection between the poet and his reader, viz. the text, the precise words that the poet used, was of less interest. Hence no doubt the curious multiplicity of textual corruption that was tolerated in the popular Victorian anthologies and reprints. What the poet actually wrote, his exact meaning, did not really matter, provided an exciting stimulus was immediately available. It is true that a minimum of meaning *was* the indispensable precondition – even Poe provided that. And on these premises an exciting misreading of one's author might even be preferable to the original text's manifest or demonstrable intention.

A nice example of such semantic insouciance is A. E. Housman's extraction of a line from Milton's *Arcades* out of its context (which he

[1] *Language* (1933), p. 139.    [2] 'Thoughts on Poetry and Varieties' (1859).

describes as 'blithe and gay') that then becomes an entirely different one-line poem:

But in these six simple words of Milton –

      Nymphs and shepherds, dance no more –

What is it that can draw tears, as I know it can, to the eyes of more readers than one? What in the world is there to cry about? Why have the mere words the physical effect of pathos when the sense of the passage is blithe and gay? I can only say, because they are poetry, and find their way to something in man which is obscure and latent, something older than the present organization of his nature.[1]

The pathos of Milton's six simple words presumably derive for Housman from the last two of them. As Shenstone had pointed out in the middle of the eighteenth century, 'the words "no more" have a singular pathos; reminding us at once of past pleasure, and the future exclusion of it'.[2] But Milton's injunction to the nymphs and shepherds was not, in fact, to stop dancing, but to 'dance no more By sandy *Ladons* Lillied Banks'. The nymphs were only to transfer their dances from Arcadia to Harefield in Middlesex (where an 'entertainment' was being presented to the Dowager Countess of Derby).[3] Housman's tears came from taking Milton's line out of its context and giving it a meaning it was never intended to have.

Housman, a brilliant textual critic in English as well as Latin and Greek, knew what he was doing. The more usual situation is unconscious mis-interpretation to adapt the poem to one's expectations and preferences. A familiar example of this process is Blake's lyric 'And did those feet in ancient time', which has now established itself as a non-denominational hymn as well as being the official anthem of the English Women's Insti-tutes. Its 'dark Satanic mills', which we tend to visualize as the factories of the Industrial Revolution, were meant by Blake to symbolize the churches of his time, and they are not 'dark' from smoke or soot but because darkness is Blake's recurrent symbol for oppression. If we must visualize the mills, the image should be of handmills operated by slave labour similar to those in which Samson toiled after Delilah's treachery. It is natural, too, to take the 'feet' of the first line as Christ's, but Blake is as likely to be referring to Albion – 'our Ancestor, patriarch of the Atlantic Continent, whose History preceded that of the Hebrews'. In Blake's epic

---

[1] *The Name and Nature of Poetry* (1933), p. 46.    [2] *Works*, vol. ii (1764), p. 187.
[3] Housman's mistake has already been pointed out by Kenneth Muir. See 'Three Hundred Years of Milton's Poems', *Penguin New Writing*, No. 24 (1945), p. 140.

*Jerusalem* Albion's 'awful' genitals precede a passage similar in its imagery to the third stanza of the lyric:

> in his burning hand
> He takes his bow, then chooses out his arrows of flaming gold;
> Murmuring, the bowstring breathes with ardour; clouds roll round the
> Horns of the wide bow.[1]

And Jerusalem? Jerusalem, the symbol of the free poetic imagination, is at the mythological level the daughter of Albion and the 'bride' of Jesus – and a lyric in *Jerusalem* has two lines which seem to identify the mysterious 'feet' as in some sense hers:

> She walks upon our meadows green;
> The Lamb of God walks by her side. . . .

No doubt at a more literal level Jerusalem is simply the Holy City. What is certain is that underlying Blake's allegory and myth is the legend – accepted as sober historical fact in the eighteenth century and referred to as such by Milton in *Areopagitica* – that Pythagoras had derived all his learning from the early Druids. The alleged dependence of English culture upon that of the Mediterranean was therefore for Blake and the other Druidists of his time the exact reverse of the truth, the real cradle of civilization having been England: 'All things begin and end in Albion's ancient Druid rocky shore.'

Since capitalism is felt to be vaguely discreditable nowadays and the smoke-polluted factories of Lancashire and Yorkshire were particularly unpleasant examples of it, the modern reader, uninstructed by editorial notes, naturally assumes that this is what 'dark Satanic mills' must mean. Opposed for him to the mills is the green and pleasant countryside of his weekend excursions, and the whole poem – reinforced by Parry's stirring tune – adds up nowadays to a patriotic version of Morris's *News from Nowhere*. And, as with Housman's distortion of Milton's line, a case of a kind can certainly be made for this socialist back-to-the-land distortion of Blake's original intentions. The elaborate allegory, the private myth and the underlying pseudo-history of Blake's meaning *may* seem to be unnecessary complications. But then Nahum Tate's refusal to allow Cordelia to die in his adaptation of *King Lear* (1681) has also had its enthusiastic admirers.

The Romantic reader's liberty of interpretation usually resolves itself into simplification by modernization. 'Poetry', a recent Headmaster of Rugby School has pronounced, 'is really a very simple affair, simpler than

[1] Plate 95.

prose, very often much simpler than life itself' – a generalization that is itself a simplification by modernization. P. B. H. Lyon,[1] this particular headmaster, was under the impression that when Milton described poetry as 'less subtle and fine, but more simple, sensuous and passionate' than rhetoric, what was meant was *simple* in its modern sense. What Milton really meant was not 'easy' but posssessing 'that unity which enables one to think of the poem as a whole', that is, the quality Coleridge was to call *esemplastic.*[2] Horace's *Ars Poetica* had provided the classic formula for every work of art, whatever the subject-matter: *Sit quidvis, simplex dumtaxat et unum.*[3]

Whatever is not immediately intelligible is still liable to such vulgarization in the interest of poetic rapture. The exact meaning of four familiar lines in Marvell's 'To his Coy Mistress' is far from clear:

> Let us roll all our strength and all
> Our sweetness up into one ball,
> And tear our pleasures with rough strife
> Through the iron gates of life.

The standard edition of Marvell by H. M. Margoliouth suggests that the 'ball' is a pomander ('a mixture of aromatic substances, usually made into a ball', *O.E.D.*); I have myself proposed cannon-ball (a common seventeenth-century meaning) as more appropriate for the second couplet. (According to Thomas Blount's *Academy of Eloquence*, 1654,[4] there was a fashion for military metaphors at the time.) Inevitably, however, the Romantic reader modernizes the image. 'If I try to visualize it', C. Day Lewis admits, 'I see nothing but two lovers feverishly trying to squeeze an india-rubber ball through the bars of an iron gate.'[5] Day Lewis is sufficiently sophisticated to realize that the rubber ball will not do, and he tries to explain away the incongruity by an unconvincing theory that Marvell's images are 'abstract' and intended to discourage any visualization. But with the metaphors unvisualised the lines reduce themselves to a crude account of the sexual act, and the detached decorum so essential to Marvell's poetic procedure has been lost.

The watering-down of 'meaning' that is typified by these examples of

---

[1] *The Discovery of Poetry* (1930), p. 14.

[2] See W. P. Ker, *Form and Style in Poetry* (1928), p. 178. Milton's definition of poetry is in his tractate *Of Education* (1644).

[3] l. 23. The Latin *simplex* had as its original sense the notion of a 'simultaneous enfolding'.

[4] p. 34.

[5] *The Poetic Image* (1947), p. 72. Tennyson told Palgrave 'that he could fancy *grates* would have intensified Marvell's image' (*Memoir by his Son*, vol. ii, 1897, p. 501), though he did not explain why.

the critical behaviour of English readers, common and not so common, of the Romantic School culminates in its partial or total repudiation by several twentieth-century critical theorists. A characteristic passage will be found in Robert Bridges's essay 'Poetic Diction' (1923):

It might be urged that with Milton and Shelley, who were educated by Hellenic models and had come by reading and meditation to have panoramic views of history and truth, it was natural to write at that height – their poetic diction may be the spontaneous utterance of their subconscious mind – but that it is nevertheless regrettable because common folk whom they might otherwise delight and instruct cannot understand it. This is a wrong notion. It was not Dr Johnson's ignorance or deficient education that made him dislike *Lycidas*. It was his unpoetic mind that was at fault, and his taste in music or painting would probably have been at the same level. Moreover, children do not resent what they cannot understand in poetry, and they generally have a keener sense for beauty than Dr Johnson had – indeed, if he would have become again as a little child, he might have liked *Lycidas* very well.

Bridges's implication seems to be that children and 'common folk' respond to the beauty of 'Lycidas' without understanding it, whereas Dr Johnson, who did understand the poem, got nothing out of it. The way to learn to appreciate Milton is not to consult the editors and the diction-aries and so discover what Milton meant, but to 'become again as a little child'.

The significant thing about Bridges's anti-intellectualism is the casual-ness with which meaning is disposed of. It is all so taken for granted. Of course the child's mind is more poetic than Johnson's. Of course poetic diction may be the spontaneous utterance of the subconscious – though this is the exact opposite of Wordsworth's Account of 'Poetic Diction' in the Preface to the third edition of *Lyrical Ballads*. These propositions did not have to be proved in the 1920s; they were apparently self-evident.

The most down-to-earth account of the unimportance of meaning in poetry is that provided by A. E. Housman in *The Name and Nature of Poetry* (1933). For the Beatific Vision and the desirability of becoming again as a little child Housman substituted a condition approaching phantasmagoria, whose poetic authenticity is guaranteed by the presence of certain physical symptoms. The list includes such phenomena as the skin bristling and a shiver running down the spine; or the reader's throat will feel constricted and tears will come into his eyes; or a piercing sensa-tion will make itself felt in the pit of the stomach. These, however, are only the effects of poetry; when it comes to describing what poetry is in itself, Housman can only talk round the problem. At one point in the lecture he seems to identify the meaningless poetry that he values most with 'sensations' that are less strictly physical. 'The Haunted Palace', he says, 'is one of Poe's best poems so long as we are content to swim in the sensations it evokes and only vaguely to apprehend the allegory.' Have these *sensations* been provoked by memories of an actual sensuous experience? The nearest we come to a description of the poetic experience without meaning is in a comment on Blake's 'My Spectre around Me Night and Day' (one of the later poems in Blake's Notebook):

I am not equal to framing definite ideas which would match that magnificent versification and correspond to the strong tremor of unreasonable excitement which those words set up in some region deeper than the mind.

It will be remembered that the six words Housman detached from 'Arcades' produced a similar effect.

Two points seem to emerge. The first is that for Housman the experience of his favourite poems is incommunicable ('definite ideas' are inadequate for the purpose); the second is that an irrational excitement is nevertheless 'set up' by Blake's 'words'. The communication process works, but in a special limited way. Since Blake's poem is meaningless – at least for Housman, though he admits it 'probably possessed for Blake a meaning, and his students think that they have found it' – it seems likely that we must take the 'words' referred to in this passage quite literally; the source of the unreasonable excitement is not in Blake's sentences but in the single words and phrases detached from their grammatical context. Read piecemeal in this way 'My Spectre around me' (which is full of Blake's private terminology as well as of his symbolic system) might well translate itself into a nightmarish phantasmagoria. The only difficulty is to understand why such a phantasmagoria should be accompanied by any profound excitement.

The air of bravado with which Housman enunciated his paradoxes – his own poetry bears little or no resemblance to the meaningless masterpieces he belauds in the lecture – is not unlike the tone that Huxley's and Waugh's heroes adopt in their speculations about poetry. What all three have in common is an attitude to poetry not unusual among writers and critics in adolescence. One of the best descriptions ever done of a boy's discovery of poetry is in Forrest Reid's forgotten autobiography *Apostate* (1928), and the excitement Reid experienced soon after his voice broke when reading Tennyson's 'Mariana' and Poe's 'Ulalume' is strikingly similar to Housman's adult testimony as well as to that of Waugh's Dennis. Reid even uses the same metaphor to describe it that Waugh was to use later: 'A single line, sometimes even a single word, was sufficient to produce this peculiar effect, as of a drug acting not upon the senses but on the imagination.' (One such word was 'Hebrides'.) And there is a similar playing-down of the actual meaning of the favourite poems:

The words said nothing; I only knew that they entered into my mind, lulling it to a kind of quiescent state, a state of receptivity in which things came and went.

The adolescent intoxication with poetry that Forrest Reid describes was also experienced by T. S. Eliot at fourteen or so, when an accidental exploration of FitzGerald's *Omar Khayyam* induced what he was to describe as 'a craving for poetry':

It was like a sudden conversion; the world appeared anew, painted with bright, delicious and painful colours. Thereupon I took the usual adolescent course with Byron, Shelley, Keats, Rossetti, Swinburne.

But Reid and Eliot – unlike W. P. Trent, Housman and the others – emerged in due course into adult attitudes to poetry, when, as Eliot put it:

we cease to identify ourselves with the poet we happen to be reading; when our critical faculties remain awake; when we are aware of what one poet can be expected to give and what he cannot. The poem has its own existence apart from us; it was there before us and will endure after us.[1]

The change is essentially one from a subjective to a more objective attitude to poetry. A poem has its meaning for the adolescent, but it is such a different kind of meaning from that experienced by the adult that a refusal to use the same word for the two experiences is comprehensible. Eliot has complained that many people never advance beyond the adolescent attitude to poetry. No doubt Professor Trent of the Beatific Vision was a case of such delayed development. Housman's is a more complicated case. In his profession as a classical scholar, he was the critical adult, always eagerly insistent on the criterion of meaning; it was only as a reader of English poetry that he remained an adolescent. The meaning that he denied to Blake, and also to 'Take O take those lips away', is taken for granted in the editions of Manilius, Juvenal and Lucan.

## II

Meaning, then, in one sense or another, is indispensable in poetry. The moral objections to the pleasure-principle as the crucial criterion can now be supplemented by a closer analysis of the logical implications of poetic meaning. We may agree that meaning, whatever its form, whether it is

[1] *The Use of poetry and the Use of Criticism* (1933), pp. 33–4.

adult or adolescent, is necessarily more or less subjective. 'A fool sees not the same tree that a wise man sees.' What the word 'Hebrides' meant to Forrest Reid was a private experience, incommunicable in its totality, whatever its external origins may have been. The sounds that are articulated when a poem is read aloud can be recorded on a tape or a disc – just as they can be translated into spatial symbols by the pen or the printing-press – but such physical accompaniments, records or alphabetical equivalents are not, strictly speaking, the poem. A poem is a mental event, not a physical object. The proposition cannot very well be disputed. Nevertheless it is natural to think of a poem as being in some sense 'out there', an independent entity that does not change its nature each time that it is read. Meaning is or ought to be public as well as private. Though there are bound to be subjective variations between the tree as seen by the wise man and the fool, still if they speak the same language wise man and fool will be likely to use the same words, more or less, to describe the same object. In other words, there is always the possibility of *inter-subjective* agreement. The process of learning its language, indeed the whole of its programme of education, is primarily a society's way of maintaining and extending the area of intersubjective agreement between its members.

It is in such terms as these that the problem of poetic meaning is best approached. Bloomfield's limitation of meaning to the speaker's 'situation' and the hearer's 'response' omits the essential *tertium quid*, viz. the linguistic conventions both speaker and hearer are committed to observe as members of the same speech group. An English speaker must speak more or less correct English if English hearers are to understand him, and his meanings cannot be separated from the words and the pronunciation in which they are communicated. It is not even certain that there can be any meanings that are not verbal meanings. Unlike Kipling's Mowgli, the few human children who have been brought up by animals are all said to have turned out idiots.

With such considerations in mind Matthew Arnold's definition of the function of literary criticism as the effort to see the literary object 'as in itself it really is' becomes a usable concept. Strictly speaking, there *is* no literary object. There is, however, the possibility of an increasing inter-subjective agreement about the common experiences which constitute a particular work of literature. And the possibility of such agreements refutes the old cynicism of *de gustibus non est disputandum*. Such disputation is both possible and desirable. The criteria of interpretation and evaluation can never, it is true, be absolutely authoritative, if only because the subjects who contribute to the intersubjective interpretation or judgment are always changing, just as the society to which they owe their allegiances is continually evolving. But a measure of literary agreement is possible, just as a measure of linguistic agreement is possible on the right way to pronounce a particular English word. The language-literature parallel is more than an analogy. Coleridge's 'homely definition' of poetry as 'the best words in the best order', whatever its ultimate limitations, is irrefutable as far as it goes. After all, once the words are eliminated from a poem what is there left? In the last analysis, then, the words *are* the poem. And it is at least a reasonable assumption – one to be explored in further detail in later chapters – that the 'best' words and word order of Coleridge's definition of poetry are at bottom an extension or perfection of just those qualities that distinguish 'good' English, for example, from English that is merely comprehensible or at best grammatically and verbally 'correct'.

What is a poem for? The question with which the preceding section opened is beginning to find some tentative answers, and it is time to ask a more difficult question. The critical reader of a poem is an embryonic literary critic, who must now ask himself with Arnold if the poem as he has experienced it is the poem 'as in itself it really is'. This may sound an alarming prospect, but, as Eliot once reassuringly put it, 'criticism is as inevitable as breathing'.[1] The difference between the professional critic and the rest of us is simply a matter of degrees of critical consciousness. A thriller that the reader cannot put down has been given, whether the reader is aware of it or not, a favourable criticism. In one respect, indeed, the silent or solitary reader of poetry is in a more favourable critical position than, for example, a dramatic critic. In addition to being implicitly a critic he is also, by the fact that he must read the poem himself and not have it read to him or acted before him, the author's mouthpiece. The dual relationship has the inevitable effect of increasing the self-consciousness of the experience. Ideally he will be reciting the poem – aloud or *sotto voce* according to the circumstances – as he believes it should be recited to maximize its meaning or value. And he is also listening to such a recitation with the proper degree of attention to comprehend all the subtleties of the poem's meaning and the proper emotional response to the imaginary situation that the meaning has communicated.

The two aspects of the reader's function derive from the different mental processes required. When we read a poem we must first of all translate the visual and spatial symbols we meet on the page into their oral and temporal equivalents, i.e. into their proper sequence of conventional sounds. A second and similar translation follows when the conventional sounds are translated into the meanings we have learnt to associate with

[1] *The Sacred Wood* (1920), p. 43.

them. But the two translations, though similar in their mode of operation, are not identical. The difference makes 'literature' (that which is recorded *literally*, in the form of letters) a radically different art form from an oral epic, a fairy story or a nursery rhyme. It is necessarily more intellectual and more sophisticated, because the first level of translation being merely one of intellectual transposition is emotionally neutral (apart from oddities like poems of diminishing line length arranged to look like hearts, etc.). The second level, on the other hand, being made up of the same linguistic material as speech, introduces with the words as they sound in everyday life all the affective associations of whatever words and phrases are common to life and to literature. And inevitably, with poems read to oneself, the first translation influences the second. It follows that such poems are partly immunized from the context of real-life emotion to which the auditors of a play or any other oral recitation are exposed. And other factors combine to de-emotionalize the poetry reader's reactions. In the theatre he is exposed to the apparent physical reality of an actor-speaker, but when he is alone – that is, when *he* is the actor – the words naturally lose much of this immediate physical impact. And the risk of confusing *word* with *thing* is reduced still more by the silent reader's ability to stop the 'performance' in the middle of a sentence or to go back at his will to an earlier page. Thus the poem as read to oneself is in a sense more artificial than the oral poem, but because immediate intelligibility is no longer essential it can be more compressed, more elliptical, more meaningful – though there may sometimes be a compensating loss of impact and illusion.

The distinction suggests a difference between meaning in literature and meaning in speech. Bloomfield's two contributors to his definition of meaning (in speech), the co-operating speaker and hearer, are internalized whenever a poem is read to oneself. But for such a reader a similar balance of complementary rôles is necessary if the full poetic experience is to be achieved. The reader-speaker, for his part, must present the poem's meaning correctly and effectively, and the reader-hearer must react to what is presented sensibly and sympathetically. The adolescent who allows the words of a poem to lull his mind, as Forrest Reid did, to 'a kind of quiescent state' – like the adult who cultivates, as W. P. Trent did, 'that more or less passive state we call rapture' – is allowing the rôle of passive internal hearer to predominate over that of active internal speaker. The poem's meaning is then being sacrificed to such feelings as may – or more probably may not – be stimulated by it. It is clear that Housman, for example, and the type of reader he represents, sentimentalized his favourite English poems by a slovenly preliminary speaking/reading. The physical and emotional excitements that Housman obtained from 'Take O take those lips away' were illegitimate because they were not the proper consequence of the song's grammatical meaning (which he was apparently too lazy to work out). The situation is comparable to that of the movie-addict who wants a good cry or a good laugh and who gets it irrespective of the proper emotional justification that the particular film actually provides. Such sentimentalists tend to eliminate the speaker-reader part in the poetic process. By the time they have reached the condition of Huxley's and Waugh's heroes single lines and phrases may well be sufficient to release the feelings originally stimulated by the poems read as wholes. The disconnected verbal fragments float into the consciousness apparently without the intervention of the active part of the mind; meaning seems to have been attenuated almost to the point of non-existence. In fact, however, even the adolescent raptures depend upon earlier active pursuits of meaning. And they are soon self-exhausting. A single narcotic word like Forrest Rcid's 'Hebrides' – presumably the fragmentary relic of earlier readings of 'Lycidas', 'The Solitary Reaper' and the 'Canadian Boat Song' – ultimately turns stale on the poetic palate.

Meaning, then, is prior to feeling in both a temporal and a logical sense. In the internal theatre of the mind the reader-actor must know his part before he can act it, and between his speaking of the poem's words and the appropriate emotional response of the reader-audience the latter must register what is spoken first of all as a series of sounds, then as a series of words and sentences, and lastly by a suspension of disbelief as a series of human situations, Aristotle's *muthos*, to which we react intellectually and emotionally more or less as we should to a comparable situation in extra-poetic reality. And the nature and degree of the final response depend in every nuance upon a previous comprehension of the meanings and semantic inter-relationships of the poem's words.

There are, it is true, two qualifications to add: (1) a poem whose meaning does not when fully understood stimulate any feelings at all, or feelings that are not in some sense pleasurable, is an unsuccessful poem; (2) such terms as *proper, appropriate, sympathetic, extra-poetic reality* beg an important question – that of the relationship of literature to the society of which it is the product. It will be for the remaining chapters of Part I of this book to look into these issues more closely.

A provisional summing-up may now be attempted. The ultimate objection to a Romantic theory of poetry is the moral one. If the account it professes to provide of the processes of composition and communication is a true one, then the traditional esteem accorded to poetry throughout the world has not been deserved. The Romantic game of art *is* a conjuring trick, if it is not a mental narcotic, and the responsible reader rejects with disgust the propaganda that offers him an alleged Beatific Vision practically for nothing. If poetic rapture is so easily available it cannot be the genuine article. Housman's bristling skin and constricted throat prove nothing in themselves, except that it is human to err. A creaking floorboard in the middle of the night has induced similar physical reactions in many a respectable householder. Even the ecstasies of poetic adolescence, though no doubt partly the product of puberty, have to be earned intellectually by a new interest in the phenomena of language. And such adolescents, as Eliot has insisted, are always the exception rather than the rule.

How is the adult, on the other hand, to earn the special rewards that poetry offers? The problem is almost always evaded, but it is clearly of the first importance to recognize one moral direction at least from which a solution to it may be expected.

Otto Jespersen, speaking as a linguist, has suggested a natural hierarchy in the use of speech: (1) the merely comprehensible, (2) the entirely correct, (3) the more than 'correct' – the 'good'.[1] Thus a foreigner's broken English will be comprehensible without being correct, while a native's correct English may occasionally achieve the racy, pithy, memorable use of idiom that consitutes good English. And good English, as exhibited, for instance, in the conversational triumphs of Dr Johnson that are recorded by Boswell, is to speech what the best English words in the best English order are to poetry. The judgment is in both cases a two-sided one – a judgment of the individual hearer or reader that is confirmed by the judgment of society (a speech-group or a culture). The individual speaker is entitled to say, with the Romantic reader, 'This verbal series gives me pleasure'; but he cannot say 'This verbal series is good' unless his judgment has in some sense been ratified by the society to which he belongs. On the other hand, a sentence that is merely correct is essentially a form of words imposed by society on the individual – without his assent to it being involved. We obey the rules of grammar as we obey the obligation to drive on one side or the other of the public way.

The next step in the critical thesis that the following chapters will explore and illustrate more fully will be to try to pinpoint the linguistic or stylistic novelty that has given pleasure to its author and his earliest readers and to relate to it the dominant forces of change in their society. What is new in the poetry, say, of Sir Thomas Wyatt is an impersonal egotism that is reflected stylistically in the number of times that he uses the first person singular instead of some such locution as 'the lover'. Wyatt's poetic egotism was welcomed by the English Renaissance – perhaps because it

[1] *Mankind, Nation and Individual* (1946), pp. 132-3.

expressed verbally the competitive individualism that was the dominant social novelty in the Tudor Court as well as on the contemporary economic plane. The poems that gave pleasure to Wyatt and his friends received their social sanction in the process; they became the 'good' poems of the time.

The critical implications of such a procedure are that if we are to discover the qualities that make a poem good rather than merely pleasurable we must read it in its original social context and relate the meaning of the poem to the social forces operative at the time of its composition. If it is objected that the society in which we live today is very different from that, for example, of the Renaissance and that our canons of criticism cannot always allow us to endorse as 'good' now what was 'good' then, the reply will be that human nature and human institutions do not change as much as they may seem to do to the casual eye, and to be able to detach oneself occasionally from the biases of our own century is one of the objects of a humane education. A sophisticated reader will encourage the reader-reciter in him to identify himself with the original situation, however historically and sentimentally remote, of the poem's composition, just as it will be for the reader-hearer in him to resist such an identification in the interest of those different values we hold especially precious today. And in the interplay of past and present meanings a more permanent critical verdict may eventually be attainable.

### III

A return can now be made to some technical aspects of the cult of poetic unintelligibility. Two separate theories were advanced in the final phases of the English Romantic Movement to justify the minimization or even total exclusion of meaning, in the ordinary sense of the word, from serious poetry of all kinds. One can be called the Suggestion Theory, the other the Pure Sound Theory.

According to the Suggestion Theory poetry is not concerned with what words mean but with what they suggest. A good poem apparently should mean very little while suggesting a great deal. Housman's comment on Blake's 'Hear the Voice of the Bard' was: 'That mysterious grandeur would be less grand if it was less mysterious, if the embryo ideas which are all that it contains should endue form and outline, and suggestion condense itself into thought.'[1] It is essential, in other words, for the success of this poem that the ideas remain in embryo, so that its meaningless grandeur can 'work' upon the reader.

---

[1] *The Name and Nature of Poetry* (1933), p. 42.

A simple example of the Suggestion Theory is Shelley's 'champak' in the 'Lines to an Indian Air':

> The wandering airs they faint
> On the dark, the silent stream –
> The champak odours fail
> Like sweet thoughts in a dream.

A champac is a kind of magnolia with fragrant orange-coloured flowers, and it is alleged that the knowledge of what a champac is spoils Shelley's poem. According to E. D. Snyder,[1] the 'peculiar effectiveness' of these lines derives from the reader not knowing – and not wanting to know – what the odours are. Unknown the 'champak' suggests mysterious illimitable possibilities; known, it is implied, the line contracts to a visit to a botanical garden.

There are perhaps three comments to be made on the Suggestion Theory. The first is that a word's connotation is as much a part of its meaning as its denotation. If Shelley thought of the champac vaguely as a fragrant Indian tree, that was its meaning for him, and it is all that an editor's footnote needs to detail. The indefiniteness of Romantic poetry is an essential part of its meaning, and to describe it as meaningless because it is imprecise is a misuse of words. A second objection to the Suggestion Theory is that a word's connotation is dependent on its denotation. Unless he knows where Troy is and what happened there (Troy's 'meaning') the reader cannot respond to the 'suggestion' in such a line as Yeats's

> Troy passed away in one high funeral gleam. ('The Rose of the World').

Moreover even words whose precise denotations the reader does not need to know, like the champac, or the 'sweet *Infanta*' of Herrick's 'The Primrose', can only be used successfully in contexts in which all the surrounding words are completely intelligible. Poets therefore like Swinburne, who suppress all denotation in order to exploit connotation, are cutting the ground away from under their own feet. A general blurring of 'meaning' inevitably entails a blurring of 'suggestion' too. The third objection that the Suggestion Theory invites is that, though relevant as a *raison d'être* of Romantic poetry, it can have no general application. A central concept of Romanticism is the primacy of the subconscious mind. The technical problem, therefore, that the Romantic poet had to solve was how to establish a relationship between the instinctive energies of his own private subconscious mind, the Freudian *libido*, on the one hand, and the system of communal conventional sounds which constitutes language,

[1] *Hypnotic Poetry* (Philadelphia, 1930), p. 45.

on the other. To put it bluntly, the *libido* does not speak English. The Romantic poets were impressed and excited by the hints that dreams gave of a reality that was deeper and older than the communal life to which they found themselves committed by the accident of birth.[1] Since it is impossible to translate the language of the *libido* literally – accurate transcriptions of dreams being either dull or ludicrous – the attempt was made to render the *qualities* of dream-experience, its strangeness, its remoteness, its inexplicability. It is significant that Romantic poetry contains a much higher proportion of negative propositions than earlier or later poetry. This may be because the easiest way to define the activities of the subconscious mind is to say what they are *not*. The alternative is to convey the impression, by the use of vague imagery and a 'suggestive' vocabulary, that life in the *libido* is something like everyday life, only more intense and more rarefied. Shelley's odours ('like sweet thoughts in a dream') are prevented from becoming the real scents of a real garden by the interposition of the mysterious 'champak'. The word 'suggests' the grotesque and slightly sinister vegetation of the East, and the 'suggestible' reader registers at the back of his mind banyans, upas trees, and mandragoras.

The Suggestion Theory need not detain us any longer. It is clearly valid for the special purposes of Romantic poetry, but it has little general relevance and the meaning that it excludes, the precise, scientific, 'dictionary' meaning of words, is after all only a part of the normal semantic content of poetry. A Homer, Dante or Shakespeare uses connotation and denotation simultaneously and in approximately equal proportions.

The Pure Sound Theory is related to the Suggestion Theory – Poe's and Mallarmé's 'pure poetry' seems to be an amalgam of both – but there is much less to be said for it. It has four subdivisions which can be considered separately: (i) verbal music (self-sufficient patterns of sound accidentally present in certain arrangements of words), (ii) melopœia (sound for creating a meaning complementary to the sense), (iii) onomatopœia (sound reinforcing the sense by adding a physical echo of it), (iv) hypnotic poetry.

*Verbal Music.* The writing of poetry, according to this theory, consists in 'the conscious and deliberate construction, upon a theme in itself utterly indifferent, of a musical pattern of words which gives delight'. Its 'purity'

---

[1] It is significant that the adjectives *deep* and *old* appear much more often in Romantic than in earlier poetry. *Deep* is used by Shelley more often than any other adjective except *sweet*; *old* is a favourite of Wordsworth's, only *good* occurring more frequently. Other adjectives that are common in Romantic poetry and relatively rare earlier are *bright* (common in Wordsworth and Keats), *dark* (a favourite of Shelley's), and *long* (common in Tennyson). I derive these facts from Josephine Miles, *Major Adjectives in English Poetry* (Berkeley, 1946).

lies in 'its absolute independence of subject'.[1] Poe's doctrine of 'sonorousness' was an earlier formulation of the theory.[2] Ezra Pound has recommended the appropriate exercises:

Study 'cadences', the finest that you can discover, preferably in a foreign language so that the meaning of the words may be less likely to divert your attention from the movement. Saxon charms, Hebridean folk-songs, Dante, and the lyrics of Goethe and Shakespeare (apart from their meaning) are especially recommended.[3]

It is odd that this kind of thing can ever have been taken seriously, but echoes of the theory can still be heard in French criticism and in that of English and American critics who have undergone French influence. From time to time too one comes across reports of children who have responded rapturously to poetry recited to them in a language they did not understand. It always transpires, however, that the reciter *did* understand the poems, and that the language in which they were written was cognate to the children's own language. To demonstrate the existence of verbal music, i.e. of beautiful word-sounds completely detached from meaning, the ecstatic response must clearly be to a poem in a language that is (i) unconnected with the subjects' own language, and (ii) unknown to the reciter. Otherwise there will always be the danger of some meaning seeping through. A phonetic transcription of a Chinese poem, which is then recited by an Englishman totally ignorant of Chinese, might provide the basis of such an experiment in this country. The fact that no such experiment has been recorded strongly suggests that there is no such thing as verbal music.[4] The illusion of its existence is attributable to the Suggestion Theory. Mallarmé had been one of the first to exploit methodically the connotations of words, and with the submergence of denotations it was easy to attribute the verbal associations not to the original meanings of the words but to their sounds. This is what Housman seems to have done. In *The Name and Nature of Poetry* he contrasts the 'suggestion' in

[1] J. Middleton Murry, 'Pure Poetry', *Countries of the Mind*, 2nd series (1931), p. 19. Herbert Read is perhaps the foremost English exponent of the verbal music theory. In *Poetry and Anarchism* (1938), p. 37, Read says of English poetry, 'Its greatest beauty is inherent in its sound: it too is a kind of music.' A similar passage will be found in his *Collected Essays* (1938), p. 100.

[2] In 'The Raven' Pallas's bust was introduced because of 'the sonorousness of the word Pallas itself', and the word *nevermore* was selected for the refrain because the long *o* is 'the most sonorous vowel' (*The Philosophy of Composition*).

[3] See H. P. Collins, *Modern Poetry* (1925), p. 160, who was quoting from *Poetry* (Chicago), March 1913.

[4] Tennyson had been told about a Japanese poet who was deeply moved by *In Memoriam* without knowing any English. But apparently the poem had been read to him by an Englishman (*Memoir* (1899), pp. 757-8).

Blake's poems with the 'thought' and the 'celestial tune' with the 'meaning', as though each pair of terms was interchangeable. And his conclusion that poetry is 'more physical than intellectual' seems to confirm the confusion. Connotations are, of course, as intellectual as denotations. It is only 'pure sound' that is non-intellectual.

The theory of poetry as verbal music has been taken particularly seriously in America, perhaps because of the influence of Poe. R. C. Givler, an American psychologist, devoted no less than eight years to a scientific and statistical investigation of the problem, in which he measured phonetically and then tabulated eighteen thousand lines of English poetry (principally Romantic poetry). His report on the experiments is an extraordinary document.[1] Thus in order to exclude any possible influence of meaning he 'transmogrified' the line 'One faint eternal eventide of gems' (*Endymion*, ii, 225) into

Won fĕmz ē nānj ŏv dī năl tĕr ĕn tēev,

which was supposed to be a nonsensical rearrangement of the sounds in Keats's line. Not unnaturally the ideas, if any, that this suggested to his subjects were quite different from the effect produced by the original line. On the other hand, when Keats's 'The air was cooling, and so very still' (*I stood tip-toe*, 2) was rearranged as 'So cooling very still was and the air', the impressions derived from the two lines were not unnaturally found to be practically identical. Givler's tentative conclusion that the 'tonal elements of the poetic line' have 'the power of arousing a mood congruous to that of the original poem, even when torn from their positions and their rhetorical anchorage, and recast' is at best only valid for experiments of this second type. To suggest, as T. C. Pollock has recently done,[2] that the experiments as a whole prove that the sounds of poetry have a value apart from their meaning is simply not true. All that they prove is (i) that sympathetic listeners will respond to the semantic associations of words in ungrammatical or illogical contexts, and (ii) that if they meet a word they don't know and the context gives no clue to its meaning they will tend to equate it with the words that sound most like it. And this had already been demonstrated much more effectively in the Nonsense Rhymes of Lear and Carroll.

*Melopœia*. This is Ezra Pound's word for poetry 'wherein the words are charged, over and above their plain meaning, with some musical property, which directs the bearing or trend of the meaning'.[3] The claim, essentially,

---

[1] *The Psycho-Physiological Effect of the Elements of Speech in Relation to Poetry* (Princeton, 1915).

[2] *The Nature of Literature* (Princeton, 1942), pp. 109-10.

[3] *How to Read* (1931), p. 25.

is that the sounds of the words create a meaning of their own simultaneous with and complementary to the sense of the poem. A simple example is provided by the opening words of the Chorus in *Samson Agonistes*,

> This, this is he; softly a while . . .

Here, according to Robert Bridges, 'the sibilants are hushing'.[1] An even simpler example is the line from *Macbeth*,

> Tomorrow, and tomorrow, and tomorrow . . .

According to David Daiches, 'The drawn-out mournful "o" sound . . . helps to convey the emotion of quiet despair';[2] he adds that the three words are 'three relentless tolling sounds; they tend to convey a mournful effect even apart from the meaning'.[3] Is there anything in melopœia? Or is it simply, as I suspect, a case of innocent self-deception? I cannot see that sibilants are particularly 'hushing'. Tennyson, who avoided them as far as he could, called them 'hissing'.[4] And in the lines on Camilla in the *Essay on Criticism* Pope uses the sibilants to suggest the rapidity of Camilla's running (like the 'whistling' of a projectile). Nor does 'tomorrow' strike me as a particularly mournful sound. In another context it might easily sound quite gay.[5]

*Onomatopœia.* This differs from melopœia in that the meaning that the sounds create is not apprehended by the reader until *after* the sense of the words has been grasped, whereas in melopœia, the two meanings are supposed to impinge simultaneously. In onomatopœia the repetition of sounds is, literally, an echo of the sense. It is only the prior knowledge of the sense that makes possible the recognition of a parallel in the sounds. This time-gap between the sense and its echo reduces the effectiveness of the device. It is only too easy for the reader, who has just mentally translated the sounds of the words into ideas, to fail to realize that he is now expected to reverse the process and to reconnect the ideas with the sounds. Thus Pope, who regarded onomatopœia as an indispensable epic property, found it necessary to append an index, 'VERSIFICATION. Expressing in the

---

[1] *Milton's Prosody* (1901), p. 41.      [2] *The Place of Meaning in Poetry* (1935), p. 7.
[3] *Ibid.*, p. 18.      [4] *Memoir* (1897), vol. ii, p. 289.
[5] Let us imagine a poem entitled 'On being left a Fortune';
> I'm feeling as gay as a bird on the spray,
> No need now to sponge or to borrow:
> What I like I shall eat, I'll take my gin neat,
> Tomorrow and tomorrow and tomorrow.

sound the thing describ'd,' to his translation of the *Iliad* to prevent this 'beauty' being overlooked. And Tennyson, an indefatigable onomatopœist, went further and warned his reader in the text when an onomatopœia was coming:

> the children call, and I
> Thy shepherd pipe, and sweet is every sound,
> Sweeter thy voice, but every sound is sweet;
> Myriads of rivulets hurrying thro' the lawn,
> The moan of doves in immemorial elms,
> And murmuring of innumerable bees.

Obviously the only reason why we are twice told here that every sound is sweet is to prepare us for the sound-effects in the last three lines. A further objection to onomatopœia is that by breaking the thread of 'meaning' to recall the reader to 'sounds' it tends to distract his attention from what the poet is saying to the cleverness with which it is being said. Words are stubborn things and to make them ring more or less like bells through a whole poem, as Poe does, certainly evinces considerable ingenuity. But I find it difficult to believe that tricks of this kind have much to do with poetry. They are surely only the literary equivalent of 'programme music' and *trompe l'œil* paintings – ingenious but fundamentally perverse attempts to transcend the aesthetic limitations of the particular medium. It is significant that there are next to no onomatopœias in Shakespeare.[1]

*Hypnotic poetry.* This is a somewhat different matter. The device has been defined by Yeats in a characteristic passage:

The purpose of rhythm, it has always seemed to me, is to prolong the moment of contemplation, the moment when we are both asleep and awake, which is the one moment of creation, by hushing us with an alluring monotony, while it holds us waking by variety, to keep us in that state of perhaps real trance, in which the mind liberated from the pressure of the will is unfolded in symbols. If certain sensitive

---

[1] A similar objection applies to the recent fashion for seeing the word order of a poem 'enact' the meaning. F. R. Leavis has commented on two lines in Keats's 'Ode to Autumn' –
> And sometimes like a gleaner thou dost keep
> Steady thy laden head across a brook –
as follows; 'In the step from the rime-word "keep", across (so to speak) the pause enforced by the line-division to "steady" the balancing movement of the gleaner is enacted' (*Revaluation* 1936, pp. 263-4). But any such 'enactment' will not be appreciable by the reader until the sentence is completed. (Before its completion who or what is kept steady must remain guesswork.) The reader will then have to go back to the previous line to realize that anything has been enacted. Why should he – unless a similar retrogression is demanded in every sentence ? In this instance cited by Leavis it seems very far-fetched to see the sequence from one line to another – from which no poem is exempt – as a specially notable balancing act.

persons listen persistently to the ticking of a watch, or gaze persistently on the monotonous flashing of a light, they fall into the hypnotic trance; and rhythm is but the ticking of a watch made softer, that one must needs listen, and various, that one may not be swept beyond memory or grow weary of listening.[1]

It is true that professional hypnotists often use the beat of a metronome at half-second intervals, or the ticking of a clock, as the physical stimulus of hypnosis. It is also true that in Swinburne's iambic metres, when the poems are read aloud with the appropriate sing-song, the stresses recur at exactly half-second intervals, and that in the anapæstic metres the stresses recur approximately every second. And there can be no doubt that Swinburne's exploitation of the hypnotic possibilities of verse induces in suitable readers a kind of trance, like that experienced by the Indian Yogi, 'in which the emotional sensitiveness of the subject grows more and more intense, sometimes reaching the pitch of ecstasy, as his consciousness is concentrated on some one phase of life'.[2] But the fact that verse in which a heavy beat is combined with extreme regularity in the recurrence of the stresses can induce a mild condition of hypnosis is not necessarily a justification of the device. Why is it desirable for the reader to be hypnotized? What is the poetic function of Swinburnian metrics?

   The 'symbols' in which, according to Yeats, the mind unfolds under the impact of hypnotic poetry, appear to be the counterpart of 'suggestion'. As the objective correlatives of subconscious forces they seem to provide obscure hints of the *libido*'s modes of operation. Hence their interest to the Romantic poet. But, unlike the symbolism of earlier Romantic poetry, that of Blake and Wordsworth, for example, the symbolism of hypnotic poetry is disappointingly elusive:

> Before the beginning of years
>    There came to the making of man
> Time with a gift of tears;
>    Grief with a glass that ran. . . .

As T. S. Eliot has pointed out: 'This is not merely "music"; it is effective because it appears to be a tremendous statement, like statements made in our dreams; when we wake up we find that the "glass that ran" would do better for time than for grief, and that the gift of tears would be as appro-

---

[1] *Essays* (1924), pp. 195-6. The quotation is from 'The Symbolism of Poetry', which was written in 1900.

[2] E. D. Snyder, *Hypnotic Poetry* (1920), p. 31. Snyder distinguishes between hypnotic poetry, semi-hypnotic poetry and intellectualistic poetry. Almost all his examples of the first two categories are drawn from the English and American Romantic poets.

priately bestowed by grief as by time'.[1] No doubt the Romantic reader was not supposed to 'wake up'. But even so Eliot's criticism is justified. For, unless the reader is sufficiently awake to respond to the specific associations of the separate words, it is difficult to see what he can derive from his reading of the poem except an emotional blur. The connotations of 'time' and 'grief' are not identical by any means, but the partial hypnosis blunts the reader's power of discriminating response.

The most that can be conceded to hypnotic poetry is that, when not carried to excess, the lulling of the critical faculty that it ensures assists the general suspension of disbelief and release of 'suggestion' that even the best Romantic poetry requires. The rather mechanical rhythms of many familiar nineteenth-century poems might be justified on these lines.

## IV

So much, then, for the Pure Sound Theory. Verbal music and melopœia are, it seems to me, examples of metrical mythology with little or no basis in metrical fact. Onomatopœia and hypnotic poetry, on the other hand, though they are not mere figments of the Romantic imagination, are of doubtful poetical utility. They can be best described as ingenious linguistic perversions. In any case they provide no evidence whatever that poetry is meaningless. In onomatopœia the sound is the echo of the sense, and without the sense there would be nothing for the sound to echo. And the only possible justification of hypnotic poetry is not that it excludes meaning but that it modifies it, suppressing denotation and encouraging connotation.

The cult of poetic unintelligibility is based upon a misunderstanding of the nature of language, which is not a system of sounds but a system of *conventional* sounds. It is the meaning that a society agrees to attach to a specific series of articulated sound-waves that matters, and the source in the throat or a part of the mouth to which any one or more meanings is conventionally attached is of little importance. 'Dog', 'Hund', 'chien' are very different sounds, though their meanings are virtually identical. Moreover sounds change – through spelling-pronunciation, class and regional influences, etc. – without the meanings necessarily being affected in any way, and the meaning of a word can be transformed without the sound being changed at all. With the exception of the small group of onomatopœic words ('murmur', 'tomtom', 'bomb', 'cuckoo', etc.) there is no umbilical cord which connects linguistic sound and meanings.

And if poetry is language at its maximum potency, 'the best words in

---

[1] *The Sacred Wood* (1920), p. 135. Empson has desperately suggested that Time has a water-clock and Grief a tear-bottle (*Seven Types of Ambiguity*, 1937 ed., p. 165).

the best order', the rôle of sound in it may be expected to be equally subordinate. Such devices as rhyme, metre and alliteration are the servants of meaning rather than of 'music'. Their uses can indeed be reduced to three general modes of semantic reinforcement or synthesis. (i) The main function of metre is simply to provide a recurrent pattern in the background of the poem, which will act as a continual reassurance to the reader.[1] 'Here is the cosmos of mind and not the chaos of phenomena.' (ii) In alliteration, assonance and rhyme the repetition of sounds provides a semantic pointer, emphasizing contrasts and underlining connections. Thus in Pope's line from the 'Epistle to Bathurst',

> Die and endow a college or a cat,

the *d*'s hint that there is a subtle identity in the dying and the endowing (the only interest that the world takes in this particular death is in the testamentary endowments), and the *c*'s point the similarity between founding colleges and financing cats' homes.[2] (iii) Vowel quantity and the accumulation or avoidance of consonants serve as a kind of punctuation, accelerating or slowing down the reading of the poem. As Daniel Webb pointed out, in Hamlet's

> And in this harsh world draw thy breath in pain

'The breast actually labours to get through this line.'[3] In fact, the ten monosyllables and the nineteen consonantal sounds (the average for the iambic pentameter is about fifteen) provide the equivalent of a stage direction. They show that Shakespeare wanted this crucial line spoken slowly. This device – which Pope confuses with onomatopœia in the familiar passage in the *Essay on Criticism* – has been used more effectively by Milton than by any other English poet.[4]

The all-importance of meaning in poetry and the comparative insignificance of sound *per se* can perhaps be demonstrated by a brief technical

---

[1] The individual 'rhythm' of a particular poet depends partly on his choices of metre but is mainly a matter of the degree to which the rhythms of colloquial speech are subordinated to the prosodic patterns.

[2] This line also illustrates the identity of formal function in alliteration and word order. The sequence *main verb + main verb/indefinite article object* 'or' *indefinite article object* offers a pattern of repetition similar to the O.E. alliterative metre.

[3] *Remarks on the Beauty of Poetry* (1762), p. 46. Webb was also before his time in realizing that alliteration always requires a semantic justification; 'it is a fault, to suffer any one letter to take possession of the ear, or to govern entirely the sound of the verse unless, where the alliteration is brought in aid of the sense: in which case, it may sometimes become a beauty' (p. 29).

[4] See Robert Bridges, *Milton's Prosody* (1901), pp. 41-3, for an analysis, on these lines, of *Samson Agonistes*, ll. 115-31.

analysis of the 'sublime epitaph' (the phrase is Coleridge's) which Wordsworth added, with three other poems about the mysterious Lucy, to the
second edition of the *Lyrical Ballads* (1800):

> A slumber did my spirit seal;
>   I had no human fears:
> She seemed a thing that could not feel
>   The touch of earthly years.
>
> No motion has she now, no force;
>   She neither hears nor sees;
> Rolled round in earth's diurnal course,
>   With rocks, and stones, and trees.

The structural basis of the poem is clearly the contrast between the two
verses. Verse one deals with the past (there are no less than four verbs in a
past tense – *did, had, seemed, could*). Lucy had been such a vital person that
the possibility of her growing old or dying had not crossed Wordsworth's
mind. Verse two concerns the present (in addition to the *now* in the first
line there are three main verbs in the present tense – *has, hears, sees*). Lucy
is dead. The invulnerable Ariel-like creature is now as lifeless and immo-
bile as stocks and stones. And the contrast is emphasized by the repetition
of *earth*: Lucy, who had seemed immune from the passage of *earthly years*,
must now submit to *earth's diurnal course*. So far from escaping the *touch* of
years she is now undergoing a daily contact with the earth. The use of the
solemn Latinism *diurnal*, the only three-syllable word in this mainly
monosyllabic poem, completes the contrast. But the final impression the
poem leaves is not of two contrasting moods, but of a single mood mount-
ing to a climax in the pantheistic magnificence of the last two lines. How
then is the surface conflict reconciled? The metre certainly makes its
contribution. The identity of the metrical pattern in the two verses –
which is paralleled by the virtual identity of the word-order (l.5 repeats
l.1, abstract noun + verb + pronoun + abstract noun, l.6 repeats l.2, and l.8
and l.4 both have nouns but no verb) – suggests an underlying identity of
mood. The gap between the two verses is also bridged by the negatives.
There are no less than six negatives in the first six lines. Indeed, as the first
line really means 'I was not mentally awake', all the sentences are essentially negative propositions, until we reach the tremendous positive of the
last two lines. Finally, the description of the living Lucy as a *thing* has
prepared the transition to the dead Lucy who is passively *rolled*. The
rhymes have no special significance, as far as I can see, but the alliterations
should not be overlooked. The initial *s*'s in l.1 do not seem to me of much
interest (it is much the weakest line in the poem), though they may be

intentional, but the *r*'s in ll. 7–8 are masterly. There are no less than three initial *r*'s and four internal *r*'s in the last twelve words,[1] and they provide a kind of cohesive cement to the lines. The implication is that the pantheistic universe is solidly *one*. The parallel lines in verse one are without alliteration, and its absence perhaps confirms the suggestion of fragility in the living Lucy (a *thing* who can only be described in negative terms).[2]

In the famous 'Preface' that Wordsworth prefixed to the edition of the *Lyrical Ballads* that included 'A slumber did my spirit seal' he justified metre as providing a kind of sedative to the excitements of poetry by 'the co-presence of something regular'. This is essentially the semantic theory of metre that is being advocated here. It is not denied, of course, that the disembodied 'tunes' of the prosodists – the Italian canzone, for example, or the trochaic tetrameter, whose respective fortunes W. P. Ker used to delight in tracing from Dante to Arnold and from Bede to Browning – have an objective existence. So has the paper on which treasury notes are printed. But you don't collect treasury notes because of their paper, and to isolate metre from its context of meaning is at least as wrong-headed.

The importance that the Romantics ascribed to rhythm was part of their general disparagement of the reason. As John Foster put it in the admirable essay 'On the Application of the Epithet Romantic' (1805), they thought they had discovered 'something sublimer than thinking'. And unfortunately, as the nineteenth century progressed, the part played by thinking in poetry diminished. A minor poet of the period, who was later to become a distinguished novelist, has described the situation in an illuminating passage:

For a great number of years I could not read 'poetry'. I wanted to; but I could not. I used to put that down to the fact that rhymes, accent, stresses, assonances, alliterations, vowel colourings, and the other devices of poets, embarrassed me as a reader. But this was not the case. The real fact is that – the dog it was that died. I have discovered this for myself from my own practice in verse. I found that as soon as I came to write a 'poem' I automatically reduced my intelligence to the level of one purely childish. And, looking one day through the Collected Edition of my

---

[1] The *r*'s in *earth's diurnal course* are not sounded in modern English. Wordsworth, however, certainly sounded them. Hazlitt had found 'a strong tincture of the northern *burr*' in his voice when they first met in 1798 (the year before 'A slumber did my spirit seal' was written). See Hazlitt's 'My First Acquaintance with Poets'.

[2] I have not attempted more than a technical analysis of the poem. A full critical discussion would need to go into the question of Lucy's identity. I have no doubt that Lucy is in some sense Dorothy Wordsworth. It is surely time the veil was withdrawn from the quasi-incestuous relationship between Wordsworth and his sister, which almost certainly lies behind this poem. Stones and trees, of course, had a special mystical virtue for Wordsworth (cf. *Prelude*, iii, 124–6, 161–2, in 1805 text), and in associating Dorothy with them he was satisfying the two central emotions of his life.

own poems that some misguided publisher issued some years ago I was appalled. It was not so much that the stuff was rhetorical. It was just silly – with the silliness of a child of a bad type. There is hardly a poet of to-day or yesterday who ever, in his matter, his ideas and his verbal texture, attempts to soar above the level of the intellect of scarcely adolescent pupils in young ladies' seminaries. Poets in fact, once they put on their laurel crown, divest themselves of every shred of humour, irony, incisive knowledge of life as it is lived.[1]

It cannot be said that the twentieth century has yet re-established the rule of reason in poetry. Even T. S. Eliot, the type almost of the cerebral critic, has not been able to resist an occasional fling at 'meaning' – 'The chief use of the "meaning" of a poem', he writes in *The Use of Poetry and the Use of Criticism*, 'may be to satisfy one habit of the reader, to keep his mind diverted and quiet, while the poem does its work upon him'.[2] Eliot does not explain how a poem can 'do its work' upon the reader without coming to have some sort of a meaning for him. If it is not absorbed through the consciousness, how is it absorbed? The *libido*, as we have seen, does not speak English. Nor can it read English. Probably all that Eliot meant was, as he puts it later in the same book, that a poem tends to have several 'levels of significance'.[3] While the reader is concentrating on the surface-meaning (the narrative element, or the 'moral') the other meanings are enriching and complicating his impressions of the primary meaning without his fully realizing what is occurring.

Eliot's own verse raises its own problems. At its best the attentive reader should not find a meaning impossible to unravel, but there are certainly a few passages from which the essential links and pointers seem to have been omitted. It is better, I think, to admit that these passages are among Eliot's failures than to accede to the logical contortions which his admirers sometimes adopt.

The conclusion to which this chapter has been leading may now be stated in unequivocal terms. It is simply that poetry *is* meaning. Poetry *qua* poetry must be completely intelligible. The contribution that each word, image or rhythm makes to the poem must be primarily explicable in rational terms. The difficulties of poetry are not due to an irrational element attracted to or imbedded in the meaning provided by the words, but to the concentration and complexity of the particular poetic statement. Poetry differs from prose and everyday speech mainly because it says so much more in the same number of words. But this is a difference of

---

[1] F. M. Hueffer (Ford), *Thus to Revisit* (1920), pp. 132-3. He adds that none of his volumes of verse sold more than 200 copies!

[2] p. 151.  [3] p. 153.

degree, not of kind. In analysing and paraphrasing a poem we are not transposing it into a wholly different medium.[1]

[1] To Eliot the fact that 'only a part of the meaning can be conveyed by paraphrase' is evidence that 'the poet is occupied with frontiers of consciousness beyond which words fail, though meanings still exist' ('The Music of Poetry', *On Poetry and Poets*, 1957, p. 30,). But *qua* poet he should surely not have to fumble for his words like the rest of us. An important point has in fact been missed. Only a part of a poem's meaning is conveyed in a translation, but words fail the translator for the simple reason that one language's vocabulary and syntax are not the same as another's. A paraphrase is limited *a priori* as it were by a poem being by definition a unique verbal construct: unless it has achieved *le mot juste* it is not a poem – and if another word can be substituted for its words, as in a paraphrase, it cannot be *le mot juste*. But semantic approximations, all-but-synonyms, are still possible and still useful. Even the most skilful poet often has great difficulty in deciding which word *is* in a particular passage *le mot juste*, as the most casual inspection of any variorum edition sufficiently demonstrates. A factor that Eliot tended to overlook is the reader's unawareness of the complicated 'speech habits' that years of linguistic communication tend to implant. In learning to swim we at first perform the necessary motions with hands and legs consciously and deliberately, and it is only as we become adept that the same motions become more and more automatic. It would be absurd to talk of a swimmer's 'frontiers of consciousness', and there seems to be no good reason either for introducing this sort of mystification to explain the apparently spontaneous composition or 'reception' of poetry. Our final unconsciousness of the linguistic process does not alter its essential character – as, alas, becomes painfully evident when we start to learn a foreign language. The point at which 'words fail' is the point at which the individual's linguistic habits turn out to be inadequate and have to be supplemented by taking thought, e.g. by coining new words or combinations of words.

# 2

# Poetic Meaning and the Poet's Audience

I

THE meaningless 'ecstasy' experienced by the Romantic reader of poetry was a corollary of the irrational 'inspiration' of the Romantic poet. The undefinable cause had produced an undefinable effect. And if the reader were rash enough to ask why certain words in a certain order caused him to experience 'ecstasy' or 'rapture', whereas other words in other orders didn't, or didn't to the same degree, a third undefinable was introduced. This was 'magic'. This word, with its synonyms and derivatives, comes up again and again in Romantic discussions of poetry. In Coleridge's famous description of the poet 'in ideal perfection' in *Biographia Literaria*[1] a 'magical power' is specifically ascribed to the poetic Imagination. And 'natural magic' was, of course, one of Matthew Arnold's principal critical counters. Moreover the two words Arnold uses to define the 'romantic element' in modern poetry in *On the Study of Celtic Literature*[2] are 'magic' and 'charm'. Tennyson's tribute to Keats – 'there is something magic and of the innermost soul of poetry in almost everything which he wrote'[3] – suggests that if he had attempted a formal definition of poetry it too would have been in terms of 'magic'. Indeed, in 'Merlin and the Gleam' – the poem intended as Tennyson's literary autobiography – he uses Merlin's magic as the basis of the allegory.

Though not definable 'magic' was exemplifiable. And from the instances and specimens – hardly ever more than two or three lines long – provided by the Romantic critics it is clear that 'magic' was a quality of poetic style rather than of poetic structure. According to Lascelles Abercrombie, 'magic' – or, as he prefers to call it, 'incantation' – is the basic element or *sine qua non* of *all* poetry. In *The Idea of Great Poetry*, a discussion of the long poem, Abercrombie begins by asking what the irreducible poetic minimum is:

> What is the first thing which we require of all poetry – not merely in order to be great, but to exist at all? I will call it, compendiously, 'incantation': the power of using words so as to produce in us a sort of enchantment; and by that I mean a power not merely to charm and delight, but to kindle our minds into unusual vitality, exquisitely aware both of things and of the connexions of things.[4]

[1] At the end of chap. xiv.    [2] Chap. vi.
[3] *Memoir by his Son* (1899 ed.), p. 127.    [4] *The Idea of Great Poetry* (1925), p. 18.

Here we seem to be on the threshold of a definition. In the final phrase the metaphors look for a moment as though they were condensing into a generalization. But it is as far as Abercrombie gets. Instead of defining 'incantation' he pats its back. We are told, for example, that the poet

must, out of the subtly adjusted sound and sense of words, contrive such a texture of intensities and complexities of meaning, of unsuspected filaments of fine allusion and suggestion, as will enable these gossamers to capture and convey into our minds just those fleeting, gleaming qualities of experience which elude the hold of everyday straightforward language.[1]

But to be told, as Abercrombie in effect tells us here, that 'incantation' is the quality that differentiates the language of poetry from the language of everyday use is not really very helpful. We want to know *how* the differentiation is effected. How is the sound adjusted to the sense? How do the allusions and suggestions operate?

Abercrombie, both as poet and critic, was one of the later Romantics. In the heyday of Romanticism the questions that he raised – even if he did not find answers for them – would have seemed impertinent and irrelevant. To the Victorian critics, with their implicit confidence in the inspiration of the subconscious mind, anything approaching *technical* criticism of poetry was abhorrent. Ideally, for them, a poem wrote itself – like 'Kubla Khan'. The conscious intervention of the poet was limited, according to Shelley, to the 'artificial connexion of the spaces between [the inspired passages] by the intertexture of conventional expressions'.[2] It is not surprising, therefore, to find E. S. Dallas, one of the most intelligent and sensitive of the mid-nineteenth-century critics, writing as follows:

Among the systematic writers of modern times, from Scaliger downwards, criticism is almost wholly devoted to questions of language. . . . They have studied figures of speech and varieties of metre, with little care for the weightier points of action, passion, manner, character, moral and intellectual aim. In simile and metaphor, in rhyme and rhythm, they have seen rules and measures, and they have reduced all the art of expression to a system as easy as grammar; but they have not sought to methodize the poet's dream, they have not cared in their analysis to grasp his higher thought.[3]

Dallas had not realized that a poet's higher thoughts are not detachable, like the roof of a house, and can only be grasped *through* the figures of

[1] *Ibid.*, p. 23.
[2] *A Defence of Poetry.* Shelley's MSS throw a curious light on this avowal. In *Epipsychidion*, for example, the original draft has many lines that are completely blank except for the rhymes. See C. D. Locock, *An Examination of the Shelley Manuscripts in the Bodleian Library* (1903), pp. 3–13.
[3] *The Gay Science* (1866), vol. i, pp. 26–7.

speech, etc., in which they are expressed. Hence, in spite of his intelligence, the obscurity into which his treatise has fallen. It is at two removes from reality – not about particular 'poems' but about what 'poetry' is *supposed* to be about. If during the last thirty years or so there has been a partial return, if not to Scaliger, at least to that detailed discussion of particular poems and passages that is to be found in the best Neo-Classic critics, it is because we now know too much about the subconscious mind to accept the Divine Right that the Romantics accorded to it. The subconscious mind *can* do wrong, in poetry as in life. Its magic may be black magic. And it is surely of the first importance to the reader of poetry, as to the critic of poetry, to know the answer – however general and tentative its formulation may have to be – to the question Lascelles Abercrombie raised. What is the quality that poetry must have 'not merely in order to be great, but to exist at all'? What is it that creates the dividing line betwen poetry and verse, between the poet and the poetaster?

If the argument of the preceding chapter was valid, our answer must be capable of statement in terms of meaning and not of sound. As a first step towards the definition of poetic meaning it will be worth while taking a good look at the six examples Abercrombie provides of 'incantation' in *The Idea of Great Poetry*. Here are six short passages that a competent critic has guaranteed to be poetry. Is there a single principle common to all of them? If so, what is it?

Abercrombie's first example is from 'The Knight's Tale'. It is a line (italicized in the following quotation) from the account of Arcite's funeral pyre. Chaucer is employing the rhetorical figure *occupatio* (a refusal to describe or narrate) and has just said that he will not go into details about the trees that were felled for the pyre:

> Ne how the goddes ronnen up and doun,
> Disherited of hire habitacioun,
> In whiche they woneden in reste and pees,
> Nymphes, fawnes, and amadrides;
> Ne how the beestes and the briddes alle
> Fledden for fere, whan the wode was falle;
> *Ne how the ground agast was of the light,*
> That was nat wont to seen the sonne bright.[1]

It is clear, I think, that the 'incantation' in the italicized line derives from the metaphor *agast* (terrified). The ground, no longer shaded by the trees, is exposed to the full glare of the sun, and Chaucer makes us see it recoiling in terror, like a denizen of the night in the rays of a lantern. The grotesque

[1] ll. 2925-32.

image is accepted by the reader because it is the natural climax to a catalogue of man's disturbances of nature. This was a living world into which Theseus's woodmen had penetrated. The ground is unobtrusively assimilated with the exiled dryads and the frightened birds and beasts. The effectiveness of *ground agast* (note the connective alliteration) is surely due to the delighted surprise with which the reader accepts this reconciliation of apparently unconnected units of meaning. Nothing could *seem* more unemotional than the land-surface in a forest. The gap that the metaphor had to bridge was a wide one; its memorability derives from the fact that it has succeeded in a peculiarly difficult act of synthesis.

Abercrombie's second example of 'incantation' was the first stanza of Herrick's 'Upon Julia's Clothes':

> Whenas in silks my Julia goes,
> Then, then (me thinks) how sweetly flowes
> That liquefaction of her clothes.

Although Abercrombie does not say so, it is fairly clear, I think, that the poetic magic is concentrated here in the word *liquefaction*. And the source of the word's effectiveness in this context is not really very obscure. Like *vibration* (a term from physics), which performs a similar function in the second stanza of the poem, *liquefaction* was a technical term in Renaissance science. It is essentially a 'learned' word, and the contrast between its polysyllabic latinity and the Anglo-Saxon monosyllables and disyllables of the rest of the passage, by concentrating the reader's attention on it (he is brought up sharp and compelled to linger over the word), brings into special prominence the metaphor already introduced in *flowes*. We are compelled to visualize the silks, and when we do so they become, as it were, a semi-transparent liquid in which Julia, a naked water-nymph, is floating. The sensuous paganism, always latent in Herrick, makes its impact *through* the verbal wit. Parallel to the integration of a scientific term in a context of love-compliment is the integration of primitive instincts within the framework of a seventeenth-century social occasion (a dance perhaps, or a stroll in one of the public 'gardens').

Abercrombie's remaining examples – one from *Julius Cæsar* (Casca's lion 'Who glazed upon me and went surly by'), one from Keats's *Hyperion*, and two from Giles Fletcher – are of a similar character. He did not give examples of 'disenchanted' verse to oppose to the specimens of 'incantation', but other Romantic critics have done this. The Abbé Bremond, who achieved a short-lived notoriety in the 1920s and 1930s by identifying poetry with prayer, made a great deal of play in his argument for pure poetry with the difference between the first line of *Endymion* in its original (though perhaps legendary) form,[1]

> A thing of beauty is a constant joy,

and the revision,

> A thing of beauty is a joy for ever.

The latter, according to the Abbé, has 'magie,' the former has not, though the two lines are notionally indistinguishable. It is clear, however, that the words *constant* and *for ever* are not strictly synonymous. *Constant* is a rather drab latinism, meaning here not much more than *continuous*, whereas the two words *for ever* are highly charged with emotional associations from romance ('for ever and a day') and the services of the Church ('for ever and ever, Amen'), and mean *always*. Keats is saying two different things in the two versions. The second version is better because it is bolder, and effects a syntheis across a wider semantic gap – on the one hand, *joy* (short-lived, laughing, pagan), on the other, *for ever* (eternal, solemn, Christian).[2]

In the preceding examples 'magic' has proved, under analysis, to be

---

[1] There is no authority in the MSS of *Endymion* for 'constant joy'. The phrase derives from Henry Stephens, a fellow medical-student and a close friend of Keats's. According to Sir B. W. Richardson (*The Asclepiad* (April 1884), pp. 148-9), Stephens as an old man used to recount the following anecdote about Keats; 'In a room, Mr. Stephens told me, he was always at the window peering into space, so that the window-seat was spoken of by his comrades as 'Keats's place'. Here his inspiration seemed to come most freely. Here, one evening in the twilight, the two students sitting together, Stephens at his medical studies, Keats at his dreaming, Keats broke out to Stephens that he had composed a new line;

> '"A thing of beauty is a constant joy."

'"What think you of that, Stephens?"

'"It has the true ring, but is wanting in some way," replies the latter, as he dips once more into his medical studies.

'An interval of silence, and again the poet;

> '"A thing of beauty is a joy for ever."

'"What think you of that, Stephens?"

'"That it will last for ever."''

Richardson only knew Stephens from 1856 to 1864 (when Stephens died), and so an interval of some forty years must separate the actual occurrence of the episode, if it did occur, from its relation to Richardson. And Richardson did not *record* the anecdote until twenty years after Stephens's death.

[2] Two well-known passages by Pope and Tennyson also exploit the associative values of *for ever*:

> The meeting Points the sacred Hair dissever
> From the fair Head, for ever and for ever!
> *Rape of the Lock*, iii, 153-4.

> But not by thee my steps shall be,
> For ever and for ever.
> *A Farewell.*

nothing more mysterious than the successful collocation of contrasted or conflicting 'meanings'. The process is essentially, I suggest, one of *semantic synthesis*. Two or more detached units of human experience have been symbolized in language in such a way that the final impression left on reading the poem is of a wider unity which has included and absorbed the separate items.

What is essentially the same point, though more vividly phrased, was made by T. S. Eliot in his essay on 'The Metaphysical Poets':

When a poet's mind is perfectly equipped for its work, it is constantly amalgamating disparate experience; the ordinary man's experience is chaotic, irregular, fragmentary. The latter falls in love, or reads Spinoza, and these two experiences have nothing to do with each other, or with the noise of the typewriter or the smell of cooking; in the mind of the poet these experiences are always forming new wholes.[1]

The notion is, indeed, one of the commonplaces of criticism. Its history seems to begin with Aristotle's discussion of metaphor in the *Poetics*[2] – 'a good metaphor', in Bywater's translation, 'implies an intuitive perception of the similarity in dissimilars'. It reappears in Hobbes's definition of 'fancy' in *Leviathan*,[3] from which Dryden derived his theory of 'imagination' or 'wit'. And Dr Johnson's *discordia concors* is only a variant of the same doctrine. Its most elaborate statement, however, is the passage on the Imagination in Coleridge's *Biographia Literaria* that has already been referred to because of the use there of the word 'magical'. Familiar though it is the passage is perhaps worth quoting in its entirety:

The poet, described in ideal perfection, brings the whole soul of man into activity, with the subordination of its faculties to each other according to their relative worth and dignity. He diffuses a tone and spirit of unity, that blends, and (as it were) *fuses*, each into each, by that synthetic and magical power, to which I would exclusively appropriate the name of Imagination. This power, first put in action by the will and understanding, and retained under their irremissive, though gentle and unnoticed, control, *laxis effertur habenis*, reveals itself in the balance or reconcilement of opposite or discordant qualities: of sameness, with difference; the individual with the representative; the sense of novelty and freshness with old and familiar objects; a more than usual state of emotion with more than usual order; judgment ever awake and steady self-possession with enthusiasm and feeling profound or vehement; and while it blends and harmonizes the natural and the artificial, still subordinates art to nature; the manner to the matter; and our admiration of the poet to our sympathy with the poetry.[4]

In the phrase 'the balance or reconcilement of opposite or discordant

---

[1] *Homage to John Dryden* (1924), p. 30.          [2] Chap. xxii.
[3] Chap. viii.          [4] Chap. xiv.

qualities' Coleridge made a crucial addition to the earlier definitions. By distinguishing between 'balance' and 'reconcilement' on the one hand and 'opposite' and 'discordant' on the other, Coleridge pointed the way to a differentiation of degrees of synthesis. The more 'balance' approximated to 'reconcilement', i.e. the more the separate units of meaning are fused together, the more *complete* the synthesis would be; the nearer the 'discordant' units of meaning came to being 'opposite' the more *valuable* the synthesis would be. The second criterion might be called the Principle of the Semantic Gap. Although Coleridge was, I believe, the first to relate it to the theory of poetic synthesis, the principle itself was an old one. John Hoskins, a sixteenth-century poet and critic, had formulated it as follows: 'you shall most of all profit by inventing matter of agreement in things most unlike, as London and a tennis court: for *in both all the gain goes to the hazard*'.[1] In other words, the more heterogeneous and unassimilable the two 'meanings' appeared on the surface to be, the greater the poetic triumph if a synthesis could be achieved. And Hoskins's example provides an exact parallel to the specimens of 'incantation' already analysed. It was because of the gap in meaning between the soil in Theseus's forest and the human emotion of fear that Chaucer's *ground agast* was so triumphantly 'incantatory'. And a similar gap explained the effectiveness of Herrick's *liquefaction* and Keats's *for ever*.

It follows from the two criteria of 'reconcilement' and 'opposition' that the Principle of the Semantic Gap can be transgressed in two ways. On the one hand, the gap can be too wide to be easily synthesizable. According to Dr Johnson this was what was wrong with the Metaphysical Poets; and it is a criticism that has been made in our own time of Jules Laforgue,[2] and of Laforgue's poetic disciples in English – especially Ezra Pound and T. S. Eliot.[3]

On the other hand, the gap may be too narrow. The reconcilement in this case will not be difficult enough, because the qualities are insufficiently discordant, the 'meanings' too much *in pari materia*. Poetry that one tends to dismiss as merely graceful, pretty or pleasant – that of the minor Victorians, for example, or such Georgians as W. H. Davies or John Freeman – will generally be found to suffer from a narrowness of the semantic gap. As T. S. Eliot has put it in a comparison between some lines in Cowley's *Davideis* and Dryden's parody of them in *Macflecknoe*: 'The passage from Cowley is by no means despicable verse. But it is a commonplace description of commonly poetic objects; it has not the element of *surprise* so

---

[1] *Directions for Speech and Style*, ed. H. H. Hudson (1935), p. 18.
[2] See G. M. Turnell, *Scrutiny* (Sept. 1936).
[3] See John Sparrow, *Sense and Poetry* (1934).

essential to poetry, and this Dryden provides.'[1] The evocation of surprise in the reader is not, of course, the only symptom of a successful observation of the Principle of the Semantic Gap. Its engenderment, indeed, tends to show that the gap has only just been bridged. The surprise is the product of a feeling of relief that all is still well, the chain of meaning unbroken. In the masters of Semantic Synthesis – Chaucer, Shakespeare or Keats, for example – exaltation rather than surprise is the predominant accompaniment. In Acts IV and V of *Antony and Cleopatra* – the highwater mark perhaps of English poetry – the unpredictable connections are made with such assurance and such success that the grain of scepticism implicit in 'surprise' is no longer warranted.

## II

The reduction of Verbal Magic to Semantic Synthesis carries with it a further implication. If poetry is only a form of synthesis, there can be no difference of kind between the poet and the non-poet. Synthesis, with its opposite analysis, is after all a normal function of thought. At almost every moment of our lives we are either abstracting from the *data* of experience (analysis) or building up our abstractions into a new unity (synthesis). Unless the syntheses of the poets can be shown to have no more than a formal resemblance to the syntheses of everyday experience, another critical tenet of the Romantics will be imperilled. This is the theory of the Genius: *poeta nascitur, non fit*. A fundamental assumption of Romanticism was that poets, the inspired agents of the divinity within us, were not as other men. The undefinability of poetry was the complement of the poets' essential superiority to other human beings. 'Magic' implied the magician.

But, like 'pure poetry' and 'incantation', the theory of the Genius will not stand up to close examination. Recent attempts to rehabilitate it have been on the lines of attributing a 'reality' to the visions of the poet that the abstractions of the scientists and philosophers do not possess. C. S. Lewis has summarized the argument with his usual clarity:

The difference between scientific or philosophical language and poetical language is emphatically not that the first utters truths and the second fancies. On the contrary everything that is concrete is real, and some suspect that everything real is concrete. The abstractions used by science and philosophy may or may not be the names of universals which are timeless realities as Plato thought; but they are not the names of 'real things' in the popular sense – things that occur in space and time. In space and time there is no such thing as an organism, there are only animals and vegetables. There are no mere vegetables, only trees, flowers, turnips, etc. There are

[1] *Homage to John Dryden* (1924), p. 16.

no 'trees', except beeches, elms, oaks, and the rest. There is even no such thing as 'an elm'. There is only *this* elm, in such a year of its age at such an hour of the day, thus lighted, thus moving, thus acted on by all the past and all the present, and affording such and such experiences to me and my dog and the insect on its trunk and the man a thousand miles away who is remembering it. A real elm, in fact, can be uttered only by a poem.[1]

A somewhat similar point of view has also been elaborated by T. C. Pollock who distinguishes three uses of language: (i) Phatic Communion ('How do you do?' and similar almost meaningless social gestures), (ii) Referential Symbolism (the abstract language of science), (iii) Evocative Symbolism (the communication of private experience in its concrete actuality).[2] The danger of such distinctions is that they attribute to poetry 'something sublimer than thinking' – in this case a mystical *photographic* capacity to reproduce phenomena in their original complexity. No linguistic medium can possibly do this. Lewis's elm may be a less general term than tree, vegetable or organism, but it is just as much an abstraction. His hypothetical poet is not only restricted to abstractions by the nature of his medium (basically all words are abstract), but the experience he is communicating, the isolation of this particular elm from the flux of his sense impressions, is itself an abstraction. It is only indeed by a process of abstraction that the poet can give meaning, a scale of social values, to the chaos of individual experience.

The syntheses of poetry, then, are essentially the same as the syntheses of our everyday intellectual life. The difference between the poem and ordinary conversation is due (i) to the rarity in poetry of the complementary process of analysis, and (ii) to their different social functions. The first of these characteristic *differentiae* determines the *form* of poetry, the second explains its *content*.

The spoken language is the vehicle of the two-way intellectual traffic (analysis and synthesis) of practical social life. Although both analysis and synthesis have tended to develop a special vocabulary (the language of science and 'poetic diction'), most of the words and virtually all the word combinations that they use derive from colloquial speech. The special linguistic problem of their practitioners, therefore, has been to protect themselves and their readers from the incursion of the opposite faculty, from synthetic implications in works of pure analysis and analytic implications in works of pure synthesis.

The danger to poetry has come primarily from grammar. Grammar is a codification of the analytical (logical) forces in the spoken language.

[1] C. S. Lewis and E. M. W. Tillyard, *The Personal Heresy* (1939), pp. 109-10.
[2] *The Nature of Literature* (Princeton, 1942).

Instead of the synthetic unity of the poetic statement grammar tends to prefer a step-by-step syllogistic process. In the sentence 'The cat is eating the mouse' the grammarian distinguishes three separable semantic elements (i) cat, (ii) eating, (iii) mouse, whereas for the poet, there is a single complex image of cat-eating-mouse. Many of the formal devices of poetry seem to derive from the necessity for a defensive strategy against grammar. Inversion in poetry is usually simply an anti-grammatical gesture. ('You have been warned that this is not prose or the language of conversation.') It is therefore particularly frequent at the beginning of poems, as in these opening lines of a sonnet by Drummond of Hawthornden:

> With flaming horns the Bull now brings the year;
> Melt do the horrid mountains' helms of snow;
> The silver floods in pearly channels flow;
> The late-bare woods green anademes do wear.

The word order in the second line might have been expected to be:

> The horrid mountains melt their helms of snow.

Grammatically this is better, because the sentence structure will now be parallel in the four lines, but it is certainly no improvement poetically.

The positive function of the various formal devices of poetry – metre, alliteration, metaphor, verbal repetition, etc. – is to ensure that the poem achieves a unity of impression. They are all fundamentally 'esemplastic', to use Coleridge's word. The continuous verbal links, interconnections and references back (i) prevent the reader from relegating to his memory the beginning of the poem before he has reached its end, and (ii) are continual reminders that each sentence in the poem must be read against a background of awareness of the whole poem in all its semantic complexity. Without realizing what is happening we find ourselves forced, in fact, to retain the whole poem in our consciousness all through the process of reading it.

The sense in which poetry is opposed to science should be clear in the light of the preceding discussion. One way of putting the difference between the step-by-step processes of analysis and the comprehensive unity of synthesis would be to say that science collaborates with time whereas poetry is a continuous struggle to abrogate time. In the sentence 'Tom hits John' the grammatical order of the words is the same as the temporal sequence of events. First of all one has the mental picture of Tom, as it were, in repose. This is followed by a picture of Tom striking the blow (the fist, as it were, in mid-air). Finally, a fraction of a second later, the blow impinges on John. To the poet, on the other hand, the whole episode is a single event, involving Tom, John and the delivery and reception of the blow *simultaneously*. Poetically it makes no difference if the word order is 'Tom hit John' or '(it was) John Tom hit,' or 'John (was) hit (by) Tom,' though grammatically these distinctions can be all-important.

This *simultaneity* of poetry may explain the relative unimportance of stanza order in many poems. Wotton's 'You meaner beauties of the night' is a poem which survives in a number of different printed and MS texts.[1] In the version printed in most anthologies the second verse is the one beginning

> You curious chanters of the wood.

There is, however, equally good authority for making this the third verse and printing as the second verse the one beginning

> You violets that first appear.

As poetry one version is as good as the other. Both verses are needed in the poem, but the order in which they appear doesn't really matter.[2]

The same point could perhaps be made in connection with Landor's 'Rose Aylmer'. Does it really make any appreciable difference to the poem as poetry if the order of the two verses is reversed, and we read:

> Rose Aylmer, whom these wakeful eyes
>     May weep, but never see,
> A night of memories and of sighs
>     I consecrate to thee.
>
> Ah what avails the sceptred race,
>     Ah what the form divine!
> What every virtue, every grace!
>     Rose Aylmer, all were thine.[3]

Shelley seems to have been feeling his way to some such conclusion in *A Defence of Poetry*:

[1] See J. B. Leishman, *The Library* (Sept., Dec. 1945), pp. 99-121.

[2] In Nashe's poem suggested by the 1593 plague, which includes the famous stanza beginning 'Beauty is but a flower', the verses, according to F. P. Wilson (*Elizabethan and Jacobean* (1945), p. 57), 'are linked together not by argument but by mood and theme, so that the six stanzas might be rearranged without destroying the poem'.

[3] Another two-stanza poem in which the order of the stanzas can be reversed without any essential loss is Congreve's 'Song', beginning
> False though she be to me and Love.
No doubt there are other examples.

A poet participates in the eternal, the infinite, and the one; as far as relates to his conceptions, time and place and number are not. The grammatical forms which express the moods of time, and the difference of persons, and the distinction of place, are convertible with respect to the highest poetry without injuring it as poetry; and the choruses of Aeschylus, and the Book of Job, and Dante's Paradise, would afford, more than any other writings, examples of this fact, if the limits of this essay did not forbid citation.

Some of the incidental implications of these conclusions will be explored later in this book in the discussion of individual poems. In the meantime it will be desirable to say something about the opposition between poetry and prose. The distinction between the poetic statement and the prose of science is clear, but what about poetry and the novel or the drama in prose? These are obviously in some sense synthetic *genres*, but their individual sentences are generally indistinguishable formally from the prose of science and philosophy.

Two differences between poetry and fiction or the drama have often been remarked upon. One is that poetry is virtually untranslatable. The only poems that can be successfully translated into the poetry of another language are those with a large 'story' element. Most poems, satires and philosophical poems as well as lyrics, when translated into the poetry of another language, become not only bad poems but to all intents and purposes new poems. On the other hand, most novels and plays can be translated with little or no loss. The second difference is that poetry is very much easier to memorize than prose. This is as true of blank verse, and even of so-called 'prose poetry' – Whitman's *Leaves of Grass*, for example – as of rhyming or metrical verse. Poetry seems to *want* to be remembered, whereas prose as such *wants* to be forgotten.

The two differences are perhaps different sides of the same thing. It is what is untranslatable in poetry that sticks in the memory. And, on the other hand, the quality that makes prose easy to translate is exactly what makes it easy to forget.

Poetry has, indeed, been defined as 'memorable words'. But this is to put the emphasis in the wrong place. Memorability cannot be made the criterion of poetic merit. If the best poem was the most memorable poem a jingle like Peacock's 'The War-song of Dinas Vawr' or Poe's 'Bells' would be preferred to Keats's odes or Milton's sonnets. The primary function of the various poetic devices and figures of speech is not mnemonic, though their secondary effects often are. What the poet *qua* poet is trying to do is to 'synthesize', i.e. to say several things at the same time. The things, though apparently disconnected and even contradictory, are really related, and it is their interrelationship that is the point of the poem.

The poet's problem is to get the reader to think of several separate things all at once, and not one by one, in a temporal and logical sequence. The mnemonic devices make this possible, *positively*, by linking the different stanzas, sentences and words together in a variety of ways, so that in Stanza III the reader is continually being called back to Stanzas I and II, and *negatively*, by reminding the reader from time to time that this is *not* prose and that he must hold in abeyance for the moment the thought processes that prose has encouraged him to apply to written words. Memorability, therefore, is only a by-product of poetry. All the poet requires is the reader's retention of the poem in his consciousness during the process of reading. Once that is completed the ability to repeat the poem parrotwise has no special point. Indeed it might be argued that exceptional facility in quotation, the Macaulay kind of memory, is a symptom of mental indigestion. The mind when functioning properly absorbs experience selectively, rejecting from the total impression left by a poem whatever is not relevant to its own requirements. The healthy response to the mental experience provided by the conscientious reading of a good poem is not to be word-perfect in it but to make it something of one's own. This incorporation of the poem into one's own consciousness is to 'criticize' it. By 'criticize' I do not, of course, mean 'find fault', nor do I wish necessarily to suggest a formal stocktaking in the manner of Dr Johnson. The right reaction to a poem will often be a single phrase, like Arthur Symons's description of Clare's songs of childish humour, 'made out of bright laughing sound',[1] or Tennyson's admirable comment on Shelley's 'Life of Life' – 'He seems to go up into the air and burst'.[2]

The reason why poetry is so difficult to translate will now be clearer. The translator has to find the equivalents in another language not only of the words of the poem, with their special associations (which may derive from a connection of *sound* with other words), but also of the incidental alliterations, the more important verbal and grammatical repetitions, and the deliberate deviations from a prose vocabulary or sentence structure. Prose, on the other hand, is fairly easy to translate because it is 'analytic'. The separate statements are detached and complete in themselves. There are no complicated interrelationships between one sentence and another, and it is not in the least necessary to help the reader to retain the whole of a chapter in his consciousness while he is reading it. Prose is difficult to memorize because there is no point in doing it. Once an episode is

---

[1] *Poems by John Clare* ( 1908), p. 24.
[2] This raises the whole question of the teaching of English poetry. At present most examinations in English literature, including the Final Schools at the Universities, are essentially an invitation to the candidates to quote, quote, quote.

completed all that it is necessary to retain in the memory is a skeletal sum-mary of it. The actual words in which the episode has been described have fulfilled their function when the reader has translated them into 'ideas'. All that need be remembered is the synthetic element in the novel or play, and that is generally embodied in the plot and characterization rather than in the individual words and sentences.

Poetry, therefore, is always 'the best words in the best order'; prose, on the other hand, though it begins in words, loses its verbal envelope in the process of reading, until it impinges on the consciousness simply as a mental picture. In a good novel or a good play the actual words should be absorbed by the reader or spectator almost without being noticed. In a poem, on the other hand, the words must be in the forefront of the reader's consciousness all the time. There are, therefore, two different arts of reading and the difficulty of combining them when reading aloud or reciting is what may make Shakespeare's best plays so 'thin' on the stage. In the study it is possible to pass from Hamlet the 'character' to Hamlet the speaker of poetry, and back again, in the course of a single line. But only the greatest of actors can achieve a similar agility. The broadcasting of an epic or narrative poem raises the same problem. Almost inevitably either the prose elements or the poetry will be overemphasized.

A rough-and-ready definition of the novel (or play) might be analytic form plus synthetic content. A poem, on the other hand, is synthetic in both form and content (which tend to be more closely identified in poetry than in fiction). The invention of printing has helped to differentiate the two *genres*. During the Middle Ages the memorability of verse was an economic asset. Owing to the rarity of manuscripts and readers a story that was not in verse was at a competitive disadvantage and could only achieve a limited circulation. Hence the multiplication of romances, alliterative and tail-rhymed, in which the verse has a mnemonic function only. Poetry benefited by the invention of printing, because the diffuse-ness that the prospect of recitation imposed was no longer a necessary evil. The listener only hears a line once – unless the metrical scheme requires its repetition, as it tended to do in such medieval forms as the rondeau, the rondel and the triolet – and, if he is to carry it in his mind until the end of the poem (as he must, on our definition of poetry, if the poem is to succeed), the line must not be too tightly packed with meaning. With the printed poem the reader can stop and look back at an earlier line if he has a momentary difficulty in remembering it. This permits a greater concentra-tion of meaning and the opportunity for subtler verbal effects (such as the elaborate rhetorical figures so dear to the Renaissance). The decreasing diffuseness of sixteenth-century poetry can be attributed very largely to the growth of a *reading* public, which had only been made possible by Caxton and his successors. The long-term trends have also been in the same direction. With negligible exceptions novels and plays are no longer written in verse, and the long poem is becoming rarer, the epic being apparently extinct. The complexity of modern poetry may not be entirely attributable to the fact that it is rarely read aloud, but it is certainly one of the relevant factors.

### III

A fourth undefinable factor in Romantic poetic theory was *taste*. *De gustibus non disputandum erat*. To the Romantics, with their predilections for 'ecstasy' and 'magic', poetic preferences were necessarily reduced to a matter of private or personal taste. There was thus no theoretic basis for any critical standards at all. On one man the 'magic' worked; on another it didn't. But the only way to decide if it was the man who was at fault or the 'magic' was to count heads – a procedure that can be applied fairly easily to the poetry of the past but that it is impossible to apply to poetry that has just been written. Homer's 'magic' was guaranteed by the fact of the *Iliad*'s and the *Odyssey*'s survival. But what about Blake's or Clare's? Palgrave and Tennyson (who assisted him in the selection of the poems) played for safety by leaving them both out of *The Golden Treasury*.[1]

At no period in the history of literature has the poet, as distinguished from the poetaster, had a harder struggle to achieve recognition than in the nineteenth century. There will be no need to recite more than one or two of the familiar facts. Thus in spite of the reviews and counter-reviews Keats's poems made no impression whatever, as poems, on the contemporary reading public. When Rossetti 'discovered' Keats in 1845 he supposed he had found an unknown writer. So did Holman Hunt, who found a copy of the 1820 *Poems* in a book-bin labelled 'This lot 4d' about the same time.[2] Even Tennyson, the poetic bestseller, 'was so far persuaded that the English people would never care for his poetry, that, had it not been for the intervention of his friends, he declared it not unlikely that after the death of Hallam he would not have continued to write'.[3]

But in the poetical slump versifying boomed. Scott's and Byron's narrative poems sold like hot cakes. Tom Moore was paid £3,000 for the

---

[1] The 1890 edition – in which Palgrave again acknowledges 'the advice of that distinguished Friend, by whom the final choice has been so largely guided' – adds Blake, Campion, Darley, the Earl of Essex, Lyte, Henry Norris, Quarles and Smart, but not *inter alios* Skelton, Donne, King, Crashaw, Rochester, Beddoes or Clare.

[2] See G. H. Ford, *Keats and the Victorians* (1944), p. 94.

[3] *Memoir by his Son* (1899), p. 83.

milk and water of *Lalla Rookh*. And Tennyson's sales were equalled or excelled by Martin Tupper's *Proverbial Philosophy*, Sir Lewis Morris's *The Epic of Hades*, and Sir Edwin Arnold's *The Light of Asia*. At no other time has the bad poet 'got away with it' so successfully. Essentially, as we can see now, the Victorian poetasters wrote prose disguised as poetry. In terms of meaning their mode of progression is additive rather than synthetic. The verse form is an irrelevant trimming to the narrative or ethical content. But their success, which was by no means confined to the 'Mudie' public, was the inevitable consequence of Romantic poetic theory. Without objective critical standards it had become as difficult to reject the fake poem as to acclaim the original poem. In their absence, by an aesthetic Gresham's Law, the bad poetic money drove out the good.

A standard of poetic taste can only be maintained in a society where the poet and his audience are in direct and intimate contact with each other. The Principle of Semantic Synthesis works both ways. It assumes a reader prepared to respond to the poet's stimulus as well as a poet with the wish to stimulate. And the units of meaning that are to be synthesized must not only be intelligible to the reader but must assume in the process of reading the same order of importance that they have to the poet. Finally, the width of the semantic gap must be implicitly agreed between them as well as the methods necessary for its bridging. It might almost be said that the reader must be the poet's *alter ego*. He must be sufficiently like the poet to think, feel and see as he does, and yet sufficiently unlike him for the act of communication involved in the writing of the poem to be worth while.

The fulfilment of these conditions was made difficult and often impossible during the nineteenth century by the increasing individualism of the period. In its final Paterian form Romanticism shivers on the brink of solipsism. Unless the world is your creation, what *right* have you to burn in it with a hard gemlike flame? But the trend is there from the first. It is no doubt a literary counterpart of the political liberalism and *laissez-faire* capitalism of the nineteenth century. The Romantic poet was not the spokesman of the social group so much as its martyr (Shelley), its exile (Blake), its victim (Coleridge), or its prisoner (Tennyson). Wordsworth is sometimes cited as the exception. But, with all his social consciousness, Wordsworth's sense of social reality was erratic in the extreme. He was fond of distinguishing between the 'public' and the 'people', the 'public' being the middle classes, Arnold's Philistines, who wouldn't buy his poems, whereas the 'people' were the peasantry, among whom, as he told Wrangham, he hoped his poems would circulate in chap-book form.[1] In fact 'We are Seven' was the only one to achieve this distinction, and

[1] Letter of 5 June 1808.

Canon Rawnsley found that his humbler Westmorland neighbours had never read Wordsworth at all. 'Well you see, blessed barn, there's pomes and pomes, and Wudsworth's was not for such as us.'[1] In the end it was the 'public' from whom the Wordsworthians were recruited, but the initial isolation was as complete in his case as in that of the other Romantic poets.

Poetry, in any of its normal manifestations, involves four factors: (i) the poet, (ii) his readers or auditors, (iii) a common language, and (iv) a literary tradition shared by the poet and his readers. Remove any one of the four factors and poetry ceases to be possible. Upset the balance between them and poetry, though possible, becomes more difficult to achieve. The Romantics, in their theories at any rate, consistently over-looked these elementary considerations. Obsessed by individualism they concentrated their attention either on the poet alone (Coleridge and Shelley) or on the reader alone (Pater and Symons), although it is in the poet-reader *relationship* that the essence of poetry lies. To Coleridge, for example, 'What is poetry? – is so nearly the same question with, what is a poet? – that the answer to the one is involved in the solution of the other. For it is a distinction resulting from the poetic genius itself which sustains and modifies the images, thoughts, and emotions of the poet's own mind.'[2] This means that if you can define what goes on in the poet's mind, you will have defined poetry. Coleridge then proceeds to give his definition of the poet 'in ideal perfection', which has already been quoted. In this definition Coleridge only once refers to the reader's share in poetry. (I presume the *we* implied in 'our admiration of the poet' and 'our sympathy with the poetry' is the poet's readers, though it is not clear why a reader would find the two things necessarily opposite or discordant.) But without some much fuller indication of the reader's rights and responsibilities a definition of poetry is obviously seriously incomplete. It is the reader who must fuse *his* separate faculties and reconcile the qualities that *he* would normally find discordant. Without the reader's cooperation the poem might just as well not exist. A comprehensive definition of the poet's function *must* include a summary of the processes by which he secures that cooperation. The first thing the poet must know is whom he is writing for. Until he has located his audience the question of the modes and *media* of communication cannot arise. But did Coleridge know whom he was writing for? Would any of the Romantics have been able to identify that ghostly 'gentle reader' they are so fond of addressing?

---

[1] *Trans. Wordsworth Soc.* (1884), vi. Rawnsley was quoting the ex-garden boy at Rydal Mount. The ex-page's verdict was even more devastating: 'There's no doubt but what he was fond of quality, and quality was very fond o' him.'

[2] *Biographia Literaria*, chap. xiv.

Take the case of Keats, the greatest potentially of the Romantic poets. At one period he was writing apparently for the mere sake of writing. 'I feel assured', he wrote to Woodhouse in October 1818, 'I should write from the mere yearning and fondness I have for the beautiful even if my night's labours should be burnt every morning, and no eye ever shine upon them.' And Lord Houghton's account of Keats's habits in 1819 confirms this. 'Shorter poems were scrawled, as they happened to suggest themselves, on the first scrap of paper at hand, which was afterwards used as a mark for a book, or thrown anywhere aside.'[1] We may say that these poems were written for *nobody*. At an earlier stage Keats had been writing primarily for Leigh Hunt and the Hampstead coterie, but by 1819 he had become ashamed of this dependence. 'I have done nothing', he wrote to Haydon in October, '– except for the amusement of a few people who refine upon their feelings till anything in the un-understandable way will go down with them – people predisposed for sentiment.' Later it was apparently posterity that he was addressing. ' "If I should die," said I to myself, "I have left no immortal work behind me – nothing to make my friends proud of my memory – but I have lov'd the principle of beauty in all things, and if I had had time I would have made myself remember'd." '[2] It is clear that the posterity he has in mind here is not a remote one, because his friends are expected to be still alive when he is 'remember'd'. Presumably it was the mid-nineteenth-century reading public, who, as it turned out, were to read Keats with more ardour than any of his contemporaries. (The 1850s were the turning-point in his reputation.[3]) For the reading public of his own day Keats expressed loathing and contempt. 'The more I know what my diligence may in time probably effect; the more does my heart distend with Pride and Obstinacy – I feel it in my power to become a popular Writer – I feel it in my strength to refuse the poisonous suffrage of a public.'[4] But this is not the only note. On one occasion he told Haydon: 'I have no cause to complain because I am certain any thing really fine will in these days be felt.'[5]

Keats's contradictions and confusions can be paralleled in all the other nineteenth-century poets. Rossetti only melodramatized their uncertainty when he buried the MSS of his poems in his wife's coffin in 1862 and dug them up again in 1869. With Flecker, a typical late Romantic, who dedicated his poems 'To a Poet a Thousand Years Hence',

---

[1] *Life and Letters of John Keats*, World's Classics ed., p. 176.
[2] To Fanny Brawne, Feb. 1820.
[3] See G. H. Ford, *Keats and the Victorians* (1944).
[4] To Reynolds, 24 Aug. 1819.
[5] To Haydon, 3 Oct. 1819.

> O friend unseen, unborn, unknown,
>   Student of our sweet English tongue,
> Read out my words at night, alone:
>   I was a poet, I was young.

we may contrast Dryden's dedications 'To the Right Honourable the Earl of Abingdon, etc.', 'To His Grace the Duke of Ormond', 'To the Most Honourable John, Lord Marquis of Normanby, Earl of Mulgrave, etc., and Knight of the Most Noble Order of the Garter', etc. The seventeenth and eighteenth centuries were free from the doubts and difficulties which beset the nineteenth and twentieth centuries. The Augustan poets knew exactly whom they were writing for. They knew that 'the Readers of Poesie', as Hobbes put it, 'are commonly Persons of the best Quality',[1] and their eyes were firmly fixed, during the process of composition, on the 'great', the 'polite world', the 'best companies', the 'people of fashion', 'upper life', and the 'beau monde' (to quote some of their synonyms for their ruling class). Their difficulties arose not from any uncertainty who their audience was, but from an internal contradiction in that audience itself.[2]

Criticism has not paid sufficient attention to this problem of the poets' audiences. As it is fatally easy to hypostatize 'poetry', it will be safer to limit this discussion to 'poems', The first point, then, that must be made is that a poem only becomes a poem, in the ordinary sense of the word, when it is read. Up to that stage it is only so many black marks on a piece of white paper. (The psychological processes inside the poet as a result of which the black marks are on the paper include so much that is not recorded there that they cannot be equated with the poem, though they are, of course, related to it.[3]) The actual process of reading falls into four stages: (i) the reader translates the black marks into words (meaningful sounds); (ii) the separate words are combined into phrases or detached statements (units of meaning); (iii) the associated phrases and statements are

---

[1] 'To the Reader concerning the Vertues of an Heroique Poem', *Homer's Odyssey* (1675).

[2] The Augustan philosophy of life was based on 'common sense', the rational faculty that is shared by all human beings except children and lunatics. But this egalitarianism was contradicted by the rigid class-divisions that the aristocracy imposed upon eighteenth-century society. See p. 121 below.

[3] See, e.g., Robert Graves's account of the composition of 'The General Elliott' in *On English Poetry* (1922), pp. 55-62, or the equally illuminating passage in *Poetry for You* (1944), pp. 35-9, by C. Day Lewis, which describes the genesis of his poem beginning

> Children look down upon the morning-gray
> Tissue of mist that veils a valley's lap.

Both accounts include a variety of personal experiences and reminiscences that are quite irrelevant to the appreciation of the completed poem. See also the detailed 'Birth of a Poem' by Robert Nichols (appended to Rosamond E. M. Harding's *An Anatomy of Inspiration*, 2nd edn. [1942]). The poem in question is Nichols's own 'Sunrise Poem'.

linked up so as to form a complex statement or sentence (the poetic unit); (iv) the various complex statements or sentences are connected together in the mind and *their* interrelations worked out (the composite meaning which is the poem).

Of the four stages the third is clearly the complement of the poet's Semantic Synthesis ('magic' in the terminology of the Romantic critics) that was discussed in the preceding section. In the line, for example, that Abercrombie quoted from Chaucer,

> Ne how the ground agast was of the light,

the reader has in effect to repeat the poet's bridging of this particular semantic gap. There are already two phrases or units of meaning in his mind, (i) the ground exposed to the light, (ii) 'agast' (the emotion of fear), and by synthesizing them the reader *recreates* Chaucer's metaphor.

An identical process of synthesis operates, in fact, at all the four stages. In the first two stages habit, i.e. continuous practice, has made the process almost wholly unconscious, though any unusual spelling or unfamiliar word that threatens to interrupt the synthetic continuity will always bring it back into the full light of consciousness. These two stages are, of course, common to the reading of prose and poetry. It is only at the third stage that the two modes of statement-response diverge. Opposed to the 'esemplastic', synchronous synthesis of phrases characteristic of poetry is the analytic temporal sequence of phrases in prose.[1] The fourth stage is not met by the reader of science or philosophy, but the reader of fiction, or the spectator of drama goes through it in much the same way as the reader of poetry. If a metaphor, such as that of 'ground agast', is typical of the third synthetic phase, the fourth phase is typified by the literary resolution of a psychological conflict. The synthesis in this final stage may be, in the case of poetry, *formally* of poetic units (such as metaphors), but *materially* it is made up of items of human experience (such as the sense-impression, in the example from Chaucer, of the treeless wood and the emotion of fear). It must therefore necessarily have much in common with any other synthesis of human experience based upon speech, such as the catharsis of Greek tragedy or the 'happy ending' of a sentimental novel. A fuller discussion of the fourth phase must await the treatment of the content of poetry in the next chapter. On the whole, in this phase, considered in critical isolation, matter predominates over manner, whereas in the third phase poetic manner (style) tends to predominate over poetic matter. For most purposes, indeed,

---

[1] For Coleridge's 'homely definitions of prose and poetry: that is, prose = words in their best order:—poetry = the *best* words in the best order' (*Table-Talk* [12 July 1827]), I would like to substitute the following equally homely definitions: *Prose is saying one thing after another; poetry is saying two* (or more) *things at the same time.*

the third phase can be identified with the 'figures of speech' of rhetoric.

At each of the four stages the possibility of variant interpretations arises. A letter may be misprinted, a word may be understood in more than one way (e.g. the 'ball' in Marvell's 'Coy Mistress'), a phrase may be construed in a variety of senses (e.g. Blake's denunciation of the 'dark Satanic Mills'), and there may be several interpretations not only of the separate poetic units (e.g. the relevance of a 'metaphysical' metaphor), but also of the whole poem considered as a semantic entity (examples will be found in the poems analysed in Part Two of its work). Such problems cannot always be resolved because the conclusive evidence is not always available. But the principle involved is a simple one, though its implications are far-reaching. It bases itself on the interconnectedness of the four synthetic stages. In the case of a disputed word, for example, the reader will tend to prefer the interpretation that is most compatible with the meaning of the rest of the poem. If the rest of the poem is in English, a sense the word bears in English will be preferred to that which it has in French or Latin. If the rest of the poem is in English of the mid-seventeenth century a sense the word had then will be preferred to one it has acquired later. And if the poem is addressed to the 'Persons of the best Quality' of that period a sense that was current in Charles II's court will be preferred to one only found among his seamen. Similar considerations, though they are necessarily more complex, apply to the third and fourth synthetic stages. Such familiar poetic devices as metaphor, simile, paradox and symbolism have in fact very different functions at different periods.[1]

In other words, the better the poem is and the more there is felt to be 'in it' (i.e. the more *meaningful* it is), the closer the modern reader will unconsciously tend to try to identify himself with the poet's original readers. (Bad poems can generally be seen through without all this trouble because they are fundamentally *meaningless*, i.e. nothing is synthesized.) The ultimate criterion, therefore, in poetic interpretation is not 'what the poet meant' *tout court*, i.e. what was going on inside the poet during the composition of the poem (which is largely either unknowable or irrelevant), but 'what the poet meant to his contemporaries', i.e. the way his poem would have been understood by the particular social group to whom it was primarily addressed:[2]

[1] See Part Two of this book.

[2] The point could be made in a number of ways. Rosemond Tuve has recently demonstrated – in *Elizabethan and Metaphysical Imagery* (1947) – that Renaissance imagery is rooted in the training in rhetoric and logic that the schools and universities then provided. Nineteenth- and twentieth-century criticism of Sidney and Donne, overlooking this, has been in continual danger of misreading their poems. The writing of Latin verse at school had a similar influence on Augustan poetry that has not yet been properly documented.

It takes two people to say a thing – a sayee as well as a sayer – and by parity of reasoning a poem's original audience and environment are integral parts of the poem itself. Poem and audience are as *ego* and *non ego*; they blend into one another. Change either, and some corresponding change, spiritual rather than literal, will be necessary in the other, if the original harmony between them is to be preserved.[1]

This conclusion has a number of important consequences. The first is its delimitation of the information about a poet's personal life that the modern editor needs to give in his notes. Since poetry only exists in the poet-reader relationship, and the ideal reader approximates as closely as possible to one of the more intelligent of the poet's original readers, all that it is necessary for us to know about the poet is the personal information that he could take for granted in his contemporaries. In the case of a Byron or a Pope that was, of course, considerable. Most poems, however, are quasi-anonymous to their original readers and the question of the personality and even the identity of their authors often hardly arises. Such works therefore as *The Road to Xanadu*, or B. I. Evans's detailed investigation of what was in Keats's head when he wrote the sonnet 'On First Looking into Chapman's Homer'[2] (a beautiful bit of detective work), fall outside the province of strict criticism. They are contributions of great interest to the psychology of literary creation, but they have only incidental *critical* value. This is not necessarily to decry 'source-hunting'. A proper understanding of a poem must entail an appreciation of the literary allusions that the ideal contemporary reader would have detected. To go further than this, however, is to desert literary criticism proper for the history of ideas. A similar caveat must be made against the investigators of the authorship of anonymous or disputed work with their paraphernalia of metrical tests and verbal clues. Occasionally the successful attribution of an anonymous poem to a known author or the bringing together of evidence that a certain poem has been misattributed may effect a reorientation of our views on who its original readers were, but more often the new factual information makes no poetic difference. The game of attribution, as played by J. M. Robertson, Charles Crawford, Dugdale Sykes, etc., in the field of minor Elizabethan and Jacobean drama, is an enjoyable sport, with its own elaborate rules, but it should not now be mistaken for criticism.

A second critical corollary that follows from the general principle of the primacy of 'what the poet meant to his contemporaries' is that the modern editor's initial duty is to identify the audience for whom a poem or group of poems was originally intended. The more precise the identification, the

[1] Samuel Butler, *The Iliad of Homer Rendered into English Prose* (1898), Preface.
[2] *Essays and Studies*, English Association (1930).

easier it will be for the modern reader to recapture the meaning of a poem in its pristine totality. But for this to be achieved more is required than a mere descriptive label of the individuals or the social group to whom the poem was, explicitly or implicitly, originally addressed. We need to know a good deal about this audience's habits and assumptions at each of the stages that reading involves. What were the *words* that they expected to meet in a poem, and what meanings did they attach to those words? What were the kinds of *statement*, or combination of words, that they looked for in poetry? Finally, what sort of general *relationships* between the separate statements were they accustomed to find in poetry? In reading a modern poem such questions hardly arise, because the poem is addressed to *us*, and it naturally conforms to *our* semantic habits and *our* literary tradition. But we cannot take such a conformity for granted in the poems of the past.

The history of English criticism includes a series of Awful Warnings – Rymer on *Othello*, Johnson on Milton's sonnets, Macaulay on Restoration comedy, Eliot on Hobbes,[1] Leavis on *Samson Agonistes*,[2] C. S. Lewis on Donne.[3] These and similar *gaffes* were not failures of taste so much as *misreadings*, condemnations based on misinterpretations. And in each case the root of the error has been the isolation of a body of writings from its original context – in other words, the neglect of the 'reader' element in the original poet-reader relationship. The wise man will follow Sainte-Beuve's advice and humbly try to cultivate 'cette faculté de *demi-métamorphose, qui est le jeu et le triomphe de la critique, et qui consiste à se mettre à la place de l'auteur et au point de vue du sujet qu'on examine, à lire tout écrit selon l'esprit qui l'a dicté'*.[4] That at any rate remains the ideal. How exacting it can be, how difficult of attainment, Sainte-Beuve himself has unconsciously demonstrated in this very passage. The quotation with which he ends is an adaptation of Pope's famous couplet in the *Essay on Criticism*:

> A perfect Judge will read each work of Wit
> With the same spirit that its author writ.

Pope, however, did not in fact mean to recommend a *sympathetic* reading, but, as the quotation from Quintilian in his note on the passage proves,[5] a *careful* reading ('spirit' meaning *energy, vivacity*). Without realizing it,

---

[1] *For Lancelot Andrewes* (1928).     [2] *Revaluation* (1936), pp. 64-7.

[3] *Seventeenth-century Studies presented to Sir Herbert Grierson* (1938), pp. 64-84.

[4] 'Diderot', *Causeries du Lundi*, ser. 3. Sainte-Beuve would certainly have included the original reading public in the *point de vue du sujet qu'on examine*.

[5] Dilgenter legendum est, ac pæne ad scribendi sollicitudinem; nec per partes modo scrutanda sunt omnia, sed perlectus liber utique ex integro resumendus (*Inst. Orat.*, x, i, 20).

therefore, Sainte-Beuve has committed the very error against which he is warning others – in this case, of making Pope speak the language of nineteenth-century relativism.

A continuous alertness is certainly necessary. Some knowledge of the history of the language is virtually indispensable. An acquaintance with social and economic history is highly desirable. The 'perfect Judge' will not make the mistake of thinking poetry simple. But some signposts can be erected for his guidance. We have already discovered one criterion of semantic relevance. The meaning of a poem is the meaning that it had for the ideal representative of those contemporaries of the poet to whom the poem, implicitly or explicitly, was originally addressed. But this is only a first stage in the enquiry. The next step will be to consider the *content* of poetry.

# 3

## Poetry and Society

IT will be as well at this point to try and summarize the course of the argument in the two preceding chapters. Chapter One, it will be remembered, was devoted to a demonstration of the primacy of meaning in poetry. It was not denied that the spoken word is sounded, or that the sounds of poetry can be utilized by the poet either as a mimetic echo of the sense or as a mild form of hypnotism. But in poetry, as in language generally, sound is always *primarily* semantic. Words, like bank-notes, are in general use in the civilized world because they are convenient symbols. In both cases their social utility does not derive from their physical properties, but from what they symbolize. A word is 'an intellectual thing', and to fail to recognize this elementary fact is as irrational as to imagine that the value of a bank-note lies in the paper that it is printed on.

Poetry, then, is meaning. But poetic meaning is not the only kind of meaning. In Chapter Two it was suggested that *formally* a poem is a verbal synthesis, a complicated, simultaneous, unified whole, and that the familiar technical devices, such as rhyme and metaphor, should all be considered the agents of poetic meaning, either defeating the reader's temptations to divagate into analysis or reinforcing the synthetic habits that he or she carries over from everyday life. The last question to be asked was 'Meaning to whom?' In the final section of Chapter Two the suggestion was made that a poem only comes to have meaning in the poet-reader relationship. Although the poet need not be fully conscious of it, the fact is that his poems are only written with a view to being read. The readers, therefore, that the poet is implicitly addressing *determine* to a considerable degree the kind of poem that he is writing. It follows that to understand a poem's meaning today we need to be able to identify ourselves as far as possible with its original readers, the poet's contemporaries, whose ideal response to the poem in fact constitutes its meaning.

Poetry, finally, represents a specialization of normal speech. It is an act of communication, and so far from being restricted to the inspired few, is always, as Wordsworth insisted, 'a selection of the language really spoken by men'. The basis of the selection is not, however, the exclusion from poetry of certain allegedly non-poetic words,[1] but the mitigation of the word order of grammar with its rigid syllogistic patterns.

It now remains to consider the *content* of poetry. What are the meaningful elements that are synthesized in the poem? How many of such elements will there normally be? What relation, other than that of mere juxtaposition, will the separate elements bear to each other?

The content of poetry is often said to be coextensive with the range of human interests, *quidquid agunt homines*. To Wordsworth, as long as they concern us 'as enjoying and suffering beings', poems could be about almost anything:

> The remotest discoveries of the Chemist, the Botanist, or Mineralogist, will be as proper objects of the Poet's art as any upon which it can be employed, if the time should ever come when these things shall be familiar to us, and the relations under which they are contemplated by the followers of these respective sciences shall be manifestly and palpably material to us as enjoying and suffering beings.[2]

But the Wordsworthian formula of 'enjoying and suffering beings' is unsatisfactory. Two objections immediately suggest themselves:

(i) Do purely *physical* pleasures and pains, however intense or prolonged, ever form the basis of major poetry? Poems are not, in fact, written about toothaches or Parisian cooking. Even the poetry of intoxication derives its essential *élan* from the thirst that from the soul doth rise.

(ii) Is poetry limited to enjoyment and suffering, as the words are ordinarily understood? Wordsworth has surely overstressed its emotional elements. Much of his own poetry, for example, is contemplative rather than emotional. Such admirable things as the 'Cumberland Beggar' and 'Peter Bell' do not provoke the smile or the lump in the throat so much as the reflection, 'How odd, how very odd, human beings are!'

I am inclined to believe that the content of poetry is best defined as *human nature in its social relations*. The purely private emotion and reflection cannot get into poetry, because the use of language necessarily involves a socialization of individual experience. All poems are therefore in the last analysis public poems. And, other things being equal, the poems that seem to 'come off' best with their original readers, those with the maximum semantic exchange value, tend to be those where a large amount of common ground is shared by the poet and the reader. This is another way of saying that the constituents of poetry tend to be

---

[1] This is the *negative* theory of poetic diction. The earlier Augustan critics, such as Hobbes, Dryden and Dennis, had merely tried to ban technical terms and words with vulgar associations. The *positive* theory of poetic diction – that certain words are poetical in themselves – is implicit in Collins and explicit in Goldsmith and Shenstone. Both theories are defensible in certain special circumstances, but neither has any general validity.

[2] 'Preface' prefixed to *Lyrical Ballads* (1802).

What oft was thought but ne'er so well express'd.

It follows that the contribution of the poet is limited to 'expression', i.e. the selection and synthetic arrangement of the social units of meaning.

By 'a social unit of meaning' I mean a social attitude, i.e. one of the series of relations that one human being can take up, or find himself in, or be forced into, *vis à vis* one or more other human beings. In most poems the theme, content or subject-matter turns out under analysis to consist of the juxtaposition of *two* contrasted or conflicting social attitudes. This is true at both the third and fourth stages of poetic synthesis (as distinguished in the preceding chapter). At the fourth stage the concept becomes a particularly useful critical tool. The typical poem can be thought of at this stage as a miniature drama in which two 'sides' meet, come into conflict and are eventually reconciled.[1] In Wordsworth's 'A slumber did my spirit seal' (see p. 29 above) the two sides' could perhaps be labelled 'humanism' (Wordsworth *ought* to have had 'human fears') and 'pantheism' (the mysticism of 'rocks, and stones, and trees'). The vague living-Lucy of this poem is opposed to the grander dead-Lucy who has become involved in the sublime processes of nature. We put the poem down satisfied, because its last two lines succeed in effecting a reconciliation between the two philosophies or social attitudes. Lucy is actually more alive now that she is dead, because she is now a part of the life of Nature and not just a human 'thing'.

The two contrasted social attitudes need not be -isms. In the following poem, in which a great deal of meaning is condensed into the four lines, the opposition is at a less abstract level:

> Western wind, when will thou blow,
> The small rain down can rain?
> Christ, if my love were in my arms
> And I in my bed again![2]

Here ll. 1-2, addressed to the west wind, are a prayer for rain for the growing crops, and ll. 3-4, addressed to Christ (the exclamation has the effect of a vocative), are a prayer for the return of the lover. And the parallelism of form overcomes the contrast of content. The effect is to

---

[1] I derive this metaphor from Cleanth Brooks who has elaborated it in *Modern Poetry and the Tradition* (1939) and *The Well Wrought Urn* (New York, 1947).

[2] The MS in the British Museum that has preserved the only text of this anonymous poem includes pieces by William Cornish and other professional musicians at Henry VIII's Court. The lines, however, are so different in style that they suggest an earlier date and a popular origin. E. K. Chambers has suggested that the poem is a fragment – perhaps a variant first verse of the well-known ballad 'The Unquiet Grave' (*English Literature at the Close of the Middle Ages* (1945), p. 157).

suggest that the lover whose return is desired so passionately is also involved in the natural cycle of the seasons. In spite of appearances to the
contrary spring will eventually come again, and the speaker tries to
attribute a similar certainty to the return of the lover. By a blasphemous
implication Christ is in effect assigned the rôle of a fertility spirit. The
'sides' in this poem are therefore (*a*) the non-human processes of growth,
and (*b*) human self-fulfilment in sexual love. To define the content of the
poem in more abstract terms would be to distort its meaning.

The Principle of the Semantic Gap assumes a peculiar importance at this
final level of synthesis. However brilliant the details no poem can be
considered a good one unless the basic social attitudes implied or expressed
are genuinely 'opposite' or 'discordant'. It is the absence of any fundamental conflict of human attitudes that accounts for the emptiness of
many nineteenth-century anthology pieces. I seem to detect just such a
deficiency in the familiar lines that Landor prefixed to *The Last Fruit of an
Old Tree* (1853):

> I strove with none, for none was worth my strife.
> Nature I loved, and, next to Nature, Art;
> I warmed both hands before the fire of Life;
> It sinks, and I am ready to depart.

The arrogance surely is oversimplified. The social attitude struck in the
first line is maintained too consistently, so that Landor seems guilty of
attitudinizing. The love of Nature and of Life which might have provided
the counter-attitude is not developed sufficiently. It was for his own selfish
gratification, we feel, that he loved them. The image of warming the
hands before the fire, though vivid, is too reassuring, emphasizing, as it
does, the agreeable sensation felt by the hands rather than the mysterious
forces of the fire and the surrounding blackness.

A poem that can be compared with Landor's because of the similarity
of form and content, and that 'comes off', it seems to me, whereas his just
doesn't, is Herrick's 'The comming of good luck':

> So Good-luck came, and on my roofe did light,
> Like noyse-lesse Snow; or as the dew of night:
> Not all at once, but gently, as the trees
> Are, by the Sun-beams, tickel'd by degrees.

The contrast that gives this poem its attractively idiosyncratic flavour is
between the beneficiary of Good Luck, the jolly Devonshire clergyman
whom we know, and Good Luck itself, a curiously impalpable figure. But
the contrast operates at two separate levels. In the four lines we are told
five things about Good Luck: (i) it is personal, something with a purposive

existence of its own (it *comes* and *lights*, instead of being brought or dropped); (ii) it is a natural phenomenon, like dew, snow or sunbeams; (iii) it insinuates itself gradually, noiselessly and when there is nobody about – like snow or dew at night, or the early morning sunshine (*tickel'd* implies the rays of the sun *under* the leaves and twigs); (iv) it is beneficent, refreshing and enlivening what it touches; (v) it is local, lighting upon the house instead of the occupier of the house.

Good Luck, it is clear, is not a Robin Goodfellow so much as a semi-supernatural semi-natural being like Will-o'-the-wisp, and, although there is a faint suggestion of *lares et penates*, it is primarily an English deity unconnected with the Goddess Fortuna. The initial contrast between Herrick and Good Luck, i.e. between human and non-human nature, is therefore *duplicated* in the complexities of Good Luck's own make-up. As compared with Landor's poem Herrick's is much more 'meaningful'.

An additional requirement is that the two social attitudes be more or less equally matched. A poem of which the outcome is a foregone conclusion, in which one of the 'sides' is manifestly a man of straw, cannot engage the reader's interested cooperation to the same degree. Perhaps another four-line poem, Prior's 'The Lady Who Offers her Looking Glass to Venus', may be held to exemplify this social lopsidedness:

> Venus, take my Votive Glass:
> Since I am not what I was;
> What from this Day I shall be,
> Venus, let Me never see![1]

The poem gets its effectiveness from the contrast between what the lady says and the poet's implied comment on it. At first we take the lady at her word and accept her logic. Yes, as the sight of her wrinkles distresses her, she will be well advised to get rid of the mirror. In this way she will be able to bring the march of time to a halt. But a moment's reflection reminds us that this is really a *non sequitur* and we swing over to Prior's side. Unfortunately getting old is not just a matter of seeing oneself do it. The lady's gesture is a futile one. The comedy of the poem derives from the contrast between the lady's apparently perfect logic and its real fallacy. Like the great comic figures – for example, her own contemporary Lady Wishfort in Congreve's *Way of the World* (1700) – she exposes herself by what she herself says, and not as the result of what other people say about her. But the comedy borders on satire because there is not even a sug-

---

[1] Text from *Poems on Several Occasions* (1718). The poem is a translation from an epigram attributed to Plato which is reprinted in Johnson's *Rambler*, No. 143. A reference to the poem in 'Cloe Jealous' suggests a date in the late 1690's, when the majority of Prior's poems to 'Cloe' (Jane Ansley) were written.

gestion of pity for the lady's very human failing. The poem might have been a better one if it had not been so heavily weighted against her.

The attempt here made to restrict the content of poetry to human nature in its social relations has received some confirmation in recent investigations into the way children learn to speak. M. M. Lewis, who is the Director of the Institute of Education at University College, Nottingham, has now demonstrated that the incentives to linguistic communication can be either 'manipulative' (serving the practical activities of society and its members) or 'declarative' (in which the social response is an end in itself):

The child uses speech manipulatively when it is an instrument to secure the satisfaction of his primary needs: to remove discomfort, to obtain pleasant experiences or to prolong them once they have begun. At the beginning the child in discomfort vaguely strives to rid himself of it; the contortions of his body, the thrusting out of his arms and legs, and not least his cries – these are all of them different ways in which his striving shows itself.[1] Then, as he comes to recognize that the possession of a particular object, for instance food, relieves his discomfort, his vague striving may change into a directed reaching-out to secure this object. In the same way, catching sight of some plaything, for instance a bright ball dangling from his cot, he gurgles with pleasure and reaches out towards it. But it is of course a long time before he is physically capable of achieving his intention; this is when the group intervenes to help him. His cry is heard and food is brought to him. Or his mother hears his gurgle of delight, and her sympathetic hand swings the ball towards him. Thus his utterance becomes the instrument of achieving his intention, an instrument used blindly and fumblingly at first, but with a clearer understanding of its use as time goes on. It is a social instrument – a means by which instead of directly manipulating his physical environment, the child manipulates his social environment, which in turn manipulates his physical environment for him.

In its declarative function language plays a different part. Often it is evident that the child is not so much attempting to seize hold on some portion of his physical environment as simply to express its effect on him, and that his satisfaction comes from securing an appropriate expressive response from someone else. For instance, the child lying in his cot and gurgling with pleasure at the dance of light and shade on the ceiling becomes happier still when his mother points to the dancing pattern and also expresses her delight. Soon it is clear that he is intentionally trying to secure this response from her, that he declares his pleasure in order to enhance it by effective communion with her. In this declarative use of speech the child seeks to obtain from others, not some manipulation of his physical environment, but simply an expressive response. Speech is still a social instrument, but now it is directed, not to secure some change in the physical environment, but social response as an end in itself.[2]

---

[1] This is Darwin's account of the origin of expression in *Expression of the Emotions* (1872).
[2] *Language in Society* (1948), pp. 23-4.

In terms of adult life, the 'manipulative' function of language is especially prominent in business, politics and science, whereas the 'declarative' function ranges from 'phatic communion' (talk about the weather, etc.) to the art of literature.

The relevance of Lewis's distinctions to the definition of poetry will be clear. Poetry is obviously the declarative function in its purest and most concentrated form. Poetry makes no attempt to manipulate the physical environment; hence the futility of didactic poetry and the inferiority of partisan political verse. In its essence it is simply the expression in language of the sense of social solidarity, the linguistic equivalent of flags, national anthems and emblems, or symbolic figures like Saint George, John Bull and the reigning constitutional monarch. *Das Volk dichtet* – the formula of ballad origins attributed to Jacob and Wilhelm Grimm – can be applied to poetry generally in the sense that a social group, by virtue of its possession of a special highly developed instrument for its own internal communication in its own language, is the indispensable precondition for the composition of poetry. Without the group you cannot have a living language; without a living language you cannot have poetry. Poetry, however, is something more than an alternative outlet of the herd instinct. Because of the intimate interconnections between language and thought it is at its best the herd instinct at its point of maximum consciousness, the synthesis of a particular social order, in which that society achieves its most significant self-expression – and ultimately its historic meaning. Andrew Fletcher of Saltoun's 'wise man', who 'believed if a man were permitted to make all the ballads, he need not care who should make the laws of a nation', was making the same point in more homely terms. In the long run, and by a curious paradox in spite of their untranslatability, it is by its poems above all that a country is remembered by the rest of the world. And it is right that this should be so. As man, the political animal, is most himself in a selfless service to the community, so the community fulfils itself most completely, not in war or commerce or religion or science (impermanent and transient occupations infected by the physical environment, soon lost in the mist of time), but in that assertion of its own *idea* which constitutes poetry.

II

In the light of the foregoing considerations the old problem of the *utile* and the *dulce* can be seen to be a quarrel between half-truths. Instruction can never be poetry's primary purpose, because the impartment of instruction is a practical activity, involving a use of language that is 'manipulative' rather than 'declarative'. Poetry is only useful in the sense that it is not self-regarding, a disinterested activity. In its essence it is simply a part, in some respects a culmination, of the process of social living, one of those things, like law-abidingness and politeness, voting at a General Election, or reading the newspaper, that life in a human community necessarily involves, and it is no more useful, strictly speaking, than any other purely social activity. On the other hand, it is equally misleading to insist on the delightfulness of poetry. No doubt most poetry does incidentally delight both its writers and readers, but to make delight the basis of poetry is as wrong-headed as making happiness the basis of virtue. Delight is generally a by-product of poetry, just as happiness is generally a by-product of virtue. But you do not live a good life in order to be happy, and you should not write or read poetry primarily because of the pleasure it will give you.[1] Poetry has a more honourable function than the titillation of the aesthetic sense. It is written or read because one is a member of a social group, because one is expected to do so by the group, because it enlarges one's consciousness of the group and one's relations with it, because in the last analysis the operation of a social sense in oneself makes it impossible not to. The reading and writing of poetry is, in fact, a natural function of man the political animal. To insist on its delighting us as individuals, as the Romantics did with their demand for 'ecstasy', is a kind of perversity comparable to perversities of the natural function of sex.

The reading of poetry and the writing of poetry are *both* social duties, essential acts of citizenship. The two things are complementary. A proper reading of poetry is not possible unless one is at least a writer of poetry *in posse*. The process of verbal synthesis that is demanded of the reader of poetry differs only in degree from the synthesis of poetic creation. To claim, as Ben Jonson and others have done, that 'To judge of poets is only the faculty of poets; and not of all poets, but the best',[2] is to mistake the function of criticism, which is the formulation of the *reader*'s reaction in the poet-reader relationship. Poets are not necessarily the best readers of poetry, not even of the poems they have written themselves. And they may well be unaware of the social element in criticism. How important that is can be gauged from Sainte-Beuve's note on the French reading public:

[1] Cf. I. A. Richards (*Principles of Literary Criticism* (1928), pp. 96-7); 'Pleasure and unpleasure are complicated matters arising in the course of activities which are directed to other ends. . . . It is the poem in which we should be interested, not in a by-product of having managed successfully to read it.'

[2] *Timber: or, Discoveries* (1641), p. 129. Landor thought that 'Great poets are the only judges of poets' (*Imaginary Conversations*, 'Lord Chesterfield and Lord Chatham'), and T. S. Eliot has made a similar claim in the English Association's *Essays and Studies* for 1936. Dryden's position is more plausible; 'Poets themselves are the most proper, though I conclude not the only critics' (preface to *All for Love* [1678]).

Car en France, notez-le bien, on ne veut pas surtout s'amuser et se plaire à un ouvrage d'art ou d'esprit, ou en être touché, on veut savoir si l'on a eu droit de s'amuser et d'applaudir, et d'être ému; on a peur de s'être compromis, d'avoir fait une chose ridicule; on se retourne, on interroge son voisin; on aime à rencontrer une autorité, à avoir quelqu'un a qui l'on puisse s'adresser dans son doute, un homme ou un corps.[1]

In Sainte-Beuve's time the English reader had not got beyond 'knowing what he liked'. Even today, there is a prejudice against 'knowing what one ought to like', though Arnold, Eliot, and Leavis, and some other propagandists for criticism, have done much to break it down. But the desirability of there being somebody about to guide the amateur reader to the best poets is, one would imagine, obvious. And the poets themselves usually have other things to do.

Such a guide must base his operations upon the contemporary poets of his own social group. The usual thing today is to start by introducing the beginner to the poets of the past. He has then to work his way slowly and painfully up to his own contemporaries. But this is to put the cart before the horse. The dead poets did not write for us but for their own countries and their own generations. A process of mental adjustment is needed before we can understand what it is exactly that they are saying. With our own contemporaries, however, such problems do not arise to the same degree. They are talking to us in our own language about the things that we too are interested in. If they are any good at all – and the proportion of good poets is more constant than is often thought[2] – they must have things to tell us that we need to hear. Relations between poet and reader of the same generation and the same social group – what Wordsworth meant to Mill, what Pope meant to Horace Walpole, what Auden means to us – are necessarily far more intimate and stimulating than any contacts between the living and the Mighty Dead can ever be. And they are the only possible base from which to conduct raids into the Dantes and Shakespeares. The man who is not prepared to understand the poetry of his own time *must* be incompetent to appreciate that of the past. This may seem a desperate conclusion, but are not many even of the best academic critics of today and yesterday – men like Oliver Elton, W. P. Ker, H. W. Garrod, F. L. Lucas, J. Dover Wilson, and F. P. Wilson – a standing proof that learning and a lucid prose style are not enough? The essential connection between the literature of the present day and the literature of the past was pointed out by T. S. Eliot in the now famous passage in 'Tradition and the Individual Talent';

---

[1] *Causeries du Lundi*, vol. xiv, p. 209.  [2] See p. 195 below.

No poet, no artist of any art, has his complete meaning alone. His significance, his appreciation is the appreciation of his relation to the dead poets and artists. You cannot value him alone; you must set him, for contrast and comparison, among the dead. I mean this as a principle of aesthetic, not merely historical, criticism. The necessity that he shall conform, that he shall cohere, is not one-sided; what happens when a new work of art is created is something that happens simultaneously to all the works of art which preceded it. The existing monuments form an ideal order among themselves, which is modified by the introduction of the new (the really new) work of art among them. The existing order is complete before the new work arrives; for order to persist after the supervention of novelty, the *whole* existing order must be, if ever so slightly, altered; and so the relations, proportions, values of each work of art toward the whole are readjusted; and this is conformity between the old and the new.[1]

The academic critics, through their failure to realize that several new works of art have arrived in the last twenty or thirty years (the poetry of Eliot himself, for example, or that of Auden, who is likely to prove the most influential English poet since Keats), have not appreciated that the existing monuments have been modified pretty considerably. In discussing Shakespeare or Spenser or Donne from their Edwardian standpoints they are talking about something that is no longer there. Hence – in spite of the occasional critical shrewdness, the learning gracefully worn, the brilliant literary detective-work – the feeling of ultimate futility that their books generate. A. C. Bradley is out of date now, but he can still be read on Shakespeare because the Shakespeare he discusses did once really exist. Dover Wilson's Shakespeare is not even a ghost.

### III

But the concept of poetry as a society at its point of maximum consciousness is too general to be used as a critical tool. We need to know, in addition, (i) what constitutes a society (what are its spatial and temporal boundaries?) and (ii) what the social elements are that get into poetry (is poetry a reflection or a distillation of social life – if the latter what is the process's formula?).

The two problems are closely related and can be best approached via

[1] *The Sacred Wood* (1920), pp. 44-5. Eliot may perhaps be accused of using unnecessarily mystical terms. The essential point is that, by virtue of being a member of a particular social order, the modern reader of poetry necessarily has mental habits and prepossessions different from those of readers of the past. A mental adjustment is therefore necessary in his case if he is to undergo the *demi-métamorphose* into a contemporary of Shakespeare's, for example. As the metamorphosis cannot be complete, the twentieth-century reader's reactions to Shakespeare must be different from the nineteenth-century reader's. In other words the poet-reader relationship 'Shakespeare' has *changed*. In so far as a man fails to read the best poems of his own day he is an *incomplete* member of his own society – in the terminology of ancient Athens, an ἰδιώτης.

the spoken language, of which, as we have seen, poetry represents a specialized form. A society, whatever else it is, is the sum of the individuals speaking the same language. Its boundaries are determined therefore by the speakers' consciousness of differences between one side and the other of a fence created by (i) national allegiances, (ii) regional differentiations, (iii) class distinctions, and (iv) the lapses of time.

In modern times a society, in the sense of a linguistic unit, rarely over-flows the political boundaries of the nation-state. The borderline cases in the history of English poetry are the Scotsmen, the Anglo-Welsh and the Anglo-Irish. Before 1603 few if any natives of Scotland aspired to be members of an English social group, but in the seventeenth century a certain number of Scottish aristocrats were assimilated into the English ruling class, and in the eighteenth and nineteenth centuries large numbers of middle-class Scots became to all intents and purposes Englishmen. Drummond, Thomson, Scott and Stevenson are obviously on the English side of the fence, whereas Dunbar, Ramsay and Burns obviously aren't. The social attachments of the Welshman and the Anglo-Irish are perhaps less clearcut, because the English that they speak is essentially our English, though modified by Celtic influences. On the whole an Irishman's brogue and a Welshman's accent are not felt as social barriers, since the semantic content of their speech is more or less identical with our own (another instance of the primacy of sense over sound).[1]

The existence of clearly differentiated regional and class dialects in England is evidence of the coexistence of a number of separate social groups within the nation-state. But the paucity and inferiority of the poetry that most of them have left behind, at any rate since the fifteenth century, suggests that there can have been little vitality in their social life. At any one period, indeed, there would seem, on the evidence of the poetry, to have been only one social group in England that was function-ing healthily. This was generally, but not always, what is vaguely called

---

[1] The important difference between the native English writer and the *métèque* (the writer with a non-English linguistic, racial or political background) is the latter's lack of respect for the finer points of English idiom and grammar. This allows the Anglo-Irishman (like George Moore) or the Anglo-Scot (like Stevenson) to attempt effects of style, sometimes successfully, that the English writer would feel to be a perverse defiance of the genius of the language. In the field of eighteenth-century poetry there are the cases of James Thomson (of *The Seasons*) and 'Ossian' Macpherson. More recently there have been Yeats, the Anglo-Irishman, and Eliot, the Anglo-American. Although there can be no doubt that Yeats's and Eliot's lack of linguistic inhibition has extended the range of modern English poetry, the influences of the native poets, Hopkins, Hardy and Owen, will probably prove to have been healthier in the long run. In second-rate writers on the linguistic fringe – Anglo-Jews like Guedalla, Anglo-Scots like Compton Mackenzie, Anglo-Welshmen like Emlyn Williams – there is a particular temptation to bogus slickness. On the other hand, the disregard of the organic overtones of the language often enables the *métèque* to achieve a peculiar lucidity in prose.

the ruling class. The ruling class's speech set the standards of 'correctness' of the moment, to which careerists and parasites born outside its ranks tended to conform. Linguistic correctness being the outward and visible sign of social conformity, its essential criterion is not spelling or pronunciation but meaning (social intention). Quantitatively, therefore, a society, in the sense in which the word can be used to define English poetry, is the sum of the individuals whose semantic speech-habits conform to those of a dominant group. Qualitatively, however, a society *is* the dominant group within the nation-state, since this group's characteristics are the shibboleths which determine the admission of others to its ranks.

A society's effective life can be measured in economic and political terms, but the history of the language provides a more sensitive index to the births and deaths of the dominant groups. It is generally agreed, for example, that the 1650s are a social watershed in English history. They mark, among other things, the end of the inflationary period, the degradation of the monarchy, the abolition of feudal tenures, the end of centralized government, a new colonial expansion, a struggle against Dutch maritime supremacy, the beginning of religious and racial tolerance, the foundation of what was to be the Royal Society, and a trend to a scientific agriculture. Taken singly, however, each of these changes wears something of an accidental look. There was no *special* reason why any one of these things had to happen in the 1650s. But where politics and economics offer only tentative approximations, the linguistic evidence is conclusive. Indeed, the revolutionary character of the 1650s might almost be demonstrated from the history of one word – the word *romantic*. Until 1650 no need seems to have been felt for an adjective for the common word 'romance'. But between 1650 and 1659 the word *romantic* is used by no less than seven writers – T. Bayly (1650), J. Bourne (1650), S. Sheppard (1651), J. Evelyn (1654), W. Lower (1656), the anonymous translator of Pierre de Marmet (1658) and H. More (1659).[1] On most of these occasions the word would seem to have been an independent creation. No less than four other attempts were also made during the 1650s to create an adjective for the word 'romance': *romance* (as adjective, 1653), *romanical* (1653), *romancy* (1654), *romancicall* (1656).[2] None of these forms were in use as adjectives before 1650. In the light of this evidence it is clear that in the 1650s a general need suddenly made itself felt for a special word to distinguish the kind of fiction retailed in Sidney's *Arcadia*, with its

[1] See F. Baldensperger, *Harvard Studies and Notes in Philology and Literature*, vol. xix (1937), pp. 13 ff., and W. L. Ustick, *Times Literary Supplement* (21 Dec. 1933).

[2] See L. P. Smith, 'Four Romantic Words' (in *Words and Idioms* [1925]). The adjective 'romancy' was used by three writers in the 1650s – Edmund Gayton (1654), Anthony Wood (1659), and (probably) John Aubrey (*Natural History of Wiltshire*, begun 1656).

deplorable tendency (as Sprat put it when using the word in 1667) 'to frame more perfect images of things, than the things themselves will bear'.[1] The nature of the needs does not concern us for the moment.[2] What is significant is the revolution in the climate of opinion to which all this word creation bears witness. Most words come into a language gradually, over a long period of years. That thirteen writers should have been feeling their way independently to what is essentially the same new word within the short period 1651-59 is evidence of an exceptional and violent disturbance of the linguistic *status quo*. A new English language was, in fact, in process of creation, and this language, as we can now see, was the mouthpiece of the 'squirearchy', the new dominant group that achieved its maximum consciousness, its ideal self-projection, in the poetry of Dryden, Swift and Pope.

What, however, is it in the social order that is projected in the poetry? It is time to come down to the brass tacks. Two recent comments on the poetry of Andrew Marvell will provide a convenient test case. Obviously the American professor who thinks that 'The Nymph Complaining for the Death of her Fawn' may represent 'an Anglican's grief for the stricken Church' is talking through his Yankee hat.[3] Obviously the Marxist who equates Marvell's 'Mower' impartially with 'the power of Love', 'the scythe of Death or Fate', 'the revolutionary armies', 'the productive classes as against the drones', and 'a pre-commercial simplicity', is also seeing things that aren't really all of them there.[4] But it is easier to feel that this sort of thing is wrong than to be able to say specifically why it is wrong. The fundamental error, it seems to me, lies in identifying a social order with the concrete particulars, human or institutional, that make up its cogs and shafts, instead of with its prime mover, the basic human incentive that is ultimately responsible for setting in motion the particular manifestations, political, economic, religious and literary.[5] The social order that finds its

[1] *The History of the Royal Society* (1667), p. 331.

[2] The intellectual climate of opinion includes (i) Hobbes's attack on metaphor, (ii) the Royal Society's campaign for one word for one thing, (iii) the Cartesian interest in the nature of truth.

[3] Douglas Bush, *English Literature in the Earlier Seventeenth Century* (1945), p. 161. It is only fair to add that this is an isolated lunacy. The book is a thorough and sensible, if somewhat superficial, guide-book to the period.

[4] Christopher Hill, 'Society and Andrew Marvell', *The Modern Quarterly* (Autumn 1946), p. 18. In spite of some rather wild identifications this is a most interesting article.

[5] It is the failure to realize this that vitiates L. C. Knights's *Drama and Society in the Age of Jonson* (1937), the most ambitious attempt since Buckle and Taine to relate English literature to the social background. Knights provides an admirable summary of English economic history, 1550-1650, and follows this with two excellent critical essays on Ben Jonson and some rather more perfunctory ones on Dekker, Heywood, Middleton and Massinger. The idea is that the economic analysis will illuminate the literary criticism. In fact, however, the two halves of the book do not coalesce, and the reader lays it down with a feeling that the claims made in the Introduction have not been justified. Knights handicapped himself unnecessarily by excluding the political and religious influences.

expression in Marvell's lyrics cannot be defined in terms of social cogs like the Anglican Church and the New Model Army. To do so is to confuse effects with their causes. Even the political and economic systems of the English Renaissance are not the essential features of its social order. The fundamental question is a 'Why'. Why was the English ruling class the agent of such systems? The formula that we need must be one that defines the human motives that controlled the social behaviour of this dominant group.

What was the motivating force *par excellence* of the English Renaissance? I believe the one-word answer to this question is 'self preservation'. The self-interest, however, of the new ruling class of the 'King's Servants', who had displaced the feudal aristocracy of the Middle Ages was neither narrow nor calculated. The sheep-farming that created deserted villages and the usury that financed piracy and the slave trade were accompanied by more reputable protections of the ego – among them military and athletic prowess, the art of dress, the patronage of culture, the ability to write a love poem, the ambition of universal learning, and the delights of introspection. Unlike nineteenth-century individualism the individualism of the Renaissance was not specialized or one-sided. According to the theory of the handbooks of 'courtesy', like Castiglione's *Il Libro del Cortegiano* and Peacham's *The Compleat Gentleman*, success in the competition for the Prince's favour went to the accomplished individual, the man who had brought to perfection all the different sides of his personality. And during the reigns of the Tudors at any rate the theory had a certain basis in fact. The careers of Leicester, Sidney, Ralegh and Essex were, up to a point, an exemplification of it. Even more important, however, than the many-sidedness of Renaissance individualism is its mysticism. The *étalage du moi* was not a deliberate exploitation of the anti-social instincts, but a spontaneous response to a universe that had suddenly become dangerously unpredictable. The destruction of the feudal and ecclesiastical hierarchies of the Middle Ages had knocked the bottom out of the 'chain of being' explanation of the world and its associated doctrines.[1] On the political plane, instead of the hierarchical series of villein/manorial lord/ feudal magnate/king, or family/tithing/hundred/county/kingdom,

> There was naught but a naked people under a naked crown.

And Protestantism was also busy removing the theological intermediaries

---

[1] E. M. W. Tillyard (*The Elizabethan World Picture* [1943]) and Hardin Craig (*The Enchanted Glass* [1936]) stress the persistence of the theory. It survived in the sense in which the Christianity of *Hymns Ancient and Modern* survives today – as popular mythology, part of the fabric of thinking. Its fantastic correspondences (flames, blood, gold, mint, crocodiles and swans were some of the things that were 'solary', i.e. attracting to oneself the virtue of the sun) were a gift to the poets, but only the cranks took them seriously.

– Pope, saints and angels – between God and the individual worshipper. In the end, indeed, there were only four certainties left – God, the Prince, the head of the family and the ego. In every other province of human life *anything* might be true. Hence the omnivorous curiosity and credulity of the Elizabethans. Hence too the new fear of witchcraft and the growth of interest in alchemy and astrology. The wildcat speculations and the financial extravagance, the travellers' tales and the sensational news-sheets, the eccentric religious sects and the 'Heath Robinson' inventions were only different aspects of the same exuberant irrationality. It was a world in a state of nature in which everything was possible, if only four things were certain.

It was this world picture that was displaced in the 1650s by the man-made world of the scientists and of 'common sense', in which probability was the guide of life and there were no certainties outside mathematics. Here is the background against which Marvell's lyrics must be read. They were written in the late 1640s and early 1650s by a man whose heart and head were divided. Marvell's heart was with the old world of mystical individualism which he associated with the unconscious life of young growing things (flowers, fawns, children, and grass, especially grass) and with their custodians, the mowers and gardeners. His enemies were those who interfere with nature – the lovers who cut their names on trees, the architects who 'square and hew' the green trees of the forest, the troopers who shoot the nymph's fawn. It is all summarized in 'The Mower, Against Gardens':

> Luxurious man, to bring his vice in use,
>   Did after him the world seduce,
> And from the fields the flowers and plants allure,
>   Where Nature was most plain and pure.

The heart was wild. Marvell's head was on the other side. Politically he was a Parliamentarian, intellectually he was a rationalist, temperamentally he was a satirist. And the head refused to allow the heart to take itself too seriously. The mower's case against gardens is so over-stated that it is clear it is largely only a pretext to describe their charm. Marvell's irony enabled him to have it both ways. He retained the mystical individualism of the Renaissance while recognizing its inadequacy, and as a consequence a tension is generated in his poetry comparable to that in the later poems of Yeats, who also had a foot in two cultural camps.

There may well be details in the preceding analysis that can be questioned, but it is at this level of abstraction at any rate that the social significance of Marvell's poems, and indeed of all poems, must be determined. The principle is inherent in the nature of poetry. The subject-matter of poetry is not 'things', but conflicting moods and attitudes, *human nature in its social relations*. Even important 'things', like an economic or political system, cannot be the subject-matter of poetry except as the objects of human emotions and reflections. The inner meaning of a poem is the synthesis of conflicting attitudes and not the conflict of institutions. To interpret a poem as an allegory of incidents on the political scene, like the Puritan attack on the Anglican Church, or on the economic scene, like the struggle between capitalism and pre-commercial morality, is really to condemn it as poetry and reduce it to *roman à clef*. All that the poet can do *qua* poet is to dramatize the basic human attitudes that have been institutionalized as Anglicanism or Puritanism or whatever it is. This is what Marvell has done in 'A Dialogue between the Resolved Soul and Created Pleasure', a poem with far more strictly social significance than 'The Nymph complaining for the Death of her Fawn' or the 'Mower' poems. In this poem Marvell introduces a 'Soul' which rejects *seriatim* the temptations dangled before it by 'Pleasure'. The temptations begin with the pleasures of the senses (taste, touch, smell, sight and sound in that order) and conclude with the lusts for feminine beauty, gold, power and knowledge. The poem is clearly intended to symbolize Marvell's rejection of the Renaissance world (it was to satisfy precisely these lusts that Faustus had sold his soul to Lucifer), and it is reasonable to describe it as an exposition of an intellectual Puritanism. But this is a very different thing from the disguised history of the Civil War that the writers I have referred to wish to ascribe to him.

My conclusion, therefore, is that the social content of poetry must not be identified with the concrete particulars of everyday life. There is no reason why teapots, Proportional Representation and the Crystal Palace should not be introduced into a poem, but again there is no reason why they should be. The imprint of the social order must be looked for at a higher level of abstraction, and to the casual reader it may easily not be visible at all. It will normally be concerned with the basic incentives, the human prime mover, that a particular society offers its members. In English Renaissance poetry its centre of interest seems to lie in variations round the theme of a precarious mystical individualism.

# 4

## Schools of Poetry

### I

EXCEPT by implication little or nothing has been said in the preceding pages about the literary tradition. Of the four essential elements of poetry, the removal of any one of which from a poem is literally impossible without the poem ceasing to exist, distinguished in Chapter Two – viz., the poet, the reader, a common language and a common literary tradition – it is the one that usually receives disproportionate attention. There are books and articles galore on the history of the English sonnet, the evolution of blank verse, Elizabethan tragedy, Restoration comedy, the poetry of natural description, poetic diction, satirical and mock-heroic poetry, *et hoc genus omne*. They make dreary reading because it is all so unreal and external – the form without the content, and the form treated not as meaning but as a sort of envelope. The history of the sonnet, for example, is reduced almost entirely to a matter of rhyme schemes (*abbaabbacdecde* fighting it out with *ababcdcdefefgg*). To all such Dryasdusts I commend the dilemma with which, according to Robert Bridges, Professor J. J. Sylvester posed a poor translator of Horace: 'If he thought the original was like that, what can he have seen in it to make him think that it was worth translating?' If the important thing about Milton's sonnets is the rhyme schemes – their discussion occupies two-thirds of the commentary devoted to the sonnets in the best recent edition of Milton's shorter poems[1] – why do you expect us to read them?

The futility of the literary historians derives from the vicious circle of their assumption that literature can only be explained in terms of itself. If you exclude all unliterary factors from the comparison, virtually the only thing that the sonnets of Surrey and the sonnets of Shakespeare will have in common is the rhyme schemes and the Petrarchan conceits. As Fluellen learnedly concluded in another sixteenth-century comparison, 'there is salmons in both'.

The literary historian who draws an indelible line between poetry and life, is faced with the problem of explaining how a literary tradition begins.[2] The standard solution, in the textbooks of English literature, is

---

[1] *Shorter Poems of John Milton*, ed. B. A. Wright (1938).

[2] Even Walter Bagehot, who certainly didn't live in an Ivory Tower, has to ascribe the cause of change of literary style to 'accident'. See *Physics and Politics*, chaps. i and iii.

'foreign influence'. Even W. P. Ker, who was much more than a writer of textbooks, was apparently satisfied with this easy answer:

> In the larger fashions of poetry, the fashions of thought and imagination, and diction and ornament – not merely the fashions of verse – there is seldom any great change without some foreign influence, sometimes France, sometimes Italy, while at the back there are always the ancients, the poets of Greece and Rome; and at any age in English poetry there is always the possibility of new study of the ancients and new inferences to be drawn from them.[1]

And, according to J. M. Robertson,[2] 'The dramatic efflorescence of the last fifteen or twenty years of Elizabeth's reign was one of the results of a rapid fertilization of the English intelligence by a variety of forms of foreign culture'; and the decline of the drama in the seventeenth century was because 'culture did not pour in as before'.

Such pronouncements skate on very thin ice. To those who say that a *genre* is transmitted from one literature to another by a kind of process of infection the obvious rejoinder is: (i) How did the process ever start? (English allegory derives from the French, and the French get it from the late Latin poets, who derive from Virgil, who derives from Homer, who derives from. . . . ?). (ii) Why is a country more susceptible to a particular infection at one time than another? No purely literary answer to the two questions is possible. As Brunetière found, *l'évolution des genres* is ultimately only explicable in social terms. It would be premature, however, to attempt such an explanation of the evolution of English poetry before the literary pattern has been defined.

There is, in my opinion, no good history of English poetry. This is not because our literary historians are particularly incompetent; they are not (indeed, the intelligence diverted into 'research' in the 1900s and 1920s that might then have reorganized British industry provides a nice social problem), but because, strictly speaking, there is no such thing as 'English poetry'. The *corpus poetarum anglorum* – *all* the English poems of *all* the English poets, from Cædmon to Dylan Thomas – cannot be treated historically, since the only unity it possesses is accidental and superficial. A history is only possible if there is an organic relationship between the component parts, and there is no such relationship between Old English poetry, and that of the present day, or indeed between any two schools of English poetry, except where one school immediately preceded or succeeded another. Such surveys as there are generally consist of a series of isolated and detachable chapters, each of which is devoted to a separate

---

[1] *Form and Style in Poetry* (1929), p. 194.
[2] *Elizabethan Literature* (1914), pp. 242–3.

'period', 'movement', or 'school'. G. H. Mair's excellent little manual *English Literature: Modern* in the 'Home University Library' can be taken as typical. It consists of chapters on 'The Renaissance', 'Elizabethan Poetry and Prose', 'The Seventeenth Century', 'The Age of Good Sense', 'Dr Johnson and His Time', 'The Romantic Revival', 'The Victorian Age', and 'The Present Age'. The particular labels used by Mair may not always strike one as happy (the *differentia* is sometimes political, a reign; sometimes chronological, a century; sometimes cultural, a dominant trend; and once it is attached to a particular writer, Johnson), but his general formula is obviously sound. The only concrete realities, about which historical propositions can be made, are the English poems (or novels or plays, etc.) of a *limited* period. English poetry in its entirety, like the English town or the English character, is too wide a field for profitable historical treatment.

The existence of schools of English poetry was recognized by the Elizabethan critics. Puttenham, for example, distinguished between the 'new company of courtly makers' (Wyatt, Surrey, Vaux, etc.), who 'sprong up' towards the end of Henry VIII's reign, and 'an other crew of Courtly makers' (Sackville, Sidney, Ralegh, etc.), who 'sprong up' in Elizabeth's reign. And an explicit recognition of the connection between schools of poetry, the language and the social order is to be found in Sir Kenelm Digby's note 'Concerning Spencer':

It is true that the vicissitudes of things (change being a necessary and inseparable condition of all sublunary creatures) and the inundations of barbarous nations, may overgrow and overrun the vulgar practise of the perfectest languages, as we see of the forementioned Greeke and Latine, yet the use of those toungues will flourish among learned men as long as those excellent authours remaine in the world. Which maketh me consider that noe fate nor length of time will bury Spencers workes and memory, nor indeed alter that language that out of his schoole we now use untill some generall innovation happen that may shake as well the foundations of our nation as of our speech: from which hard law of stepmother nature what Empire or Kingdome hath ever yet bin free?[1]

But there has been little or no serious attempt made to analyse the implications of such pronouncements, or even as far as I know to collect them, though they have, of course, become increasingly frequent since Puttenham's and Digby's time.

At least three major schools of poetry are now recognized to have

[1] *The Poets and their Critics*, ed. H. S. Davies (1943), pp. 37-8. Davies dates Digby's note, which has only recently been printed, *c.* 1638, but it cannot be later than 1637 as Jonson is referred to as still alive. It was 'wrote at Mr. May His Desire,' and Thomas May had dedicated his *Tragedie of Cleopatra* to Digby as early as 1626. See E. W. Bligh, *Sir Kenelm Digby and his Venetia* (1932), p. 278.

intervened between the early sixteenth century and our own time. A recent textbook defines them as follows: (i) The Renaissance ('from Sir Thomas More to Milton, of course including both'); (ii) the eighteenth century ('The term "eighteenth century" is used here according to the usual convention to denote a period of our literature with a more or less uniform character of its own. Thus it includes Dryden, who was born in 1631, if not Waller, who was born in 1606, while it excludes Wordsworth, who was born in 1770'); (iii) the nineteenth century ('For the historian of literature the nineteenth century may be taken as beginning with the publication of *Lyrical Ballads* in 1798 and continuing well into the twentieth century').[1] A somewhat similar division was made by Peacock as early as 1820 in his *Four Ages of Poetry*. According to Peacock, the English age of gold was that of Shakespeare, with Milton standing between the ages of gold and silver, the latter ('beginning with Dryden, coming to perfection with Pope, and ending with Goldsmith, Collins and Gray') being succeeded by the age of brass of Wordsworth, Coleridge and Southey. A more accurate statement of the respective *termini a quibus* and *ad quos* would perhaps be:

(i) *Renaissance poetry:* Wyatt (1503?-42) to Traherne (1636?-74). Wyatt's earliest sonnets were written about 1528, and the last genuinely Renaissance poem of any merit is perhaps Congreve's 'On Mrs. Arabella Hunt Singing' (*c.* 1692).

(ii) *Augustan poetry:* Waller (1606-87) to Crabbe (1754-1832) or Gifford (1756-1826). Waller's 'Of the danger His Majesty escaped' was written *c.* 1624, though it was not until 1635, according to Clarendon, that he acquired any reputation as a poet; Gifford's last satire was published in 1800, and Crabbe's *Tales of the Hall* in 1819 (though several of the tales had been written by 1814).

(iii) *Romantic poetry:* Chatterton (1752-70) to Rupert Brooke (1887-1915). Chatterton's Rowley poems date from *c.* 1768; the last surviving Romantic poet of any distinction was de la Mare (b. 1873), whose last collection of poems came out in 1945.

In the foregoing summary the *termini a quibus* are probably more reliable than the *termini ad quos*. The peculiar importance ascribed by their successors to the experiments of Wyatt and Surrey, Waller and Denham, and Chatterton is well known. These men were recognized by their followers as the founders of new schools of poetry. The last poets of a decadent tradition, on the other hand, tend not to be noticed by their contemporaries, unless they survive as the figures of fun of a new school. Somebody might investigate this question of the Aunt Sallies of criticism.

[1] J. A. K. Thomson, *The Classical Background of English Literature* (1948), pp. 166, 199.

The Augustans' principal butts among their immediate predecessors appear to have been Quarles (*Emblems*, 1635), Benlowes (*Theophila*, 1652) and Flecknoe (*Miscellanea*, 1653) who were born in 1592, *c.* 1603 and *c.* 1620 respectively. The Romantics seem to have assigned a somewhat similar rôle to Erasmus Darwin (*The Loves of the Plants*, 1789), who was born in 1731. And in our own days Alfred Noyes (*The Torchbearers*, 1922-30) has served as the special scapegoat of Romanticism. Noyes was born in 1880. It will be noticed that the birth dates and the *floruits* of the 'butts' are somewhat earlier than the dates suggested above for the *termini ad quos*. The latter are therefore probably the outside temporal limits of the three schools.

Perhaps the most interesting point that emerges from this summary is that the three schools of poetry each had an effective life of about the same length. There were intervals of 133 years, 148 years and 135 years between the dates of birth of Wyatt and Traherne, Waller and Crabbe, and Chatterton and Brooke respectively. Between the writing of the first and last work in each school the intervals, taking the schools in chronological order, were 164 years, 193 years and 178 years.

The school preceding Renaissance poetry – the school of Chaucer, as it is sometimes called, from its greatest though not its most representative poet – also followed the same general pattern. After a hiatus in the early fourteenth century (when literary output was 'small in quantity' and 'negative and disappointing' in quality[1]) there was a sudden flowering of English poetry about 1350 – the approximate date of 'Wynnere and Wastere' (Langland's model in *Piers Plowman*, itself not very much later), 'The Tale of Gamelyn', and the earliest miracle plays and 'Robin Hood' ballads. The Chaucerian school petered out in Skelton, whose last poem ('Why come ye not to court') was written in 1522, thus giving it a duration of 172 years. There may have been a still earlier school, beginning in the late twelfth century with Layamon and Orm – when 'the break with the past is so sharp' that it 'would be chosen with more justice than Chaucer's time as the starting-point for a study of modern literature'[2] – and ending in the early fourteenth century, but too little verse of the period survives to make it possible to clinch the conjecture. W. P. Ker has described this poetry as 'generally directed towards the ideal of French poetry, a struggle to realize in English what had been already achieved in French, to make English literature polite'.[3] It might be called the Anglo-French school. Finally there is clearly a school of modern poetry. Its beginnings can perhaps be ascribed to a group of poets who were born in the 1840s – Hopkins, Hardy, Bridges and Doughty – and its end does not seem to be in

---

[1] K. Sisam, *Fourteenth-century Verse and Prose* (1921), p. xvi.    [2] *Ibid.*, p. 10.
[3] *English Literature Medieval*, Home University Library, p. 102.

sight yet. The more important later names seem to be those of Yeats, Edward Thomas, T. S. Eliot, Wilfred Owen, Robert Graves, W. H. Auden, and Dylan Thomas. Its earlier phases overlapped the tail-end of the Romantic school, just as the early Augustans overlapped the later Renaissance poets, and the early Romantics overlapped the last Augustans.

As a working hypothesis, we can perhaps say that a poetic school spans five generations, each of about thirty-five years.[1] The five stages might be labelled (i) the Experimental Initiators (Wyatt, Waller, Chatterton, Hopkins), (ii) the Protagonists of a New Style (Spenser, Dryden, Wordsworth, Eliot), (iii) the Assured Masters (Donne, Swift, Keats, Auden), (iv) the Polished Craftsmen (Herrick, Pope, Tennyson), (v) the Decadents, that is, men reduced to 'stunts' to get new effects out of the exhausted tradition (Cowley, Collins, Swinburne). I am not suggesting that each school conforms exactly to this pattern, but that the general trends are towards something like it. And there are naturally plenty of borderline cases. Milton *ought*, judging by the date of his birth and his place in the Renaissance tradition, to have been either a Polished Craftsman or a Decadent. In fact he is both and a good deal more. Dryden is both the Protagonist of a New Style and an Assured Master. Marvell and Cowley begin as Renaissance Decadents and end as the Experimental Initiators of Augustan poetry. And other qualifications will no doubt suggest themselves.

In each school the poetry of its third generation, the stage I have called that of the Assured Masters, may be expected to constitute its classic expression. Here is the golden moment of equipoise between the forces of development and the forces of decay. I am inclined to believe that the foregoing is the only sense in which the word *classic* can now be usefully employed in literary criticism. I find some confirmation of this belief in T. S. Eliot's essay 'What is a Classic?' (1945). For Eliot the test of a classic age is maturity:

The age which precedes a classic age, may exhibit both eccentricity and monotony; monotony because the resources of the language have not yet been explored, and eccentricity because there is yet no generally accepted standard – if, indeed, that can be called eccentric when there is no centre. Its writing may be at the same time pedantic and licentious. The age following a classic age, may also exhibit eccentricity and monotony: monotony because the resources of the language have, for the time at least, been exhausted, and eccentricity because originality comes to be more valued than correctness. But the age in which we find

[1] No special virtue is claimed for the subdivision by generations. The curve of a poetic school's rise and fall should be thought of as an arc which can be marked off in any number of equally spaced divisions. I use the five generations because they provide a simple and familiar formula.

a common style, will be an age when society has achieved a moment of order and stability, of equilibrium and harmony; as the age which manifests the greatest extremes of individual style will be an age of development or an age of decay.[1]

It is true probably that the Protagonists of a New Style tend to exhibit both eccentricity and monotony. The diction of Spenser, of the early Dryden (e.g. *Annus Mirabilis*) and of the Wordsworth of *Lyrical Ballads* can certainly be called eccentric, and their poems are sometimes in danger of becoming monotonous. It is also true that the Polished Craftsmen and the Decadents are frequently either monotonous or eccentric. Herrick, Collins and Swinburne exemplify both defects. But Eliot's conclusion, which is that neither Shakespeare nor Marlowe nor even Pope (who came nearest to it) can be called classics, does not seem to be justified. These poets may not be mature in the sense in which Virgil is mature – that is a matter of opinion (Eliot's essay was originally an address delivered before the Virgil Society) – but their writing surely exhibits as much maturity as the particular poetic tradition that they inherited was capable of. After all, if the test is to be maturity, a ripe blackberry can be as mature as a ripe peach, though it may be less luscious.

The classic moment will naturally be the central point in the cycle of a poetic school's evolution. Applying this criterion to the terminal dates of the Renaissance and Augustan schools, I get 1570 and 1680 as the dates of birth of their potentially classic poets, and 1610 and 1720 as the theoretical dates of their most classic poems. These dates fit the facts reasonably well. Shakespeare was born in 1564 and Donne in 1576, while *The Tempest* was probably written in 1611, and Donne's 'Twickenham Garden' and 'A Valediction: forbidding mourning', two of the best of his *Songs and Sonets*, and *An Anatomie of the World* and its sequel, all date from this period. The only poet I know of who was born in 1680 is William Oldisworth, a very minor poet indeed who edited *The Examiner* for some years, but Addison was born in 1672 and Pope in 1688. And the last two volumes of Pope's *Iliad* came out in 1720, a year which represents a half-way point between his early poems like *The Rape of the Lock* and the later satires. The Romantic school is less accommodating, the classic year coming out according to our formula as 1837 and the birth-date of the classic poet as 1820. Both of these dates are clearly too late; Matthew Arnold, who was born in 1822, can hardly qualify as an Assured Master. However, this exception may only prove the general rule. Most English poets have achieved their masterpieces when middle-aged, when between forty and fifty years old, but the Romantics generally wrote their best poems when

[1] pp. 13-14.

they were about thirty or even younger (no doubt because the sub-conscious mind becomes more sluggish after sexual maturity has been reached). This suggests that the standard poetic generation of thirty-five years, on which these calculations have been made, may need to be amended in the case of the Romantic school.

Finally, it is interesting to find that the application of the standard formula (thirty-five years to each of the five poetic stages) to the modern school of poetry suggests that *our* classic year is 1950 or thereabouts.

## II

Parallel with the six consecutive poetic schools – Anglo-French, Chaucerian, Renaissance, Augustan, Romantic and Modern – our hypothesis requires six distinguishable social orders whose basic incentives will provide a poetic content in the central line of evolution of each school. In terms of the source of the ultimate social influence a tabulation that commends itself to me is:

(i) The Period of Lawyers' Feudalism (Henry II – Edward III).

(ii) The Local Democracy of the Yeomanry (Edward III – Henry VII).

(iii) The Centralized Absolutism of the Prince's Servants (Henry VII – Cromwell).

(iv) The Oligarchy of the Landed Interests (Charles II – George III).

(v) The Plutocracy of Business (George III – George V).

(vi) The Managerial State (George V – ?).

The second item on this list may seem an anomaly. Clearly the yeomen of the fifteenth century were not in any sense the ruling class of the period, even in local government. The feudal aristocracy however, who were the real ruling class, had by then become a purely repressive and disintegrating force, and the social initiative in local affairs was almost invariably taken by the church-wardens, the juries of the manorial courts, the religious and charitable guilds, and similar middle-class bodies. The yeomanry and their urban counterparts were undoubtedly the centre of effective social influence, so far as the period had one at all.[1]

---

[1] 'In the political struggle of the Wars of the Roses the "great connections" found their doom. As a result of that struggle the new men, who in the preceding two or three generations had succeeded to the commanding position in rural economy, were also able to succeed to local power and political influence' (M. M. Postan, 'Some Social Consequences of the Hundred Years' War', *Economic History Review*, vol. xii (1942), p. 12). In other words, the *social* dominance locally of the 'new men' in the later fourteenth and fifteenth centuries, preceded their *political* dominance in the sixteenth century. Postan includes among the 'new men' (1) local men of the humblest origin, the 'kulaks' of the English countryside, 'who had been assembling land piece by piece for many years', (2) 'reeves, manorial officials or other officers of noble households', (3) 'merchants, clerks, or returned captains . . . the *nouveaux riches* of the war'.

Each dominant group has marked the consolidation of its power by a dramatic 'demonstration' against its immediate predecessors, which has made it perfectly clear who the new masters are. Episodes that exemplify this are the Peasants' Revolt, the Tudor Enclosures, the Expulsion of James II, the Reform Bill, and the General Election of 1945 (with the nationalizations consequent on it). Such episodes are evidence that a new class is firmly in the saddle (the Peasants' Revolt of 1381, though repressed, achieved its moral effect), and they are therefore *consequent* upon its accession to power. A period of some forty years separates most of these episodes from what I should regard as the real social watersheds, viz. the Black Death, the Fall of Wolsey (with its consequences – Protestantism, the suppression of the monasteries, and the creation of a new landed gentry), the execution of Charles I, the French Revolution and the 1906 Election. It will be seen that the dates – 1348-9, 1530, 1649, 1789, 1906 – coincide, with only minor discrepancies, with the dates of the Experimental Initiators of the various schools of poetry. But both series of revolutions, political and literary, must be regarded as the reflection of more fundamental changes in the effective social incentives. It remains to define, in the most summary terms, what those changes were.

In terms of social trends the change from the Lawyers' Feudalism of the thirteenth century to the Yeoman Democracy of the fifteenth century, which was accelerated by the Black Death and the resulting shortage of manpower, was one from centralization to local autonomy and from a hierarchical class-division to egalitarianism.[1] The new motive force was still custom, but a native custom, the democratic tradition of the Saxon agricultural communities on which a Continental feudalism had been superimposed.

The sixteenth-century incentives have already been discussed, but the urban origins of its mystical individualism deserve emphasis. The contrast between the get-rich-slow economics of the Golden Age of the English Peasantry (Thorold Rogers's term for the fifteenth century) and the get-rich-quick mentality of Henry VIII's courtiers, who were largely recruited

---

[1] The economic recession of the fifteenth century – see M. M. Postan, *Economic History Review*, vol. ix (1939), pp. 160-7 – acted as an unseen Robin Hood, making the rich poorer and the poor richer. Its effects were most noticeable in the country, but egalitarian tendencies were also to be felt in the towns. 'The view of medieval town-economy as one of restriction and egalitarian monopoly, held and propagated by nineteenth-century historians, largely derives from the municipal and guild documents of the late fourteenth and fifteenth centuries: and what is sometimes regarded as evidence of a typical medieval regulation is in fact nothing else than instances of fifteenth-century departure from the freer and more speculative conditions of the earlier centuries' (*ibid.*).

from the ranks of the earlier city merchants,[1] is the key to the two periods, with inflation exerting an influence similar to that of the Black Death though in the opposite direction. (It encouraged the capitalist entrepreneur and depressed the peasantry and the craft-guilds.)

The eighteenth century represents a reversal of these trends with a decentralized régime, internal *laissez-faire*, and a dominant and prosperous countryside. Its prosperity apparently derived from the technological progress that was the fruit of a cooperative rationalism, which had displaced the mystical individualism of the Elizabethans. The system collapsed *economically* when the balance of wealth passed from the landed interests to the urban capitalists who had been the junior partners in the 1689 Settlement, and *morally* with the emergence of a half-starved overworked proletariat as a result of the rapid growth in the population.

In the nineteenth century the cooperative rationalism of the squirearchy, typified in the early membership of the Royal Society, ceases to be the dominant philosophy, and with the predatory capitalism of 'each for himself and the devil take the hindmost' there is a reversion to an urban mystical individualism. But this is a specialized individualism, suppressing important parts of the personality and over-encouraging others. The unpredictable rhythm of slumps and booms is paralleled by a pervasive irrationality in the ruling 'upper middle class' (who had retained the landed aristocracy as their political executives, but kept all the essential power in their own hands).

Today the ruling specialists, thrown up from all classes but increasingly from the working class, are primarily rationalists. Their incentive to promotion is to an exceptional degree the *intellectual* interest of the higher posts. The success of our civilization will probably depend as much as anything on the degree to which the technicians and the Civil Service can be humanized. The condition of modern poetry, uncertain in tone and somewhat irresponsible but intelligent and emotionally mature, is not unreassuring.

If we exclude the Anglo-French school of poetry and the Lawyers Feudalism with which it runs parallel – on neither of which am I competent to express any opinion – the dominant incentives of the remaining social orders, in which the *contents* of the consecutive schools of poetry tend to centre, can be summarized, in the baldest terms, as follows:

(i) Local Democracy of the Yeomanry: traditional egalitarianism based on country life. (School of Chaucer.)

---

[1] Although the lesser Tudor gentry were mainly the sons and grandsons of the fifteenth-century yeomen, the new aristocracy was almost completely non-agricultural. According to J. H. Round, the Spencers of Althorp were the only noble family that 'owed their riches and their rise neither to the favour of a court nor to the spoils of monasteries, nor to a fortune made in trade, but to successful farming' (*Studies in Peerage and Family History* (1901), p. 281).

(ii) Centralized Absolutism of the Prince's Servants: mystical individualism of complete personality based on London. (Renaissance School.)

(iii) Oligarchy of Landed Interests: cooperative rationalism (non-specialized) based on country life but revolving round London. (Augustan School.)

(iv) Plutocracy of Business: mystical individualism (subjective) based on manufacturing towns. (Romantic School.)

(v) Managerial State: cooperative rationalism (specialized) without local basis. (Modern School.)

The summary, over-simplified though it necessarily is, has the merit of bringing out some of the long-term rhythms of English social life, notably the ways in which an individualist cycle follows one in which the emphasis had been on the claims of society, and an urban cycle follows one based on country life. The sequence of rural collectivism and urban individualism may perhaps explain the affinities between Chaucer and Dryden (which Dryden himself recognized) and between Shakespeare and Keats (on which Middleton Murry has expatiated), and more generally between (i) the Renaissance and the nineteenth century, and (ii) the later seventeenth century and our own day.

### III

In the definition of poetry in Chapter Two four stages were distinguished in the process of reading a poem: (i) the translation of the printed letters into words, (ii) the combination of the words into phrases and short sentences (units of meaning), (iii) the synthesis of conflicting or contrasted phrases (the creation of the poetic unit), and (iv) the further synthesis of the separate poetic statements into the complex unity that represents the total meaning of the poem. It was then suggested that the modern reader who aspires to understand a poem of the past will need to know a good deal about the intellectual habits of its original readers at each of these stages. So far this chapter and its predecessor have been mainly concerned with the fourth and final stage of the process. But the second and third stages are also important. Unless we know not only the precise meaning the words bore to their original readers but also the kind of associations they attached to them we are in constant danger of going slightly wrong and assigning a meaning to the poem that it never had. I have discussed this problem at length in an earlier essay[1] and shall say no more about it here, confining myself to the third stage – that of poetic sentence patterns or the 'figures of speech'.

The form of poetic statement that is most characteristic of English

[1] *English Poetry and the English Language* (1934).

poetry of the Renaissance is undoubtedly the metaphor. C. S. Lewis has
said that 'a riot of images tumbling over one another to greet every single
idea was for the Elizabethans the essential faculty of the poet'.[1] M. Praz
has described the seventeenth century as 'that century in which the tendency to images reached its climax'.[2] And other testimonies to the same
effect could no doubt be assembled. But why was the Renaissance the
metaphoric period *par excellence*? C. S. Lewis has suggested that the origins
of the habit 'lie in Medieval Latin literature of the rhetorical type',[3] but
there is no need to look as far afield as this. The suggestion, indeed, is
typical of the straits into which the purely literary critic is driven when
faced with the problem of poetic change. Elizabethan imagery is not
confined to the poets; it is found everywhere – in business letters and in
Acts of Parliament, in sermons and in school books. Its sources lie, I
believe, in the mystical individualism that I have suggested characterizes
Renaissance society. John Hoskins, writing about 1599, has a definition of
metaphor which is also a characteristic example of the metaphoric outlook:

A METAPHOR, or TRANSLATION, is the friendly and neighbourly borrowing of one
word to express a thing with more light and better note. . . . The rule of a metaphor
is that it be not too bold nor too far-fetched. And though all metaphors go
beyond the signification of things, yet are they requisite to match the compassing
sweetness of men's minds, that are not content to fix themselves upon one thing
but they must wander into the confines; like the eye, that cannot choose but view
the whole knot when it beholds but one flower in a garden of purpose; or like an
archer that, knowing his bow will overcast or carry too short, takes an aim on this
side or beyond his mark.[4]

Hoskins's similes bring vividly before us the greedy eye of the Renaissance Englishman, to whom all sensual experience was equally welcome,
and the adventurous hit-or-miss philosophy of his practical life. In the
unpredictable universe anything might turn out to be the image or double
of anything else. The metaphors are the complement of the mysticism.

A metaphor is a synthetic statement (two heterogeneous meanings
fused into a new complex unity), and is therefore, according to our
definition, a miniature poem. To some critics, indeed, metaphor is the

[1] *Rehabilitations and Other Essays* (1939), p. 170.
[2] *Studies in Seventeenth Century Imagery* (1939), p. 12.
[3] *Rehabilitations and Other Essays* (1939), p. 180.
[4] *Directions for Speech and Style*, ed. H. H. Hudson (1935), p. 8. There is a useful discussion of
this passage in Rosemond Tuve's *Elizabethan and Metaphysical Imagery* (1947), p. 124. Miss
Tuve's book is much the most detailed and intelligent discussion of Renaissance imagery that
I know, though the native English trends opposed to Continental poetic theory are unduly
minimized. And the influence of the social background is not discussed at all.

basis of *all* poetry. But this is to go too far. The metaphor is not the only basic synthetic statement, just as Renaissance poetry is not the only kind of poetry. The other English poetic schools have their own basic forms of synthetic statement, their favourite 'figures of speech', which are the reflection of their own social orders, and the reader who aspires to understand the whole range of English poetry will need to familiarize himself with all of them.

If the original metaphor, the brand-new coinage of the individual poet, is the basis of Renaissance poetry, the popular simile or proverbial comparison would seem to underlie the poetry of the Yeoman Democracy of the later fourteenth and the fifteenth centuries. Langland is always saying that something is not worth a rush, a mite, a pea, a grain or even, once, a pie-crust. And Chaucer adds to this list *inter alia* a straw, a leak, a fly, a gnat, a butterfly, a haw, a bean, a toad, a hen and an old shoe. Similar catalogues could be constructed of the similes of quantity, colour, temperature, noise, ignorance, beauty, etc.

Such comparisons, which normally derive from popular usage and are never the copyright of the individual poet, add enormously to the vividness and liveliness of the poems not only of Chaucer and Langland but also of Gower, the miracle plays (especially the Towneley series), 'Sir Gawayne and the Grene Knight', the best ballads and carols, Skelton's doggerel of genius, and indeed all the genuine poetry of the period. The content of these similes is in sharp contrast with that of the metaphors of the Renaissance. For the latter, as Johnson said, the whole of nature and art were ransacked. On the whole, at any rate in the Polished Craftsman and Decadent phases of the school, the more fantastic and far-fetched their metaphors the better the Renaissance poet and his readers were pleased. Chaucer's similes, on the other hand, apart from a diminishing number derived from the French tradition of the *Roman de la Rose*, are familiar and parochial, smelling of the village green and the village ale-house rather than of the arts of poetry and the bestiaries. And some of his most characteristic effects are obtained by going one better than the popular idiom. The Monk, for example, is described in the General Prologue as regarding monastic asceticism as out of date:

> He yaf nat of that text a pulled hen,
> That seith that hunters ben nat hooly men,
> Ne that a monk, whan he is recchelees,[1]
> Is likned til a fissh that is waterlees, –
> This is to seyn, a monk out of his cloystre.
> But thilke text heeld he nat worth an oystre.

[1] 'Neglectful of duty and discipline' (Robinson).

In this passage the similes of the plucked hen and the fish out of water are, of course, popular idioms, but the grotesque oyster is Chaucer's own importation.[1] And how *right* it is!

The Augustans make little use of metaphor. One of the difficulties, indeed, that stand in the way of our appreciation of Dryden and Pope is their frequent insensitiveness to the metaphors latent in popular speech. The following passage from the 'Elegy to the Memory of an Unfortunate Lady' is spoiled for me by the mixed metaphors, though Pope and his contemporary readers probably never noticed anything wrong:

> Ambition first sprung from your blest abodes;
> The glorious fault of Angels and of Gods:
> Thence to their Images on earth it flows,
> And in the breasts of Kings and Heroes glows!

Here 'sprung' and 'flows' suggest that ambition is being compared to a stream, but it is difficult to visualize this stream flowing through the air into the images and impossible to understand why it 'glows' when it gets there. To Pope, however, it is clear that the verbs were almost abstract and had lost most of their sensuous associations. The whole trend indeed of Augustan diction was to 'the Mathematical plainness' that the Royal Society tried to exact from its members, and neither metaphor nor simile is the basic synthetic statement of its poetry. Their place is taken by *paradox*, the simultaneous advancement of two contradictory propositions both of which turn out to be true, *irony*, the apparent contradiction between what is said and what is meant, *oxymoron*, 'the rhetorical term for the combination of words, generally epithet and subject, of opposed and contradictory meanings',[2] and similar devices.

> In pious times, e'r Priest-craft did begin,
> Before *Polygamy* was made a Sin . . .

> Meerly for Safety after Fame they thirst;
> For all Men would be cowards if they durst. . . .

> Or plung'd in Lakes of bitter *Washes* lie,
> Or wedg'd whole Ages in a *Bodkin's Eye* . . .

> How vain the ardour of the Crowd,
> How low, how little are the Proud,
> How indigent the Great!

It is in such passages as these that the sceptical rationalism of the Augustans achieves memorability. The quality that they valued most in

---

[1] He had found the rhyme in Jean de Meun's *Testament*.
[2] P. Vivian, *A Dictionary of Literary Terms* (1908).

poetry was Surprise. In spite of the tameness of his own verse Addison was fully aware of the importance of a semantic gap between the two elements in a synthesis. In the essay on true, false and 'mixed' wit in *The Spectator*[1] he adopts Locke's definition ('the Assemblage of Ideas') with the qualification 'That every Resemblance of Ideas is not that which we call Wit, unless it be such an one that gives *Delight* and *Surprise* to the Reader: These two Properties seem essential to Wit, more particularly the last of them. In order therefore that the Resemblance in the Ideas be Wit, it is necessary that the Ideas should not lie too near one another in the Nature of things; for where the Likeness is obvious, it gives no Surprise.' And Johnson's definition of the Sublime ('the first effect is sudden astonishment, and the second rational admiration'[2]) in effect limits sublimity to the paradox. The Romantic Sublime – of which Burke was the first prophet[3] – was provocative, on the contrary, of *irrational* admiration.

With the mystical individualism of nineteenth-century plutocracy the metaphor comes back as the basic poetic form of statement in the form of symbolism:

There are no lines with more melancholy beauty than these by Burns:

> The white moon is setting behind the white wave,
> And Time is setting with me, O!

and these lines are perfectly symbolical. Take from them the whiteness of the moon and of the wave, whose relation to the setting of Time is too subtle for the intellect, and you take from them their beauty. But, when all are together, moon and wave and whiteness and setting Time and the last melancholy cry, they evoke an emotion which cannot be evoked by any other arrangement of colours and sounds and forms. We may call this metaphorical writing, but it is better to call it symbolical writing, because metaphors are not profound enough to be moving, when they are not symbols, and when they are symbols they are the most perfect of all, because the most subtle, outside of pure sound, and through them one can the best find out what symbols are.[4]

The Romantic symbol differs from the Renaissance metaphor in two important respects: (i) its function is not to compare one thing with another, but to provide the objective correlatives to subjective experience; (ii) unlike a metaphor it can be used more than once by the same poet

---

[1] *The Spectator* (11 May 1711).

[2] Life of Cowley.

[3] *A Philosophical Inquiry into the Origin of our Ideas of the Sublime and Beautiful* (1756).

[4] W. B. Yeats, 'The Symbolism of Poetry' (*Essays* (1924), pp. 191-2). The lines from Burns are misquoted. What Burns wrote ('Open the Door to me, oh') was;

> The wan moon sets behind the white wave,
> And Time is setting with me, oh.

though, unlike the popular similes of the Chaucerians, it is not generally transferable from one poet to another. Wordsworth's 'rocks, and stones, and trees' are peculiar to Wordsworth. Coleridge's symbolic effects of light are peculiar to him. And Blake's symbolism is so much his own that a key is needed to it as much as to his mythology.

The typical symbols of the Romantics are from wild nature. Of the forty-three animals introduced or alluded to in *Prometheus Unbound* only four are domestic (horse, dog, sheep, goat). There are no cattle, pigs, cats, rats, mice, or poultry of any description in the poem. The 'infinitude of truth' that Wordsworth demanded in poetry[1] preferred the untethered and far-ranging species as its symbols. Birds were particularly suitable. Romantic poetry without its skylarks, nightingales, cuckoos and albatrosses would be unthinkable.[2] And water in its various forms – brooks, rivers, seas, mists, clouds and sunsets – had similar attractions. The operative condition was the absence of human association. A one-time page of Rydal Mount told Canon Rawnsley that Wordsworth hadn't been interested in agriculture: 'farming, nor beast, nor sheep, nor fields wasn't in his way, he asked no questions about flocks or herds'. On the other hand; 'He was a man as noticed a deal stones and trees, very particular about trees, or a rock wi' ony character in it.'[3] Fundamentally it is a townsman's interest in the country. The country for the Romantics is not a place where men and women wrest a difficult and precarious living from the soil. It is primarily simply a place to escape to out of the towns. To one who has been long in city pent – Keats adopted the Miltonic line to open an early sonnet describing a day in the country[4] – the attraction of the country is its unlikeness to the town. The emphasis is on its wildness, its solitariness, its freedom from human contamination. The inferiority of the man-made town to the God-made country parallels the inferiority of conscious mind, the product of the social environment, to uninhibited instinct.

If the nature symbol, the synthetic link between the conscious and the subconscious mind, is the basic unit of Romantic poetry, what is it that takes its place in post-Romantic poetry? It is perhaps too soon to be sure, but I am inclined to think that modern poetry also bases itself upon the

---

[1] 'Celebrated Epitaphs Considered.'

[2] 'In a note on *Calvary* he [Yeats] explains that certain birds, "especially such lonely birds as the heron, hawk, eagle, and swan, are the natural symbols of subjectivity"' (Louis MacNeice, *The Poetry of W. B. Yeats* (1941), p. 147).

[3] *Trans. Wordsworth Soc.* No. 6 (1882), pp. 189, 191.

[4] The features of the rustic scene itemized by Keats in this sonnet sufficiently indicate the limitations of his interest in the country. They are the blue sky, the grass, a nightingale and the sunset clouds!

symbol, though our symbolism is not restricted to wild nature and makes no pretension to the mystical significances of Romanticism. As compared with Shelley's Cloud Eliot's Waste Land gives an impression of calculated exploitation. The cloud exists for Shelley in its own right, and he is merely the recorder of its exuberances. Eliot's Hanged Man, Tereus, Tiriesias, Phlebas the Phœnician and the Fisher King have a far less substantial existence. Their value to him is as shorthand transcriptions of certain facets of human experience. Essentially they are simply extensions of his vocabulary, with no more independent reality than the quotations from Shakespeare, Marvell, Dante, etc., which appear side by side with them. Our situation in fact is the obverse of the Renaissance predicament. Then every myth had potential poetic significance because they were all equally credible. In the unpredictable universe one religion was as likely to be true as another. Today every variety of religious experience is potentially significant not because it is considered objectively true now but because it has once been thought true. It is a scrap more evidence how the human mind works. 'All a poet can do today', Owen wrote in the fragmentary Preface that has become the testament of modern poetry, 'is warn. That is why the true Poets must be truthful.' The warnings must have a *factual* basis. They are necessary because of the human proneness to illusion that Romanticism had encouraged with disastrous social consequences. The crucial poetic influence of anthropology and psycho-analysis today derives from their assumptions rather than their conclusions, and particularly from their central assumption that the subconscious mind, racial and individual, is capable of rational study. Modern poetry might be described as a rationalization of Romanticism. The exploits of the subliminal self, which could do no wrong in Romantic eyes, are viewed by us in the sardonic light of a socially conscious science. Our symbols are often identical with theirs, but the synthesis is not between the subconscious mind and the non-human physical world but between the two parts of the mind, the consciousness and the subconsciousness. We are struggling towards the recovery of an integrated personality. Modern poetry is the record of that struggle; its warnings are of the dangers of a relapse.

The preceding discussion has inevitably been dogmatic and oversimplified. To attempt one-page summaries of England's literary and social evolution is to invite dissent on one count or another. They are presented as at any rate better than nothing. Here is a wood without trees. If the map of the wood is a bit crude, as I am afraid it is, part of the responsibility for its inadequacy must lie with those catalogues of trees without a wood in which my colleagues in the world of scholarship have specialized. The subject demands a *combination* of induction and deduction. The specialist investigations must build up into conclusions of general applicability and the wide-ranging generalizations must break down into a technique for dealing with concrete particulars. Until they do, however, there is a clear case for the amateur's home-made makeshift.

So far this book has been an attempt to work out a number of critical formulas. In the earlier chapters it was possible to illustrate such a formula as the Principle of the Semantic Gap by an analysis of familiar poems or passages of English poetry. But the formulas proposed in this chapter have not lent themselves to incidental illustration in the same way. Part Two of the book is intended to remedy this deficiency. Some examples will be found there of the way in which a poetic school can be divided into five phases or generations, but the formula that the discussion of most of the poems revolves round is the suggested identification of the successive poetic schools with the changes in dominant social incentives in this country since the fourteenth century.

# 11

## APPLICATIONS OF THE DEFINITION

# 5

## The Yeoman Democracy and Chaucer's 'Miller's Tale'

I⊤ was only in 1340, until recently the accepted date of Chaucer's birth,[1] that Presentment of Englishry ceased to be law. The repeal of this piece of racial discrimination relieved the hundred or township, in a case of suspected murder, of the *onus* of proving that the victim was an Englishman, in order to escape the heavy communal fine levied for the murder of a Norman. But, though the conquerors and the conquered had at last merged into one nation, it was not yet certain what language this new England would speak. The upper classes still spoke French. Higden, whose *Polychronicon* dates from this period, noted that the gentleman's child spoke French 'in the cradle', and that the snobbery of the yeomanry was making them learn French too. French was the language of the Court, of Parliament, and of the various law courts. And in the grammar schools Latin was invariably taught in French and not in English.

But the predominance of French was not to last. In 1356 it became illegal to plead cases in the London Sheriff's Courts in any language except English. In 1362 English superseded French as the spoken language of the King's law courts. In 1363 the Chancellor opened Parliament in an English speech, and, though Edward III may not have known much English, Henry IV claimed the throne before Parliament 'in Englyssh tonge'.[2] Trevisa, Higden's translator, writing in 1385, reported that by then the use of French had been entirely given up in the grammar schools, and that 'gentil men habbeth now moche yleft for to teche here children Frensch'. And William Nassyngton was able to claim about 1375,

> lerid and lewid, old and young
> All understanden English tongue.

Trevisa considered that the dividing line was the 'furste moreyn', i.e. the Black Death of 1348-9. It is probable enough *a priori* that the acceleration of economic processes brought about by the Black Death[3] would be

---

[1] The date now favoured by the experts is *c.* 1343-4.

[2] See G. G. Coulton, *Chaucer and his England* (4th edn., 1927), pp. 3-4.

[3] 'If there had been no pestilence on the scale of the Black Death, the disintegration of the manor as the result of the working of purely natural forces – the gradual permeation of a money economy: the demand of the lord for a more flexible instrument than the inelastic and cumbrous labour dues: the accumulation of capital in the hands of the servile tenants: the growth of urban markets – must assuredly have been an infinitely slower process' (E. Lipson, *The Economic History of England*, vol. i (8th edn., 1945), p. 102).

accompanied by equivalent social changes. But the rapidity and extent of the linguistic revolution has not been appreciated. It all happened in thirty years. It is as though since 1939 Cockney had suddenly displaced the King's English as the Received Standard, and we were now all trying to talk and write like the East End. The social implications of such a change can be imagined. In the fourteenth century the victory of English meant a discrediting of the whole of Norman-French culture – among other things, of feudalism, of the international church, of courtly love and of poetic rhetoric – and a partial return to the older, simpler culture based essentially on the co-operative open-fields agriculture. A new *class* was suddenly taking the social initiative. (The Peasants' Revolt of 1381 has been described by a modern economist as 'the first great struggle between capital and labour; and the first notable occasion on which the latent feeling of class antagonism was openly manifested'.[1]) Inevitably a new literature came into being as the point of maximum consciousness of this new social order, the 'yeoman minstrelsy', as Sir Edmund Chambers has called it, of the the Robin Hood ballads, the group of narrative poems on the King and Subject theme and similar writings,[2] to which the miracle plays and most of the writings in the alliterative metre can perhaps be added.

Nobody has noticed how interested Chaucer was in this contemporary class struggle. As a boy he had served as a page in the household of Prince Lionel and his earliest poems are redolent of the French culture of the court. But as he approached middle age his poetry becomes noticeably more English and more popular. The gradual change of allegiance can be measured by the decrease in the proportion of rhetorical figures in his poetry and the increase in the number of proverbs and popular idioms.[3] By the 1390s, when he was writing the *Canterbury Tales*, though he is never a partisan, his fundamental sympathies seem to be mainly with the new yeoman democracy of the countryside. It is noteworthy that the only mystical figures in the General Prologue are the Ploughman – who is presumably related to Langland's Piers Plowman – and his brother the Country Parson. But Chaucer is less comfortable with these symbols of the *ideals* of the yeomanry than with such concrete exemplars of the class as the Franklin and the Wife of Bath, and their humbler allies the Miller and the Reeve. By their side the embodiments of 'gentilesse' – the Knight, the Squire, the Clerk and the Prioress – seem unreal and ineffective, while

---

[1] Lipson, *op. cit.*, p. 121.

[2] A good specimen is *Gamelyn* (c. 1350) which there is reason to believe Chaucer had intended to retell as a tale for the Squire's Yeoman.

[3] See J. M. Manly, *Chaucer and the Rhetoricians*, British Academy (1926), and B. J. Whiting, *Chaucer's Use of Proverbs* (Harvard, 1934).

*their* poor relations the 'gentil Maunciple' and the 'gentil Pardoner' are as unedifying as they are secretly unhappy.

The 'Miller's Tale' is almost the best thing Chaucer ever wrote, but except for a passage in Aldous Huxley's brilliant but neglected essay[1] it has received little critical attention. And its heroine Alison, who is described as fit 'for any good yeman to wedde', can be regarded as the embodiment of the yeoman's philosophy of life, much as Shakespeare's Cleopatra embodies the Renaissance idea, Millamant the Restoration's, and Becky Sharp the nineteenth century's. The Tale follows the 'Knight's Tale' and the comic competition of Nicholas and Absolon for the carpenter's wife is obviously intended to provide a worldly contrast to the tragic rivalry of 'gentil' Palamon and Arcite, 'of chivalrie the flowr', for the angelic Emelye ('as an aungel hevenysshly she soong'). This social contrast is underlined in the preliminary 'wordes bitwene the Hoost and the Millere', from which we learn that, when all the pilgrims had pronounced the 'Knight's Tale' 'a noble storie',

> And namely the gentils everichon,

the Host, who has invited the Monk, another 'gentil', to contribute a tale, is interrupted by the drunken Miller, who announces

> I kan a noble tale for the nones,
> With which I wol now quite the Knyghtes tale.

The Miller, in other words, is going to give *his* (English) idea of nobility.

Characteristically Chaucer carefully dissociates himself in advance from this 'cherles tale'. He assures 'every gentil wight' that he is a mere reporter who has to record all that occurred on the pilgrimage, and recommends the prudish to turn over the page to another tale, where he will find plenty

> Of storial thyng that toucheth gentilesse,
> And eek moralitee and hoolynesse.

With this gesture to respectability – which can hardly have been meant very seriously[2] – Chaucer proceeds to his merry tale.

One's first impression is of an earthy physical solidity. This bedroom farce is firmly anchored to the real world. The contrast with the rarefied sentimentality of the 'Knight's Tale' is immediately enforced by the repetition of a line that Arcite had just used in his dying speech, as he

---

[1] *On the Margin* (1923), pp. 203–29. A somewhat fuller discussion will be found in E. M. W. Tillyard's *Poetry: Direct and Oblique* (1934).

[2] The curious figure that Chaucer cuts in his own poems presents a nice critical problem. In the *Canterbury Tales* it is pretty clear that we must not take him too seriously. His apology at the conclusion of the General Prologue for not having introduced the Pilgrims in their order of social precedence is,

> My wit is short, ye may wel understonde!

moralized on the transitoriness of a man's life, now the happy lover, now in the cold grave,

> Allone, withouten any compaignye.

In the 'Miller's Tale' the line is applied to Nicholas, the Oxford post-graduate student, sitting in his 'digs' and planning the seduction of his landlady! There are no emotional overtones in yeoman minstrelsy and there is no vagueness. We know exactly what the parish clerk, Absolon, looked like, *and* Nicholas, *and* the carpenter and his wife, and what clothes they wore. We know their respective ages and their social status. The carpenter owed his downfall to his social presumption:

> Men sholde wedden after hire estaat.

But, because he had money, old John, the simple carpenter of Oseney Abbey, had succeeded in making the young and beautiful Alison his wife. In doing this he had offended not only against the law of 'kind' (nature), which requires the young to marry the young, but also against the social values of the marriage-market. In getting Alison to marry him he had been guilty of matrimonial sharp practice, because her beauty and vitality ought to have earned her a mate higher up the social scale:

> She was a prymerole, a piggesnye,
> For any lord to leggen in his bedde,
> Or yet for any good yeman to wedde.

Alison's proper place in the social hierarchy would have been to be either a lord's mistress or a yeoman's wife. The carpenter, therefore, receives no sympathy at the end of the Tale when he breaks his arm and is made at once a cuckold and the laughing-stock of Oxford. Consistently with this his wife, who has been unfaithful to him and has also connived in the practical joke against him, escapes scot-free. It is significant that of the four protagonists she is the only one who emerges from the episode unscathed and without a stain on her character. Alison is a feminine type that recurs in Chaucer. She is related both to Criseyde and to May in the 'Merchant's Tale', and it is not impossible that she might grow up to be a Wife of Bath. Compared to the talkative males, it is true, she has little to say. Her longest speech only runs to six lines and she is usually content with a few emphatic remarks – though the last word is generally hers. But Alison is a good deal more than a young woman who knows what she wants. The long description that introduces her to the reader might be compared to Enobarbus's picture of Cleopatra on the Cydnus. Here is a whole culture, a way of life, concentrated in a single representative figure. The passage is worth examining in detail.

Although Alison lives in Oxford and so knows the value of money,[1] her looks and costume are described in a series of the similes from country life that were characteristic both of yeoman poetry and of the proverbs of the time. The portrait begins as a study in black and white. Under the white cap Alison's eyebrows are as black as a sloe, and her white smock is embroidered with coal-black silk. Her apron is as white as morning milk. And a lovely simile clinches the contrasting colours:

> She was ful moore blisful on to see
> Than is the newe pere-jonette tree.

(The pear flowers before the leaves show, and the effect in spring, when the tree is 'newe', is of white blossoms against black boughs.) But the description is not only a symphony in colours. Alison is also as slim as a weasel, as soft as wool, and the gayest creature in the world. She sings too like a swallow sitting on the barn, and is as gamesome as a kid or a calf. Her breath is as sweet as mead, or as apples stored in hay or heather. And she is as skittish as a colt. Altogether there are seventeen similes in the thirty-four lines, most of them from the animal or vegetable kingdom. The animals are all domestic and reassuring – except one. The description begins,

> Fair was this yonge wyf, and therwithal
> As any wezele hir body gent and smal.

This simile of the weasel follows a couplet in which we were told that the carpenter by marrying a young wife, had 'fallen in the snare'. Alison is the weasel, the carpenter apparently is the rabbit. The implication provides an ironical comment on the passage a few lines before:

> Jalous he was, and heeld hire narwe in cage,
> For she was wylde and yong and he was old,
> And demed hymself been lik a cokewold.

How right the carpenter was! In the end it is not the young wife but he that is in the cage. And Alison retains a suggestion of something wild, aloof and slightly sinister, a hint of a pagan fertility spirit, through the rough and tumble of the tale.

In Alison Chaucer's synthetic genius has succeeded in fusing two contradictory elements, the human and the animal. The breath of a nature red in tooth and claw blows through her, but on the whole she is the attentive wife, the compassionate lover and the ingenious practical joker. And this dual nature is communicated to the reader by the piling up of

[1] This interpretation is confirmed by the marginal note on l. 3382 in some MSS, 'Unde Ovidius: Ictibus agrestis'. Chaucer's source, which is *not* Ovid, has not yet been identified.

similes from the world of domestic animals (who are related both to wild nature and to man). When Nicholas seemed to be attempting to rape her,

> She sproong as a colt dooth in the trave,
> And with hir heed she wryed faste awey,
> And seyde, 'I wol nat kisse thee, by my fey!'

Like this young colt Alison was full of spirit, but she was potentially tameable, as Nicholas soon found. She symbolizes in her gaiety and good nature the Merry England of a yeoman democracy that had set its face against the theoretical asceticism of the Continental church, on the one hand, and the practical brutality of Continental feudalism, on the other. Its ideals were not particularly high but they were *attainable*, and the evidence of court rolls, field orders and guild records is that, in spite of the Wars of the Roses and the French wars, they were in fact attained more often in the fifteenth century than in other and more splendid periods.

# 6

## Sir Thomas Wyatt and the Renaissance

To the lower classes of the sixteenth century, looking back into the past, the England of the fifteenth century seemed above all a 'merry world'.[1] Shakespeare's John Holland who complains in *Henry VI*, Part 2, that it 'was never merrie worlde in England, since Gentlemen came up' is using the identical phrase and argument that some Oxfordshire anti-enclosure rioters were actually to employ in 1596.[2] The new ruling class of 'Gentlemen' were predominantly the sons and grandsons of the city merchants of the fifteenth century, and the capitalist agriculture that they forced on the countryside meant the end of the old rural democracy and its yeoman minstrelsy. Instead of the simple, almost anonymous 'merry tales', with their frank animalism, poetry passes into the keeping of Renaissance courtiers, learned and passionate, who

> poor Petrarch's long-deceasèd woes
> With new-born sighs and denizened wit do sing.

Sir Thomas Wyatt, courtier and diplomatist and the grandson (through his mother) of a fifteenth-century *nouveau riche*, was the originator of this new poetry. So successful was he that his friend Surrey believed that Wyatt had actually 'reft Chaucer the glory of his wit'. And Leland, the antiquary, was certainly justified in claiming, in his fluent Latin elegy, that Wyatt had initiated a whole school of court poets:

> Nobilitas dedicit te praeceptore Britanna
> Carmina per varios scribere posse modos.

The courtiers Wyatt, Surrey, Sidney, Ralegh, Donne, Carew and Suckling represent the central line in English Renaissance poetry – from which even Spenser, Marlowe and Milton are only magnificent offshoots – and its social basis deserves a more detailed examination than it has

[1] Although the primary sense of *merry* in this phrase, as in 'merry England', was *pleasant*, it seems clear that two other contemporary senses of the word are also implied, viz. *fine* (of climate) and *joyous* (as in modern English).

[2] The ringleaders promised 'a merry world shortly . . . and asked if there were not 100 good men who would rise and knock down the gentlemen and rich men who made corn so dear and who took the commons' (Cal. State Papers Dom. Eliz. (1595-7), p. 316). The phrase recurs again and again in the pamphlets and broadside ballads.

hitherto obtained. Here it will only be possible to make a few of the principal points.

The following sonnet appears to be one of the earliest of Wyatt's poems:

> Whoso list to hunt, I know where is an hind,
>   But as for me – helas, I may no more,
>   The vain travail hath wearied me so sore,
>   I am of them that farthest come behind.
> Yet may I, by no means, my wearied mind
>   Draw from the deer; but as she fleeth afore
>   Fainting I follow. I leave off therefore,
>   Since in a net I seek to hold the wind.
> Who list her hunt, I put him out of doubt,
>   As well as I, may spend his time in vain.
>   And graven with diamonds in letters plain
> There is written, her fair neck round about:
>   *Noli me tangere*, for Caesar's I am,
>   And wild for to hold, though I seem tame.

Wyatt's hind is Anne Boleyn, who was almost certainly his mistress before she was appropriated by Henry VIII. It is true J. M. Berdan[1] and others have argued that the poem cannot be autobiographical, as it is based on a sonnet of Petrarch's. But a comparison of the two poems shows that Wyatt has merely adapted Petrarch – as he also adapted Petrarch's rhyme-scheme – for his own purposes.[2] Petrarch does not *hunt* his beautiful white deer, and the deer is not Caesar's *property* but has been liberated by him. In Wyatt the hunting metaphor is the key to the poem. It is precisely Anne's elusiveness that is so aggravating. Wyatt's egotism – he refers to himself ('I' 'me' or 'my') no less than twelve times, whereas Petrarch has

---

[1] *Early Tudor Poetry* (1920), p. 483.

[2] Una candida cerva sopra l'erba
>   Verde m'apparve, con due corne d'oro,
>   Tra due rivere, all' ombra d'un alloro.
>   Levando'l sole, a la stazione acerba.
> Era sua vista si dolce superba,
>   Ch'io lasciai per seguirla ogni lavoro:
>   Come l'avaro che'n cercar tesoro
>   Con diletto l'affanno disacerba.
> 'Nessun mi tocchi', al bel collo dintorno
>   Scritto avea di diamanti et di topazi:
>   'Libera farmi al mio Cesare parve'.
> Et era'l sol gia volto el mezzogiorno:
>   Gli occhi miei stanchi di mirar, non sazi
>   Quand'io caddi l'acqua, et ella sparve.
>       (*In vita Laurae*, No. clvii.)

only four similar references – had been deeply wounded, and is only partly assuaged by the arrogant casualness of the 'and' in line 11 ('I advise you not to waste your time on this elusive creature – and *incidentally* she is the King's property'), and by the hint to Henry in the last line that even he might have trouble with Anne (as, indeed, he did). The poem is intensely personal and yet attains a certain cool objectivity – largely, I think, by the help of the hunting metaphors.

A related poem is the famous 'They flee from me, that sometime did me seek':

> They flee from me, that sometime did me seek,
> With naked foot stalking in my chamber:
> I have seen them gentle, tame, and meek,
> That now are wild and do not remember
> That some time they put themself in danger
> To take bread at my hand; and now they range
> Busily seeking with a continual change.
>
> Thankèd be Fortune, it hath been otherwise
> Twenty times better; but once, in special,
> In thin array, after a pleasant guise,
> When her loose gown from her shoulders did fall,
> And she me caught in her arms long and small,
> Therewith all sweetly did me kiss,
> And softly said, 'Dear heart, how like you this?'
>
> It was no dream; I lay broad waking:
> But all is turnèd thorough my gentleness
> Into a strange fashion of forsaking;
> And I have leave to go of her goodness;
> And she also to use new-fangleness.
> But since that I so kindly am servèd,
> How like you this, what hath *she* now deservèd?[1]

The editor of *Tottel's Miscellany* (1557), where Wyatt's poem was first printed, prefixed an elaborate title to it, 'The lover sheweth how he is forsaken of such as he sometime enjoyed'. It is not by any means certain, however, that Wyatt's poem is concerned with more than one mistress. The 'they' and 'them' of the first verse are at least partly metaphorical – deer perhaps, as in the sonnet. The vagueness is clearly intentional, and it throws the detailed picture of the second verse into greater relief. The third verse returns to the implications of the original metaphor. It appears that

---

[1] In the last line, where the original manuscript has 'I would fain know what she hath deserved', I have followed Tottel's brilliant emendation (which may derive from Wyatt himself).

Wyatt and the lady are both of them alternately hunters and hunted. (i) When Wyatt was a potential source of *danger* the lady was *gentle* and *tame*, but with his new *gentleness* she has become *wild* and is *forsaking* him. (ii) Previously she had come *stalking* him and *caught* him, but now she has begun to *range*. And Wyatt's problem, since she is treating him *so kindly*, i.e. according to the law of kind, is what to do about it? In another poem he had written

it is of kind<br>
That often change doth please a woman's mind.

His lady, he reflects, is only a wild thing after all, obeying her natural instinct to *continual change*; and to suggest that she may deserve a punishment is to invoke a moral law that would be beyond her comprehension. Wyatt is really more sorry for himself than irritated with this illogical, inconsistent woman.

This analysis should have made it clear what a sophisticated poem 'They flee from me' is. A comparison of it, and the sonnet, with the 'Miller's Tale', will bring out the essential difference between Chaucer's similes and Wyatt's metaphors. In Alison Chaucer effected a synthesis between his own humanism and the primitive nature-mysticism of the countryside. The world of man and the world of growing things, vegetable and animal, come to terms in agriculture – which is basically a *partnership* between the farmer and his fields and livestock. Alison, like the domestic animals and vegetables with which she is compared, is a link therefore between the two worlds. She represents a happy balance of the physical and the spiritual, neither denying her animal instincts nor dominated by them, a human being affectionate and intelligent, but with no pretensions to being an angel like Emelye – or Dante's Beatrice and Petrarch's Laura. Like Criseyde she might have said,

What, par dieux! I am not religious.

Nor did the yeoman democracy she typifies take kindly to the 'religious' (nuns, monks and friars). The one topic on which the yeoman minstrels – and their allies in Church and court, like Langland and Gower – are unanimous is the detestability of the medieval Church. It is usually said that only ecclesiastical corruption was attacked, and that is no doubt generally true. But the extraordinary vigour and venom of the satire suggest a profounder opposition. At bottom the yeoman democracy was still largely pagan, still maintaining the old fertility rituals with maypole and Whitsun ales, harvest and New Year festivals, moon-worship, sacred wells, and even in places the Saxon deities themselves. The Italian *pagani* had been the countrymen, and Christian asceticism, which was born in the towns of the Roman Empire, has always had an uphill fight in agricultural communities. It is significant that the Lollards made their converts in the small towns of East Anglia, the Chilterns and Somerset, and not in the villages. It is perhaps equally significant that when Chaucer tries to write like a 'religious' – in the Tale of Melibee, and the Tales of the Man of Law, the Second Nun and the Parson – he becomes a bore.

Wyatt and his mistresses belong to a different world. The synthesis that Wyatt achieves by his metaphors is between sexual love and the chase, and its implications are worth pursuing. Note first of all that the lover *qua* hunter is primarily a seducer. Love is a sport which reaches its consummation in the capture or killing of the lady. It is natural, therefore, for the deer to fly from the hunter-lover, and their occasional tameness, the rare moments when they seek him out and take bread from his hand, is not traceable to anything he has done but is a kind of miracle, for which 'Fortune' is to be thanked. The seducer, therefore, is not a calculating seducer *à la* Stendhal. His successes and failures just *happen*, without his being able to understand why or to repeat them.[1]

Here we are in the unpredictable universe of the Renaissance with its typical central figure of the Fortune Hunter. The fortune might be economic (the 4,700 per cent interest that Drake paid the investors in the *Golden Hind*), or political (the Prince's favour – an even chancier 'risk'), or religious (the lotteries of 'grace' and predestination), or sexual. But the motives and attitudes are essentially the same. Opposed to the unpredictable universe is the mystical individualist, the Renaissance man who believed in himself and in his luck, not really on rational grounds (in spite of the propaganda for education and 'courtesy'), but simply *because he was himself*. The fascination of the ego sounds through the whole of the poetry of the period from the sensualists like Marlowe to the mystics like George Herbert.

Note too that in this world each man kills the thing he loves. The chase ends in the *battue*. With the seduction completed the love affair is over. The relationship between the mystical individualist and the unpredictable universe is one, not of cooperation (as in Alison and the yeoman democracy), but of hostility. Society is a chaos of competing individuals, each for himself, with the Devil (the God of Bad Luck) taking the hindmost. And social order can only be imposed by force from above. The young Edward VI summed it all up in a schoolboy essay:

---

[1] The word *happy* acquires its modern sense in the sixteenth century. To the Renaissance *happiness*, the favour of fortune, was the supreme felicity. The earlier meaning of *happy* is taken over during the sixteenth century by *lucky*.

This is the true ordering of the state of a well-fashioned commonwealth, that every part do obey one head, one governor, one law, and all parts of the body obey the head, agree among themselves, and one not to eat another up through greediness.[1]

Edward's metaphor was, of course, as much a common-place as his argument. Indeed, as in the case of Wyatt's metaphor of the chase, the metaphor *is* the argument. Renaissance thinking is based on analogy rather than analysis, and the primary object of the analogy is not to convince but to startle or excite. The metaphors appeal to a pre-social, pre-logical level in the mind. As Eliot has put it, in a striking phrase: 'Their words [the words of Shakespeare, Donne, Webster, Tourneur, and sometimes Middleton] have a network of tentacular roots reaching down to the deepest terrors and desires.' The shimmer of the subconscious plays over the surface even of Wyatt's verse:

> It was no dream; I lay broad waking.

In the act of denying the dream he has made the poem more dreamlike. The mysterious vagueness of the setting and the actors – but a vagueness punctuated by brilliantly vivid details like 'naked foot', 'bread at my hand', and the whispered 'Dear heart, how like you this?' – takes the poem out of any social reality. The hunter-lover is not really going to shoot the hind-mistress. Anne Boleyn is safe. And so when a comparison is made between Wyatt's 'her arms long and small' and old January in Chaucer's 'Merchant's Tale,' licking his lips as he mentally undresses May ('Hir myddel smal, hire armes longe and sklendre'), it must be realized that the comparison is not *in pari materia*. Wyatt, it is true, finds it difficult to see the hind's point of view (only Shakespeare and Donne manage to do this), but he is not a vulgar sensualist like January so much as a man *imprisoned in the world of the senses*. His own phenomenal world is the only reality that he can recognize, and he lapses finally into a stoical subject-ivism:

> Then seek no more out of thyself to find
> The thing that thou hast sought so long before,
> For thou shalt feel it sitting in thy mind.[2]

The 'thing' still sits in his brilliant, disturbing but unsatisfying poems, as it once sat in the minds of the subtle and brutal courtiers of Henry VIII.

[1] *Literary Remains*, ed. J. G. Nichols (1857), vol. ii, p. 482.
[2] 'Of the mean and sure estate'.

# 7

# The Money-lender's Son:
## 'L'Allegro' and 'Il Penseroso'

To understand Wyatt's poems it is only necessary to know something of the mental climate that they reflect. The man himself is so representative that his own career throws relatively little light on the poetry. The best commentary on it is not the gossip about Wyatt's relations with Anne Boleyn but a general history of the English Renaissance. Milton's case is different. Milton, like Spenser, is an offshoot from the central trunk of English Renaissance poetry. Sidney's disparagement of the Oratory of Art sums up the critical case against both of them:

Undoubtedly (at least to my opinion undoubtedly) I have found in divers smal learned Courtiers, a more sound stile, then in some professors of learning, of which I can gesse no other cause, but that the Courtier following that which by practise he findeth fittest to nature, therein (though he know it not) doth according to art, thogh not by art: where the other using art to shew art and not hide art (as in these cases he shuld do) flieth from nature, & indeed abuseth art.[1]

Unlike the professional poet, the courtier had the advantage of inheriting both a living tradition and an intimate audience. 'Skill of a Sonet' was a recognized pathway at court not only to the mistress's favour but also to the Prince's, and the circulation of poems in MS kept the courtier-poet in constant touch with a discriminating and stimulating poetry-reading public. A momentary glimpse of that public at the end of the sixteenth century is provided by John Hoskins, a good minor court poet:

It is true that we study according to the predominancy of courtly inclinations: whilst mathematics were in requests, all our similitudes came from lines, circles, and angles; whilst moral philosophy is now a while spoken of, it is rudeness not to be sententious. And for my part I'll make one. I have used and outworn six several styles since I was first Fellow of New College, and am yet able to bear the fashion of the writing company.[2]

There in all its sophistication you have the *milieu* of the young Donne[3]–

[1] *The Defence of Poesie*, ed. A. Feuillerat, *Works of Sidney*, vol. iii (1923), p. 43.

[2] *Directions for Speech and Style*, ed. H. H. Hudson (1935), p. 39. Hoskins became a Fellow of New College in 1586. He was writing *c.* 1599.

[3] It is tempting to connect the simile of the compasses in 'A Valediction; forbidding mourning' with the period 'whilst mathematics were in requests'. Walton dates it 1611, but Walton is often wrong (see R. E. Bennett's edition of Donne [1942]).

'who leaving *Oxford*, lived at the *Innes of Court*, not dissolute, but very neat: a great visiter of Ladies, a great frequenter of Playes, a great writer of conceited Verses'.[1] Somehow or other Shakespeare also insinuated himself into it ('witnes,' as Meres said in another context, 'his sugred Sonnets among his private friends', to say nothing of *Love's Labour's Lost*). But Spenser, the journeyman tailor's son, in spite of his connection with Sidney and Ralegh, always remained on the outside of this privileged community. His accent is never quite that of the initiate, in spite of the *roman à clef* passages of court history in the poems. And, though there are a few Elizabethan MSS of his minor poems (but not of *The Faerie Queene*), they are hardly ever of any textual significance. It seems certain that Spenser preferred to present himself to his readers in the form of the printed book. This may have made for legibility, but it interposed a barrier, a social interval, between the poet and his original readers that a court poet escaped. It meant, in particular, that Spenser never quite knew whom he was writing for – he could not foresee precisely who the pur-chasers of his first editions would be – nor how much he could take for granted in the exposition, for example, of his allegories. Compared with even the minor court poets Spenser's impact on the reader is blurred and lacking in intimacy and directness.[2]

Milton told Dryden, it will be remembered, that Spenser was 'his original'. And it was as the modern Spenser that Humphrey Moseley, the publisher, introduced the author of the 1645 volume to the 'Gentle Reader':

Let the event guide it self which way it will, I shall deserve of the age, by bringing into the Light as true a Birth, as the Muses have brought forth since our famous *Spencer* wrote; whose Poems in these English ones are as rarely imitated, as sweetly excell'd.

The money-lender's son, like the tailor's son, was something of a social anomaly. Outside the family circle there was no ready-made London audience to which he could attach himself. The court was out of reach and was soon to prove itself religiously and politically obnoxious, and the commissions that his father's friend Lawes obtained for him with the Egerton family apparently led to nothing. In the end, partly perhaps through the pamphlets and partly through the connections he had made as Latin Secretary, a public was to welcome *Paradise Lost*. Between 1,300 and

---

[1] Sir Richard Baker, *A Chronicle of the Kings of England* (1643), p. 156. Baker had known Donne personally.

[2] The moral ambiguity can perhaps be also ascribed to Spenser's uncertainty as to his audience. (If the *Bower of Bliss* was destroyed by his Puritan readers, its charms had been created by the Renaissance elements in his audience.)

1,500 copies were sold in the first year and a half after publication. But Milton's relationship with these Puritan intellectuals , some of whom we meet in the later sonnets,[1] is not likely to have been creative. The 'fit audience' that he hopes his Muse will secure is one that she must 'find'. It is not there already. The only reading public that Milton was conscious of at this stage apparently was those 'vulgar Readers' whose love of rhyme is curtly censured in the note on 'The Verse' prefixed to the later issues of the first edition of *Paradise Lost*.

But there was one period in his poetic career when Milton was free from this sense of literary isolation. At Cambridge, both as an under-graduate and a B.A., he had felt the stimulating influence of an *audience*, with poet and reader acting and reacting upon each other. There are even traces of an interchange of MSS with the poets of other colleges. Milton of Christ's has

> So bucksom, blith and debonair. ('L'Allegro')

And Randolph of Trinity has

> To make one blithe, buxom and debonair. (*Aristippus*, 1630)

Obviously one of them was plagiarizing the other, and as obviously it doesn't really matter who was the plagiarist and who was the victim.

'An Epitaph on the Marchioness of *Winchester*', one of the last of Milton's Cambridge compositions, is his only poem to have been included in any of those MS collections of the period which were the normal form of circulation for court poetry. It is subscribed there 'Jo Milton of Chr: Coll. Cambr.' In the 1645 volume it is grouped with four other occasional poems ('Song on May Morning', 'On Shakespear', and the two epitaphs on Hobson), all written in the same or the previous year (1630-1), to all of which the same signature might have been appended. It 'places' their author. He is that well-known University Wit, Milton of Christ's. A number of the Latin poems of this period are also occasional. There is one on the death of the Vice-Chancellor of the University, another on the Bishop of Ely's death, and a third, which is lighter in tone, on the death of the University Beadle. All of these poems can be called *functional*.

---

[1] The composition of *Paradise Lost* began in the 1650s. At this period, according to Edward Phillips, 'he was frequently visited by persons of quality, particularly my Lady Ranalagh, whose son for some time he instructed: all learned foreigners of note, who could not pass out of the city, without giving a visit to a person so eminent: and lastly, by particular friends that had a high esteem for him, viz., Mr Andrew Marvel, young Lawrence (the son of him that was president of Oliver's council), to whom there is a sonnet among the rest, in his printed *Poems*: Mr Marchamont Needham, the writer of *Politicus*: but above all, Mr Cyriack Skinner whom he honored with two sonnets' (J. H. Hanford, *A Milton Handbook*, 4th edn. (1946), p. 52).

Milton wrote them either in response to a specific commission or because he felt that the 'meed of some melodious tear' was expected of him by his academic audience. 'Lycidas' therefore is only the last of a series. And the fact gives the poem a special interest. It is the academic terminus, a valediction. The audience that 'Lycidas' implies is in the past. King is dead and their Cambridge contemporaries, the men who got the Fellowship Milton might have had, have sold their souls in pursuit of worldly success:

> What recks it them? What need they? They are sped;
> And when they list, their lean and flashy songs
> Grate on their scrannel Pipes of wretched straw.

Verity thought these lines 'reflect on the lack not only of moral worth in the sermons preached, but also of literary grace and polish'. A more natural interpretation would be to apply them to the *poetry* of the clergy of the period – reverend gentlemen like Herrick, Corbet, Cartwright, Mayne and Strode whose love-poems were not always strictly decorous. The early pamphlets are full of denunciations of the 'libidinous and ignorant Poetasters' of the time, and Milton was always more interested in poetry than in sermons. It is not impossible, indeed, that there is a specific reference in this passage to John Cleveland, the metaphysical poet, who had been Milton's contemporary at Christ's and had secured a Fellowship at St. John's in 1634, a step that must have involved his taking orders, though Cleveland, a seventeenth-century Charles Churchill, can obviously have had no real sense of ecclesiastical vocation. Cleveland incidentally was another of the contributors to the *Justa Edouardo King*.

In 1637 (when 'Lycidas' was being written) a social chasm, the foretaste of the Civil War, yawned between Milton and men like Cleveland. And yet ten years earlier, when they had been undergraduates together, their social-literary assumptions and background may easily have been almost identical. Milton's early poetic history is one of a surrender to Cambridge, and the Renaissance world that the University stood for, followed by a profound moral revulsion from it. In this psychological drama the key poems are, I believe, 'L'Allegro' and 'Il Penseroso', though their significance has been misunderstood hitherto because they have been misdated.

Tillyard has recently demonstrated how 'academic' the two poems are.[1]

[1] E. M. W. Tillyard, *The Miltonic Setting* (1938). A useful essay, but Tillyard has failed to convince me either that the day-versus-night theme is important or that the opening of 'L'Allegro' is burlesque. The strict parallelism between the two poems would have required, in the latter case, a burlesque opening to 'Il Penseroso' – which we do not get. Cleanth Brooks has an ingenious chapter on the light symbolism of the poems in *The Well Wrought Urn* (1947), which would be more persuasive if he had taken into account (i) Milton's own weak eyesight, (ii) the Latin-Italian literary tradition of a sunshine that is always uncomfortably hot and bright.

The system of disputations – with one student maintaining in a formal Latin speech and another opposing with equal formality some familiar philosophical proposition set them by the University authorities – naturally encouraged a *pro* and *con* structure. And the elaborate mythological preludes are entirely in the style of contemporary Cambridge disputations, if we may judge by Milton's own university exercises (the so-called 'Prolusions'). According to Tillyard the poems were written in the summer of 1631 (Milton's last Long Vacation). A more probable date is the late summer or autumn of 1629.[1] They are almost certainly the pastoral poems referred to in the final couplet of 'Elegia Sexta' (a letter in Latin verse to his friend Diodati written either at the very end of 1629 or the beginning of 1630):

> Te quoque pressa manent patriis meditata cicutis,
>     Tu mihi, cui recitem, judicis instar eris.

('For you other strains too are waiting, strains oft practised, strains struck out from my native country's reeds: you shall serve as the critic to whom I shall recite them.'[2])

Unless the reference is to some English pastorals now lost,[3] Milton *must* be alluding to 'L'Allegro' and 'Il Penseroso', perhaps in an unrevised form, which had apparently been written since he had last seen Diodati.[4]

This dating of the poems gets over the difficulty of the 'Anglo-Catholic' conclusion of 'Il Penseroso'. In 1631 Milton had almost certainly already

---

[1] Some incidental confirmation of the earlier date is provided by the verbal forms and spellings. The form 'ycleap'd' ('L'Allegro' 12) is paralleled by 'ychain'd' ('Nativity Ode' 155) and 'Star-ypointing' ('On Shakespear' 4). Milton never used y- forms after 1630. The spellings 'Wher' ('L'Allegro' 60, 79), 'Streit' ('L'Allegro' 68), 'lincked' ('L'Allegro' 140) and 'Cipres' ('Il Penseroso' 35) in the 1645 text are unique in Milton and differ considerably from the *Comus* spellings. The volume claimed to have been 'Printed by his true Copies', and these forms look more like author's spellings than printer's spellings. The order of the poems in the 1645 volume is generally believed to have been roughly chronological. Milton seems to have divided the poems into three groups; (i) religious verse ('Nativity Ode' – 'At a Solemn Musick'): (ii) occasional pieces (Winchester Epitaph – Hobson epitaphs): (iii) Renaissance pieces ('L'Allegro' – *Comus*). Note that in the third group 'L'Allegro' and 'Il Penseroso' *precede* the Sonnets – the earliest of which are generally dated 1630 (Milton bought his copy of della Casa's sonnets in December 1629).

[2] This is the Columbia Edition translation (vol. I, pt. i, p. 215). The translation in the Oxford Milton is on the same general lines. Masson took the reference to be to the 'Nativity Ode' which Milton had just been describing, but the use of the word *cicuta* (invariably used in Latin poetry, in a literary context, to describe pastoral poetry) makes this impossible. I am indebted to Professor Eduard Fraenkel for assistance with this passage.

[3] This is most unlikely. Milton even preserved his schoolboy translations of Psalms 114 and 136 as well as the fragment 'The Passion' which he had abandoned 'nothing satisfi'd with what was begun'.

[4] We can be certain that Milton had seen Diodati in July 1629, when the latter obtained an M.A. degree at Cambridge. Diodati had got his Oxford M.A. in 1628.

made up his mind not to go into the Church, as it had been his original intention to do. The decision reflects a growing Puritan antipathy to the High Church trends represented by Laud and Andrewes. In 1631 stained glass-windows, organs and anthems would have been 'impossible', except as the objects of satire or denunciation. In 1629, however, Milton was still a humanist and an aesthete, and these poems are catalogues of rival 'pleasures' and 'delights', not of competing duties and contradictory obligations. There is even an occasional suggestion of comedy. For example, the cock, who

> Stoutly struts his Dames before,

or the Breughel interior of the 'up-land Hamlet', beginning

> She was pincht, and pull'd she sed,

or that delightfully casual apology for mythological incest,

> His daughter she (in *Saturns* raign,
> Such mixture was not held a stain).

The conflict between reason and passion that dominated the later Milton has not yet made its appearance. Instead we have a fusion of two elements that lay nearer the surface of his mind. They are (i) the world of classical mythology, and (ii) the English countryside.

Leavis has pointed out how the verse comes to life in *Paradise Lost* whenever there is an 'evocation of that serene, clear, ideally remote classical world so potent upon Milton's sensibility'.[1] This is true and important. But in *Paradise Lost, Paradise Regained* and *Samson Agonistes* the references to classical mythology are normally accompanied by a re- minder that it is not *true*. In many passages the reader is specifically warned that these things are 'fables' or 'fabled', and the words 'feign'd', 'erring', 'mystic', 'dreams', a mere 'name' accompany many of Milton's other allusions to classical legends. These notice-boards, as they might be called ('Warning. This way to beauty. Go back for truth'), are an indication of the arrival of Eliot's 'dissociation of sensibility'. Sprat's *History of the Royal-Society of London*, which was published in the same year as *Paradise Lost*, had contained a tart dismissal of the 'Wit of the Fables and Religions of the Antient World':

The Wit of the Fables and Religions of the Antient World is well-nigh consum'd. They have already serv'd the *Poets* long enough; and it is now high time to dismiss them; especially seeing they have this peculiar *imperfection*, that they were only *Fictions*, at first: whereas *Truth* is never so well express'd or amplify'd, as by those Ornaments which are *Tru* and *Real* in themselves.[2]

---

[1] F. R. Leavis, *Revaluation* (1936), p. 45.         [2] p. 414.

But all this was still a long way off in the 1620s. Questions of truth, and even of goodness, had not arisen yet, as Milton read and re-read 'the smooth Elegiack Poets, whereof the Schooles are not scarce. Whom both for the pleesing sound of their numerous writing, which in imitation I found most easie; and most agreeable to natures part in me, and for their matter which what it is, there be few who know not, I was so allur'd to read, that no recreation came to me better welcome.'[1]

The schoolboy's intoxication with classical mythology is one element, then, in 'L'Allegro' and 'Il Penseroso'. The poems' peculiar distinction derives from their blend of myth with the English landscape and social life. Eliot has complained that the imagery is 'all general', quoting:

> While the Plowman neer at hand,
> Whistles ore the Furrow'd Land,
> And the Milkmaid singeth blithe,
> And the Mower whets his sithe,
> And every Shepherd tells his tale
> Under the Hawthorn in the dale.

On which Eliot comments: 'It is not a particular ploughman, milkmaid, and shepherd that Milton sees (as Wordsworth might see them); the sensuous effect of these verses is entirely on the ear, and is joined to the concepts of ploughman, milkmaid, and shepherd.'[2] But this is to miss the point. In this passage Milton is providing a list of morning *sounds* – exactly comparable, as it happens, with the two catalogues of evening sounds in Wordsworth's *An Evening Walk* – and, if there are no details about the ploughman, etc., that is because the Cheerful Man is only concerned with them as *noise-producers*. How carefully the young Milton could use his eyes is demonstrated by the lines immediately following those quoted by Eliot:

> Streit mine eye hath caught new pleasures
> Whilst the Lantskip round it measures,
> Russet Lawns, and Fallows Gray,
> Where the nibling flocks do stray.

The second couplet is a masterpiece of concentrated observation. The sheep have broken through the temporary fence round the parish's fallow field, no doubt because the common pastures are 'Russet', the short-rooted grass having 'burned', as farmers say, in the hot dry weather. 'Russet' is decidedly not the epithet one would have expected for 'Lawns' (the later Milton would have preferred 'green' or perhaps 'verdurous') –

---

[1] *Apology for Smectymnuus* (1642). Columbia Edition, vol. III, pt. i, p. 302.
[2] 'A Note on the Verse of John Milton', *Essays and Studies*, English Association (1936).

nor is 'Gray' what one would have expected for 'Fallows'. Milton must have had his eye on a real field. Most fallows after the summer ploughing are brown, but this field, perhaps because the subsoil was chalk, was grey. Milton is quite as specific about it as Wordsworth could have been.[1]

Various attempts have been made to identify the scenes described in the two poems as at Horton in Buckinghamshire or in the Cambridge and Oxford districts. The significant thing is that such attempts can quite plausibly be made. Milton's landscapes at this stage are the real thing; they have not come out of books, like those in 'Lycidas'. The obvious parallel with 'L'Allegro' and 'Il Penseroso' is 'The Scholar Gipsy' and 'Thyrsis.' Arnold gives the place names and Milton doesn't, but the poetic formula, an unselfconscious blend of classical pastoral and English landscape, is the same. It is effective because it is detailed and actualized. We believe in the neat-handed Phyllis and the savoury dinner she has prepared for Corydon and Thyrsis because we can *see* that smoking cottage 'betwixt two aged Okes'.

The day-boy of St Paul's had already acquired the taste for classical mythology, but this vivid, loving, humorous faculty of exact observation was the gift of Cambridge. Cambridge provided Milton with his first glimpse of the real adult world. With the hot-house atmosphere of Bread Street left behind – unlike the Ruskins, the Miltons *père* and *mère* did not follow their prodigy to the University – Milton was at last able to stand on his own feet. The Cambridge letters or 1628 to his left-wing friend Alexander Gill – who was to find himself in hot water the next year for drinking the health of Buckingham's murderer – are one of the few pieces of first-hand evidence we have of the kind of person Milton was at this time. Their tone, humorous and self-assured, is exactly that of 'L'Allegro' and 'Il Penseroso'. A Fellow of the College has asked him to provide his (the Fellow's) verses for the next graduation ceremony, 'being himself already long past the age for trifles of that sort!' And he ends another letter with a nice mock-solemnity: 'Vale Vir Erudite' ('Farewell, Learned Sir').

But Cambridge society, though it provided the stimulus to the cool, cultured objectivity of the two poems, was too limited and fragmentary

---

[1] Milton is a much better farmer than one might have expected. The 'Taint-worm' described in 'Lycidas' as killing 'the weanling herds that graze' is obviously the intestinal worm that the modern farmer calls 'husk', which is normally only fatal, as Milton correctly says, to newly weaned calves when they start grazing. Milton's grandfather and uncle farmed at Stanton St John near Oxford, and Milton must have stayed at the farm when he was wooing Mary Powell, whose father was the squire of the neighbouring village of Forest Hill. No doubt there had been earlier visits too. Stanton St John may be the 'up-land Hamlet' of 'L'Allegro'.

to be able to satisfy Milton for long. The five elegiac couplets that are
appended to 'Elegia Septima' are the formal retractation:

> Haec ego mente olim laeva, studioque supino
> Nequitiae posui vana trophaea meae . . .

'Sex has been exorcized. The reading of Plato has quenched its fires.' This
is the gist of what is not the least remarkable of Milton's autobiographical
excursions. In striking contrast to the modesty and impersonality of
'L'Allegro' and 'Il Penseroso' here we have the ego enthroned in all its
formidable arrogance. Unfortunately the lines are undated, but they can
hardly be earlier than 1635. ('Elegia Septima' was written in 1628, and *olim*
presumably implies an interval of at least seven years.) They are perhaps
the most repellent product of that social vacuum to which Milton con-
signed himself in the reaction against Cambridge, but they are not alone.
They had been preceded many years before by the last of the Latin elegies.
The 'Elegia Sexta' (1629), in addition to the allusion to his new English
pastorals, provides a kind of parallel to 'L'Allegro' and 'Il Penseroso' in the
portraits it paints of the typical elegiac poet, who sings of love and wine,
and the typical epic poet, who tackles higher themes and must lead a more
ascetic life. The elegiac poet is Diodati and perhaps the Milton of the last
few years; the epic poet represents the new rôle in which Milton has now
cast himself:

Let him live a simple, frugal life, after the fashion of the teacher who came from
Samos [Pythagoras], let herbs offer him food that works no harm, let pellucid
water stand near him, in a tiny cup of beechen wood, and let him drink only sober
draughts from a pure spring. On such a poet are imposed, too, a youth free of
crime, pure and chaste, and a character unyielding. . . . In this way, story says, wise
Tiresias lived, after the light had been swept away from him, and Ogygian Linus,
and Calchas, exiled from his hearth, a hearth doomed to destruction, and aged
Orpheus, in the lonely grots.[1]

Here is 'The Hairy Gown and Mossy Cell' and the 'Prophetic strain' of
'Il Penseroso's' conclusion. But it is all a degree more solemn. The flavour
of irony with which the twenty-year old poet had looked forward to
spending his 'weary age' botanizing and astronomizing in a hermitage is
no longer there.

By 1631, the date of the Seventh Prolusion, the prophetic solemnity has
deepened and we are not far off the morbidities and contradictions of
*Arcades* and *Comus*. The poet, it seems, must be a polymath. If he is also
strictly chaste, the whole world of nature and universal history will be
intelligible to him. One such man can reform a whole state! Milton even

---

[1] Columbia Edition translation, vol. i (1931), pp. 211-13.

specifies the number of years it will take to acquire polymathy. Provided one starts young enough and works every day it should be possible to complete the cycle of the sciences 'within the age of Alexander the Great'.[1] Alexander died when he was thirty-three. Milton, who had fulfilled the other conditions by then, celebrated his thirty-third year by writing his first pamphlet – which nobody read. He celebrated his thirty-fourth year by taking to himself a wife – who promptly left him. The difficult years that followed were spent in unlearning the half-baked Christian Platonism of which 'Il Penseroso' provides the first glimpse. Though he was never to recapture the cool realism of 'L'Allegro', *Paradise Lost* attained its own massive objectivity. It has been compared to Joyce's *Ulysses*. Accepting the parallel one might equate *Comus* with the *Portrait of the Artist* and 'L'Allegro' and 'Il Penseroso' with *Dubliners*. The crystal perfection with which both Joyce and Milton began was short-lived precisely because it had no effective social basis. The accident of birth had deposited the Anglo-Irishman and the money-lender's son a little to the side of the central literary current of their times. The reservations that, with all their greatness, their writings continue to excite, are primarily attributable to this social accident.

Milton was unlucky in another way. By the time he reached Cambridge the classic moment in English Renaissance poetry had already passed. If he had not been the son of a money-lender he would still have been faced with the problems set by a literary tradition that was already past its prime. As it was he did not escape altogether from the limitations of the Polished Craftsman. His poetical contemporaries, the men who were more or less his own age, were men like Habington, Randolph, Davenant, Fanshawe, Waller, Suckling and Cartwright. In spite of the grace and charm of their verse – Davenant in particular deserves to be more read than he is – they are all distinctly minor poets, metaphysical *epigoni*. With the exception of Waller (who became the first Augustan) their essential achievement is limited to elegant variations in the tradition of courtly wit. The compliment that Suckling paid Davenant applies to the whole group:

> Since the great lord of it [wit],
> Donne, parted hence, no man has ever writ
> So near him, in's own way.

Milton was a good deal more than a sedulous ape, and he had no use for Donne, but his imitations, which are not always distinguishable from plagiarism, sometimes compromise the purity of the poet-reader relationship. Our admiration for the learning distracts our attention from the

[1] ibid., vol. xii (1936), p. 279.

argument. 'L'Allegro' and 'Il Penseroso' are perhaps less liable to this criticism than *Comus*, 'Lycidas' and *Paradise Lost*, in which the style often seems to have a life of its own that is independent of the poems' overt intentions. A further difference is that in 'L'Allegro' and 'Il Penseroso' the objects of imitation are English. No contemporary reader would have failed to recognize the allusion to Marlowe's 'Passionate Shepherd' and Ralegh's reply in

> These delights, if thou canst give,
> Mirth with thee, I mean to live.

and

> These pleasures *Melancholy* give,
> And I with thee will choose to live.

And the general influence of Spenser (especially in the catalogue of horrors at the opening of 'L'Allegro') and of such Spenserians as Sylvester, Browne and Wither (a favourite of Milton's headmaster Gill) is equally clear. But if the poems are in a sense literary exercises they are exercises of genius. At the age of twenty Milton had already all but exhausted the possibilities of the English pastoral. Those who have attempted it since – Pope, Gray, Cowper, Wordsworth (in *An Evening Walk*), Arnold and Blunden – have added little or nothing to the strains this astonishing young man 'struck out from his native country's reeds'.

# 8

# A Word for Waller

WALLER is the Augustan Wyatt. 'Unless he had written', Dryden owned, 'none of us could write.'[1] In the memorial volume that Rymer, the critic and historian, edited in 1688 Sir Thomas Higgons compared Waller's contribution to the English language with Petrarch's to Italian:

> The *English* he hath to Perfection brought;
> And we to speak are by his Measures taught.
> Those very *Words*, which are in Fashion now,
> He brought in Credit half an Age ago.
> Thus *Petrarch* mended the *Italian* Tongue:
> And now they speak the Language which he sung.[2]

And Atterbury paid a similar tribute in 1690:

He undoubtedly stands first in the List of Refiners, and for ought I know, last too; for I question whether in *Charles* the Second's Reign, *English* did not come to its full perfection; and whether it has not had its *Augustean Age*, as well as the Latin ... In the mean time, 'tis a surprizing Reflection, that between what *Spencer* wrote last, and *Waller* first, there should not be much above twenty years distance; and yet the one's Language, like the Money of that time, is as currant now as ever; whilst the other's words are like old coyns, one must go to an Antiquary to understand their true meaning and value.[3]

---

[1] Preface to Walsh's *Dialogue concerning Women* (1691).

[2] *Poems to the Memory of that Incomparable Poet Edmund Waller Esquire by Several Hands* (1688), p. 3. Leland had compared Wyatt with Dante and Petrarch in the same way.

[3] *The Second Part of Mr Waller's Poems* (1690), Preface. This passage appears to be the first in which the term 'Augustan' is applied to the English language. The political analogy had been drawn by Waller himself in 'A Panegyric to my Lord Protector' (*c.* 1654);

> As the vexed world, to find repose, at last
> Itself into Augustus' arms did cast:
> So England now does with like toil oppressed,
> Her weary head upon your bosom rest.

In *Astræa Redux* (1660), ll. 320-3, Dryden transferred the compliment to Charles II. The first use of 'Augustan' in connection with English literature is apparently in John Oldmixon's *Reflections on Dr Swift's Letter* (1712). Oldmixon considered Charles II's reign 'the Augustan Age of English Poetry'.

Atterbury's difficulties with Spenser were shared by many of his contemporaries. In 1687 'a Person of Quality' (who was really Edward Howard) brought out a modernization of the first book of *The Faerie Queene* in heroic couplets as *Spencer Redivivus*. It begins;

> A Worthy Knight was Riding on the Plain,
> In Armour Clad, which richly did Contain
> The Gallant Marks of many Battels fought,
> Tho' he before no Martial Habit sought.

Nor was it only on historical grounds that Waller was admired. Hume considered him the English Horace.[1] Chesterfield recommended him to his son for spare-time reading with Horace, Boileau and La Bruyère.[2] And he is frequently quoted by the two most dazzling creations of Restoration comedy – Etherege's Dorimant[3] and Congreve's Millamant.[4]

But today Waller's name is mud. The following is a typical pronouncement:

No poetical reputation of the seventeenth century has been so completely and irreparably eclipsed as that of Edmund Waller. . . . Whereas Cowley and Cleveland can still give pleasure, Waller's name calls up scarcely more than two lyrics of attenuated cavalier grace, 'On a Girdle' and 'Go lovely Rose', and a dim memory of much complimentary and occasional verse. . . . Any public or private occasion could release a stream of his lucid rhetoric. . . . For us he remains a fluent trifler, the rhymer of a court gazette.[5]

The gap between the eulogies of the seventeenth and eighteenth centuries and the modern assessment is clearly a wide one. It can only be bridged, I believe, by the application of the critical principles laid down earlier in this book. In particular we need to know what the audience was that Waller originally addressed and what that audience expected from poetry.

Goldsmith included two poems by Waller in his *Beauties of English Poesy* (1767). They were not, however, 'On a Girdle' and 'Go lovely Rose', but 'On the Death of the Lord Protector' and 'The Story of Phœbus and Daphne Applied'. And Goldsmith, in his critical notes, makes no mention of Waller's cavalier grace. What he says is: 'A modern reader will chiefly be struck with the strength of thinking.' The fact is there are two Wallers – a minor Renaissance poet and a major Augustan poet. To concentrate on the former and overlook the latter is as uncritical as it would be to identify Yeats with 'The Lake Isle of Innisfree' and then complain of his attenuated Romanticism.

Miss C. V. Wedgwood has recently accused the cavalier poets of belonging 'to the *arrière*, not to the *avant garde*':

Their whole trend of thought reached back into a receding past, away from the cold and probing realism, both in thought and politics, which was gradually submerging the older world. They were in fact anti-political, just as the King's

---

[1] 'Of the Rise of Arts and Sciences', *Essays Moral and Political* (1741).
[2] Letter of 5 Feb. 1750.
[3] *The Man of Mode* (1676), I, i (*bis*): II, ii: III, iii (*bis*): V, i: V, ii.
[4] *The Way of the World* (1700), IV, i (*bis*).
[5] Douglas Bush, *English Literature in the Earlier Seventeenth Century* (1945), p. 166.

view was anti-political – an attempt to do without politics, not an attempt to reform them.[1]

Waller at any rate escapes this indictment. He was an extremely able Member of Parliament, and after the Restoration, as Father of the House, exercised a useful restraining influence on royalist extremists. And Waller's best poem, 'A Panegyric to my Lord Protector' (*c.* 1654) is specifically political, one of the finest political poems in English. It might be described as a seventeenth-century equivalent of W. H. Auden's 'Spain', or of the 'Prologue' to his *Look, Stranger!* Although the phrasing is not as brilliant as in Marvell's famous 'Horatian Ode' (1650), it is in some ways a better poem because it makes better sense. The political advice that Marvell gave Cromwell was much of it extremely inept – the recommendation to invade France and Italy, for example, or to exterminate the Scots. Waller's prescriptions, in these two matters, were the eminently sensible ones of a balance of power policy in Europe and a union with Scotland. And the analysis of England's economic position is equally shrewd. Unfortunately the poem is too long to quote. Here instead is 'The Story of Phœbus and Daphne Applied', which Goldsmith admired and which Elijah Fenton (Pope's collaborator in the translation of the *Odyssey*) considered 'one of the most beautiful Poems in our own, or any other modern language':[2]

> Thyrsis, a youth of the inspirèd train,
> Fair Sacharissa loved, but loved in vain.
> Like Phœbus sung the no less amorous boy,
> Like Daphne she, as lovely and as coy.
> With numbers he the flying nymph pursues,
> With numbers such as Phœbus' self might use.
> Such is the chase when Love and Fancy leads,
> O'er craggy mountains and through flowery meads,
> Invoked to testify the lover's care
> Or form some image of his cruel fair.
> Urged with his fury, like a wounded deer,
> O'er these he fled; and now approaching near,
> Had reached the nymph with his harmonious lay,
> Whom all his charms could not incline to stay.
> Yet what he sung in his immortal strain,
> Though unsuccessful, was not sung in vain.
> All but the nymph that should redress his wrong,
> Attend his passion, and approve his song.

[1] 'Poets and Politics in Baroque England', *Penguin New Writing*, No. 21 (1944), pp. 129-30.
[2] 'Observations on some of Mr Waller's Poems', p. xl (appended to Fenton's edition of Waller, 1729).

> Like Phœbus thus, acquiring unsought praise,
> He catched at love, and filled his arm with bays.

The poem's success is primarily due to the series of *surprises* that the working out of the Waller-Sacharissa and Phœbus-Daphne parallel provides. The impersonality of the poem is in striking contrast to Renaissance egotism. Although in comparing himself to Phœbus Waller might be thought to run the risk of being caught blowing his own trumpet, in fact he is so detached from the whole situation that the danger does not arise. His love for Sacharissa and her rejection of it have been abstracted out of their human context and are here simply disembodied concepts that the mind can play with in the dry light of reason. Even metaphor, the fundamental Renaissance device, is adapted to non-Renaissance uses. Half-way through the poem, indeed, the metaphoric level suddenly changes. The mountains and meads begin, as it were, in quotation marks; they are simply the conventional similes of the conventional love poet. But at 'Urged with his fury' the imagery turns into real places that the poet is imagined to be actually traversing, and he is finally said to be 'like a wounded deer'. There are therefore three metaphoric levels altogether: (i) the conventional similes, (ii) Waller imagined on the mountains, (iii) Waller on the mountains compared to a deer. Though this confusion is, I think, attractive, the metaphoric sophistication it implies is an indication how far Waller is outside the Renaissance tradition. Such acrobatics would have been impossible for a poet like Donne, a fantastic, who thought in metaphors. Waller is *playing* with metaphor here in the interests of paradox.

It is tempting to compare the poem with Marvell's 'Garden'. It is even possible that Marvell's

> Apollo hunted Daphne so
> Only that she might laurel grow

derives directly from Waller's poem. But the basic attitudes to life are very different. Marvell's green thought in a green shade is sheer solipsism, even if it is tinged with irony. Waller, on the other hand, is well aware of the worldly value of a crown of bays. He is the man of sense for whom a success in one direction compensates a disappointment in another. Here there are no heart-breaks. The synthesis of man the individual and man the social unit is complete.

Waller's reputation as a poet has suffered because of his political changes of front. To Gosse he is 'the easy turncoat,' the author of 'smooth emasculated lyrics'.[1] And H. J. Massingham, after a cascade of inaccurate abuse,

---

[1] *Seventeenth Century Studies* (1914), pp. 221, 227.

sums it all up in the statement that 'his literary product is no less con-
temptible than his public career'.[1] It is true that Waller was an ardent
Royalist in the Civil War, that he made his peace with Cromwell, who
was his cousin, in 1651, and that at the Restoration he gave Charles II an
effusive poetic welcome. But in all this he was only doing what the rest
of his class were doing, if rather more noisily. The younger squires were
not believers in the Divine Right of Kings or of anybody else. Intellectually they were rationalists (Waller, Denham and Dryden were among
the earliest members of the Royal Society), and their economic roots were
not at court but in the land. Their principal political requirement was a
government that would enable them to develop their country estates without interference. Waller's objection to the abolition of episcopacy was not
religious but economic:

I look upon episcopacy as a counterscarp or outwork, which, if it is taken by this
assault of the people . . . we may in the next place have as hard a task to defend our
property as we have lately had to recover it from the prerogative. If, by multi-
plying hands and petitions, they prevail for an equality in things ecclesiastical, the
next demand may perhaps be *Lex Agraria*, the like equality in things temporal.[2]

And this was essentially the point of view taken by Cromwell and Ireton
in the Army's Leveller debates. Ireton's objection to universal suffrage
was: 'If you admitt any man that hath a breath and being . . . we destroy
propertie. . . . Noe person that hath nott a locall and permanent interest in
the Kingdome should have an equal dependance in Elections.'[3]

To Waller and to Ireton property *is* land. 'Real' estate, as it came to be
called at this period[4] in contradistinction to the intangible estates of the
merchants, provided the only rational basis of society. 'Law', as Swift put
it, 'in a free Country: is, or ought to be the Determination of the Majority
of those who have Property in Land.'[5] The conclusion reflected fairly
enough the distribution of wealth at the time. According to Gregory
King's estimate, the capital value of the country's land and buildings in
1688 was £234 million, whereas the liquid capital, including livestock,
only amounted to £86 million. As long as the balance of property retained this ratio, as Harrington, the political theorist of the squirearchy,
had shown, the ruling class was necessarily made up of the landowners, of
whom the King was only one. The balance only swung away from land
about 1800, when a new ruling class of urban capitalists emerged.

[1] *A Treasury of Seventeenth Century English Verse* (1920), p. 373.
[2] Cit. M. Dobb, *Studies in the Development of Capitalism* (1946), p. 174.
[3] *Clarke Papers*, vol. ii, p. 314.          [4] See *O.E.D.* s.v. 'real' and 'estate'.
[5] *Thoughts on Various Subjects.*

The agricultural roots are important if Augustan poetry is to be read and understood. When the King of Brobdingnag had completed his cross-examination of Gulliver on European institutions he 'gave it for his opinion, that whoever could make two ears of corn or two blades of grass to grow upon a spot of ground where only one grew before, would deserve better of mankind, and do more essential service to his country than the whole race of politicians put together'.[1] There are two points to be noted in this famous pronouncement. The first is the *animus* against 'politicians', who represent the central government – an artificial creation often at cross-purposes with the 'natural' autocracy of the Justices of the Peace. The second is the emphasis on agricultural improvement – a movement generally associated with the second half of the eighteenth century, the period of the Parliamentary Enclosures and Arthur Young's Board of Agriculture, but in fact already active, as the Royal Society's inquiries had shown, at the Restoration. The two points are complementary and they must both be borne in mind when reading the poems of the great Augustans – Dryden, Pope, Gray, Goldsmith and Cowper, as well as Swift – and the plays of Gay and Fielding.

Agricultural improvement meant the so-called 'Norfolk' or 'four-course' system, which by diversifying corn crops with roots and one-year leys provided winter fodder for more livestock while raising cereal yields at the same time. But the introduction of the system normally involved (i) costs of enclosure beyond the average farmer's purse, and (ii) a squeezing out of the smallholders. In the process the three-tier rural hierarchy emerged of landlords, tenant farmers and agricultural labourers. Lilliput, it will be remembered, had a similar class-structure. The rural elements in Augustan society were therefore anti-egalitarian and were consequently in uneasy partnership with its urban rationalism, which presupposed a measure of social equality. As against the 'private sense' of the Renaissance (alias 'enthusiasm' or 'inspiration'), the Augustans had set up 'common sense', i.e. the rational faculty that is common to all human beings, except lunatics and babies, and that distinguishes us from animals. It was in the name of this common sense that they justified the rule of landed property. The new science was also the product of common sense. And their ethical Christianity was a common-sense religion. But this community of sense was not allowed to become a community of votes, education or income. Theoretically men were all equal, but in most of the practical affairs of life a rigid social stratification determined their relations with their fellows.

[1] *A Voyage to Brobdingnag*, ch. vii.

This central contradiction is the ultimate explanation of the pretentiousness and the emptiness of much Augustan poetry. With no mystical or traditional basis of authority on the one hand, and no rational basis on the other, except in the single field of agricultural improvement, the ruling class could only justify its privileges in the eyes of the nation by being an *aristocracy*, living in the best houses, eating the best food, reading the best books and patronizing the best poets. Hence their 'ritual of conspicuous waste' – Palladian mansions that were too large to live in, Pindaric odes that were too dull to read. None of the Augustan poets entirely resolves the contradiction, and there is therefore no Augustan poem that can quite be called great, but the better poets succeed in mitigating it. Waller's 'Panegyric to my Lord Protector', Dryden's 'Secular Masque', Rochester's 'Satyr against Mankind', Pope's portrait of Lord Timon (in the fourth 'Moral Essay'), and Gray's brilliant 'On Lord Holland's Seat near Margate', go some way at any rate to salving the period's social conscience.

# 9

# Swift's 'Description of the Morning'

IT is time Swift's status as a poet was reconsidered. Although his verse is uneven and often slipshod, at his best he seems to me one of the great English poets. I prefer him to Pope. Pope is a superb *talker* in verse, endlessly vivacious and amusing, but it is difficult to take him or his opinions very seriously. His pet theory of the Ruling Passion can only be described as half-baked. Swift, on the other hand, though he restricted himself to light verse, is fundamentally one of the world's most serious poets. Even his jokes have metaphysical implications. But to understand Swift he must be read in the social context of his own time.

The 'Description of the Morning' was originally published in the ninth *Tatler* (20 April 1709), where it was preceded by a note by Steele, who explains that its realism is an attempt to avoid the usual neo-classic conventionalities (such as Dryden's description of night in *The Indian Emperor* which Rymer had recently extolled as the *ne plus ultra* of poetry[1]):

> Now hardly here and there a hackney coach
> Appearing, showed the ruddy morn's approach.
> Now Betty from her master's bed had flown,
> And softly stole to discompose her own;
> The slipshod 'prentice from his master's door
> Had pared the dirt, and sprinkled round the floor.
> Now Moll had whirled her mop with dexterous airs,
> Prepared to scrub the entry and the stairs.
> The youth with broomy stumps began to trace
> The kennel-edge,[2] where wheels had worn the place.
> The small-coal-man was heard with cadence deep,
> Till drowned in shriller notes of chimney-sweep.
> Duns at his lordship's gate began to meet;
> And brick-dust Moll had screamed through half a street.
> The turnkey now his flock returning sees,
> Duly let out a-nights to steal for fees;
> The watchful bailiffs take their silent stands,
> And school-boys lag with satchels in their hands.

The opening couplets are a straightforward parody of the heroic style. It is possible Swift had in mind a recent address to London in Congreve's

---

[1] In the preface to his translation of Rapin's *Reflections on Aristotle's Treatise of Poesie* (1674).
[2] The 'kennel' is the gutter in the middle of the street. The boy was hoping to find old nails.

*Pindarique Ode . . . On the Victorious Progress of Her Majesty's Arms* (1706):

> Rise, Fair *Augusta*, lift thy Head,
> With Golden Tow'rs thy Front adorn;
> Come forth, as comes from *Tithon's* Bed
> With cheerful Ray the ruddy Morn.

But the parody is almost immediately abandoned for a catalogue of the activities of a Saturday morning (the traditional 'scrubbing day'[1]) in the West End of London. The clue to the poem's peculiar flavour – the quality that Coleridge distinguished in Swift as *Anima Rabelaisii habitans in sicco*[2] – is the juxtaposition of what is morally neutral (the street cries, the charwoman, the boy searching the gutter), or at most venial behaviour (the careless apprentice, the loitering schoolboy), with real social evils (the sexual immorality and financial irresponsibility of the upper class, the appalling prison system). The implication is: 'This is life. Here you have a corner of London at the beginning of the daily round. You recognize the accuracy of the picture, don't you? A, B and C, men and women with immortal souls, are each carrying out in an almost instinctive way his or her particular function, side by side and yet completely independent of each other. But some of these functions, which we all take for granted, are criminal, aren't they? What sort of a society is this in which you, gentle reader, are so deeply compromised?'

A paradox emerges. Like the Yahoos, these Londoners are human beings and yet they are *not* human beings. The dissociated individual, mechanically pursuing his own professional function, irrespective of its social consequences, and oblivious of the activities of his neighbours, possesses none of the qualities that constitute real humanity. In the terminology of *The Battle of the Books*, he is a spider and not a bee.

The social order that Swift is attempting to discredit in this poem is the *laissez-faire* individualism of urban capitalism, and the moral that he is enforcing is the Christian one that we are members of one another. 'Only connect.' But behind the ethical humanism, giving it depth and force, is something more primitive – the countryman's sense of fact. It is this conviction of actuality that makes the poem refreshing instead of depressing. Bad though the state of the towns may be there is no need to despair, Swift implies, as long as it is possible to face the facts of the situation. The amoral urban automata, once seen in their true light, *must* become objects of contempt. There is also an implicit contrast between the uncreative activities of London – even the coalman and the charwoman, whose professions might be thought useful, are only engaged in

---

[1] See Gay's *Trivia* (1716), Book ii, ll. 421-4.
[2] *Table Talk*, 15 June 1830.

moving carbon from one place to another – and the rural partnership of man with nature. 'The difference is, that, instead of dirt and poison, we have rather chosen to fill our hives with honey and wax, thus furnishing mankind with the two noblest of things, which are sweetness and light.' The tonic quality of Swift's poem derives from the *sanity* of the underlying philosophy of life. Because he was insane when he died the nineteenth century dismissed everything that he wrote with which they did not agree as mad. Today it is the Victorian division of labour and the Victorian piling up of *things* that seem mad. Swift's special distinction is that he exposed *laissez-faire* capitalism, and all that it stands for, while it was still no bigger than a cloud the size of a man's hand.

To some extent Swift's satiric effectiveness derives from the attitude he adopts towards his readers. This is different from either Dryden's or Pope's, or indeed any of his contemporaries. As James Sutherland has recently pointed out in a useful pioneer survey of the poet's audience in the eighteenth century, the reading public Swift was addressing was not primarily that of the upper classes of society:

It was his practice, we are told, to have two of his men-servants brought in to listen to his poems being read, 'which, if they did not comprehend, he would alter and amend, until they understood it perfectly well, and then would say, *This will do: for I write to the vulgar, more than to the learned*'.[1] How well he succeeded may be seen on almost any page of his poetical works, where the idiomatic and familiar style carries his meaning easily and forcibly to the least learned reader. But here, as in some other matters, Swift was not wholly at one with his age.[2]

Sutherland appears to impute eccentricity to Swift. In reality, in my opinion, he was not at one with his age only because he transcended it. The poems were, of course, read by the aristocracy. The parody in the opening lines of the 'Description of the Morning' would only have been intelligible to the polite world. But Swift's uniqueness in his century lay in his ability to appeal to several social levels in one and the same work. It is this that sets him by Chaucer and Shakespeare.

Unlike Pope Swift's principal object as a satirist is not to get the reader 'on his side' against his enemies. The futility of such satire is the subject of his recurrent scorn. 'Satire is a sort of glass, wherein beholders do generally discover everybody's face but their own; which is the chief reason for that kind reception it meets in the world, and that so very few are offended with it.'[3] Swift's technique, on the contrary, is to insinuate himself into

[1] *Works* (1762), vol. i, 'To the Reader'.
[2] *A Preface to Eighteenth Century Poetry* (1948), p. 48.
[3] *The Battle of the Books*, 'The Preface of the Author'. F. R. Leavis has a brilliant exposition of Swift's satiric methods in *Determinations* (1934), pp. 79-108.

the enemy ranks disguised as a friend, and once he is there to spread all the alarm and despondency he can. 'I never wonder', he wrote in *Thoughts on Various Subjects*, 'to see men wicked, but I often wonder to see them not ashamed.' It was above all a sense of shame that he tried to inculcate in the capitalists of the middle class. In *A Modest Proposal for Preventing the Children of Ireland from being a Burden to their Parents or Country* (1729), perhaps the greatest of the prose ironies, the real object of Swift's attack is not, as is often asserted, the Irish policy of the Whig Government. The satire goes much deeper. It is an exposure of a whole social philosophy, of which the English economic discrimination against Ireland was only one instance. As in the 'Description of the Morning', which can be considered an early experiment in the *genre* perfected in *A Modest Proposal*, it is again competitive capitalism that Swift is trying to discredit, but the mode of insinuation is more carefully chosen. The satire in the 'Description' had camouflaged itself behind the parody of a recognized literary form. As such, however, it cannot have been likely to have attracted the attention of the City merchants, who were Philistines almost to a man. The trap had the wrong kind of bait. *A Modest Proposal*, on the other hand, talks the actual language of Cheapside and Threadneedle Street. It is to all appearances another essay in the 'political arithmetic' that was so popular in the City of London during the later seventeenth and early eighteenth centuries. The tone of voice, the method of argument, the statistical approach are exactly the kind of thing that the business world of the time had been accustomed to meet in the pamphlets of Sir William Petty, Charles Davenant and Daniel Defoe. Here was their old friend the Economic Man! The opening paragraphs have lulled any suspicions that Swift's authorship might have aroused, and the reader, who finds the Economic Man disposing of his surplus children to the butcher, is brought suddenly face to face with the contradiction between his own weekday and Sunday religions. It is the Augustan paradox, the familiar formula of the poetry of the squirearchy, but here it operates on a grander scale, charged with a higher intensity, than any of Swift's contemporaries were able to command.

# 10

# Gray's 'Elegy' Reconsidered

THE most popular poem in the English language has received curiously little critical attention. Thus in H. S. Davies's useful and representative anthology of criticism *The Poets and their Critics* (1943) Gray's unsatisfactory *Odes* obtain more than twice the space allotted to the *Elegy*. Matthew Arnold thought the *Elegy* had received 'a too unreserved and unbounded praise', but he seems to have made no attempt to elaborate this *obiter dictum*. Indeed, in the whole of his thirty-page essay on Gray the poem is only referred to this once. Cleanth Brooks has recently devoted a chapter to the *Elegy* in the collection of 'studies in the structure of poetry' that he has called *The Well Wrought Urn* (1947), and this is the most elaborate critical discussion that Gray's poem has received since the parodying *A Criticism on the Elegy written in a Country Church Yard* (1783).[1] (The treatment in Roger Martin's *Essai sur Thomas Gray* (1934), though detailed, I found unrewarding.) But Brooks, if always interesting, is somewhat less persuasive in this essay than on most occasions. Too often he seems to be forcing a meaning on Gray's words that isn't really there,[2] and the poetic 'structure' that he uncovers doesn't amount to very much.

---

[1] Generally attributed to John Young, who was Professor of Greek at Glasgow from 1774 to 1820, and claimed in later life to be the book's 'editor'. The internal evidence suggests to me an Englishman with an Oxford education;

(i) The author was a friend of Bowyer the printer (p. 8), of Calvert Blake (p. 38), and of Dr Curzon of Braesnose College (p. 53) – all Englishmen.

(ii) His knowledge of English poetry is impressive, especially of Thomson, Collins, Pope and Milton, but he shows little detailed familiarity with the classics.

(iii) He is a bigoted Tory and objects strongly to Gay's Whig views of Cromwell.

Though unfair to Gray the book makes decidedly interesting reading. The book's authorship is discussed by a number of correspondents in *Notes and Queries* (1857 and 1858).

[2] The identification of the numerous personifications with 'the allegoric figures, beloved by the eighteenth century, which clutter a great abbey church such as that at Bath or at Westminster' (p. 100) is most unconvincing. Nor can I detect 'brilliant irony' in the phrase *animated bust*. According to Brooks 'An "animated" bust would presumably be one into which the breath of life had been breathed – a speaking likeness endowed by the chisel of the sculptor with the soul itself. But the most "animated" bust (*anima* – breath, soul) cannot call the fleeting *anima* of the dead man back to its "mansion". And the mansion receives its qualification in the next line; it is no more than silent dust' (p. 102). This will never do. All that Gray means by *animated* surely is a good bust, a bust fulfilling the function of a bust, viz., of being an accurate portrait. Brooks's interpretation, taken literally, would mean that the dead man's soul had migrated from his body to the sepulchral bust. *Quod est absurdum*. It is only fair to add that many of Brooks's incidental comments are shrewd and relevant. They do not, however, *add up* to anything very substantial.

The dramatis personæ of the poem, apparently, are (i) the *storied urn* of the abbey church, (ii) the *shapeless sculpture* of the village churchyard and (iii) the final 'Epitaph', and there is a suggestion that the opposition between the first two is reconciled in the third. But the details are left discreetly vague.

The inadequacy of Brooks's account – which I do not wish to over-stress (the essay is much the best thing that I have met with on the *Elegy*) – is traceable, I believe, to his exclusion of the social and historical factors. It is dangerous to abstract any poem from its historical setting. In the case of a poem already two hundred years old and the product of a society so different from our own as that of the mid-eighteenth century the pro-cedure is peculiarly imprudent.

The most important fact about Gray's poem is that it was composed in two instalments. The first seventy-two lines (i.e. up to 'Far from the madding crowd's ignoble strife') were written at Stoke Poges in the summer or autumn of 1742.[1] In the Eton MS (an early draft in Gray's autograph) they are followed by sixteen lines which were later cancelled (though some of the phrases were utilized in the final version). 'And here', says Mason, Gray's literary executor and biographer, 'the Poem was originally intended to conclude.'[2] To avoid confusion I shall refer to this first draft, which constitutes a complete, self-contained poem of great beauty, as the *Stanzas*. (The Eton MS is headed 'Stanza's Wrote in a Country Church-Yard,' and Dryden's *Heroick Stanzas* on Cromwell's death, also in decasyllabic quatrains rhyming *abab*, may well have been Gray's metrical model.) The poem as we know it, here referred to as the *Elegy*, consists of the *Stanzas*, minus their last sixteen lines and plus fifty-six new lines. The new lines were completed in June 1750, though it is not known exactly when Gray began work on them. They may have been the 'few Autumnal verses' that, Gray wrote to a friend (in September 1746), then made up, with the reading of Aristotle, his 'entertainments during the fall of the leaf'.

The first critical point that must be made in any discussion of the poem is the inferiority of the last fifty-six lines.[3] Apart from the fragments salved from the rejected conclusion of the *Stanzas*, the only lines that can

---

[1] See H. W. Garrod's important 'Note on the Composition of Gray's Elegy', pp. 111-16 of *Essays on the Eighteenth Century Presented to David Nichol Smith* (1945).

[2] *The Poems of Mr Thomas Gray* (1775), p. 107.

[3] In Landor's *Imaginary Conversation* between Johnson and Tooke (*Works* (1876), vol. iv, p. 192), Tooke says; 'Expunge from his Elegy the second and third stanza, together with all those which follow the words "Even in our ashes live their wonted fires", and you will leave a poem with scarcely a blemish; a poem which will always have more readers than any others in any language'.

possibly be called great poetry are in the two verses beginning 'For who to dumb Forgetfulness a prey'. Their precise relevance, however, at this point is not clear. The preceding verse had described the misspelled inscriptions and their texts,

> That teach the rustic moralist to die.

Presumably this means that the more philosophically minded villagers, wandering round the churchyard, read the texts on the gravestones and by doing so learned to resign themselves to the inevitability of death. Between this perambulation and the ensuing death-bed scene there is a logical gap that makes me suspect that the two verses have been transferred from some other poem or fragment. The remaining verses (with the exception of the 'Epitaph') can only be described as *thin*. Their diluted humorous elegance compares unfavourably with the concentrated force of the *Stanzas*. And the pervasive 'literariness' is scarcely distinguishable from plagiarism.[1] Gray's notes point out two distant parallels in Petrarch, but omit all reference to Drummond's 'Far from the madding worldling's hoarse discords', and the 'hoary-headed Swain's' debt to the description of Jaques in *As You Like It*

> he lay along
> Under an oak whose antique root peeps out
> Upon the brook that brawls along this road,

and the echoes of 'L'Allegro', 'Il Penseroso' and 'Lycidas'. The final 'Epitaph' – that 'tin-kettle of an epitaph tied to its tail', as Landor is said to have called it[2] – is less empty and elegant, but it is clumsily written and the account that it provides of the dead man differs in several respects from that given by the Swain. (To the latter he was a sort of Scholar Gipsy, eccentric and unsociable, whereas the 'Epitaph' applauds his social virtues, his sympathy with the unfortunate and his devotion to his friend.)

If the last fifty-six lines are so inferior to the first seventy-two, why were they written? Why was Gray not satisfied with the brilliant *Stanzas* of 1742? I believe the sixteen cancelled lines, which rounded off the original poem, provide the explanation. They run as follows:

> The thoughtless World to Majesty may bow
> Exalt the brave, & idolize Success
> But more to Innocence their Safety owe
> Than Power or Genius e'er conspired to bless

[1] Gray wrote to Bedingfield, 27 Aug. 1756; '... do not wonder therefore if some Magazine or Review call me Plagiary; I could shew them a hundred more instances, which they never will discover themselves.'

[2] I have not been able to trace the source of this quotation.

And thou, who mindful of the unhonour'd Dead
Dost in these Notes their artless Tale relate
By Night & lonely Contemplation led
To linger in the gloomy Walks of Fate

Hark how the sacred Calm, that breathes around
Bids ev'ry fierce tumultuous Passion cease
In still small Accents whisp'ring from the Ground
A grateful Earnest of eternal Peace

No more with Reason & thyself at Strife
Give anxious Cares & endless Wishes room
But thro' the cool sequester'd Vale of Life
Pursue the silent Tenour of thy Doom.

Although there are one or two obscurities that a later revision would
have smoothed out – 'their Safety' is not quite *le mot juste* – there can be no
doubt about the literary quality of these lines. They are superb. But they
are also extremely personal. They remind me of the still greater Sapphics
that Cowper wrote after his attempted suicide in 1763 ('Hatred and
vengeance, my eternal portion'). Gray, too, is thinking aloud. He is
trying to cheer himself up in the face of a bitter disappointment. The
'anxious Cares & endless Wishes' are not poetical ornaments but his own
private demons, the 'fierce tumultuous Passion' of a young man who has
found 'Reason' an insufficient support in a suddenly hostile world. It will
be remembered that the *Stanzas* probably date from the late summer of
1742. In May 1741 Gray had quarrelled – irrevocably, as it then seemed –
with Horace Walpole. His father had died the following November,
leaving only a fraction of the substantial fortune that he had had a short
time before, though it was not until some six months later that Gray
finally learned that he was to all intents and purposes a pauper. And in
June 1742 Richard West, apart from Walpole his only intimate friend,
died suddenly from consumption. These facts provide the sombre autobiographical background against which the poem must be read.

They also provide a clue to the inner conflict in Gray's poem. The
opposition between the natural, almost animal life of the village (the
'lowing Herd' and the 'Plowman' merge into each other) and the futile
artificial life of the 'Proud' is the Gray of 1742 arraigning the Gray of
1741. This picture of the heartless insincerity of high life – the hypocritical
funeral anthem (l. 40), the flattery of the expensive epitaph (l. 44), the
lying and brazenness (ll. 69-70), the poetical eulogizing of the proud and
luxurious (ll. 71-2) – is a reflection of his own recent dependence on
Walpole, the Prime Minister's son. And the revulsion from his earlier

fashionable self is accompanied by a realistic recognition of what his poverty will now entail. *His* heart is pregnant with celestial fire, but chill penury will soon repress *his* noble rage and freeze the current of *his* genius. And there is no attempt to blink the consequences. The tenor of his doom must in future be 'silent' – as indeed it was. Between 1742 and 1747 – with the possible exception of the 'Autumnal verses' of 1746 already mentioned – Gray wrote no poems at all.

With so much of himself and his own private affairs in the *Stanzas* it was natural for Gray to refuse to allow their publication. They were shown to Walpole not long after their reconciliation at the end of 1745, and it is possible that their transmutation into the *Elegy* is attributable to Walpole's enthusiasm and encouragement. Essentially the addition of the final fifty-two lines was an attempt to *depersonalize* the poem. Unfortunately they only succeed in this at the expense of the poetry. The central figure is no longer Thomas Gray, the middle-class youth who had been admitted for a few golden years into the inner ranks of the aristocracy. His place is taken by a conventional literary figure, the Melancholy Man, who could not possibly be identified with anybody, and it is only in the 'Epitaph' – and then somewhat obscurely – that the real living Gray returns:

> A Youth to Fortune and to Fame unknown:
> Fair Science frown'd not on his humble birth,
> And Melancholy mark'd him for her own.

Gray was a reserved, sensitive man, and it is easy to believe that the publication of the *Stanzas* might have had distressing consequences. At least one of his contemporaries was shocked even by the *Elegy*: 'Delicacy and taste recoil at the publication of internal griefs. They profane the hallowedness of secret sadness; and suppose selected and decorated expression compatible with the prostration of the soul.'[1] On the other hand Gray was right in thinking that the poem would be of public interest to the England of his time. He had not written it entirely as an act of private catharsis. The poem was a protest, a *cri de cœur*, not only against his own personal misfortunes but also at the social order that had made them possible.

Like Pope's *Elegy to the Memory of an Unfortunate Lady* – the poem that seems to have been Gray's principal model – Gray's poem is partly an indictment of the ruling aristocracy. The condemnation of 'Pride' (l. 71) and 'ye Proud' (l. 37), which is also found in the *Ode on the Spring* and the *Hymn to Adversity* (both written in the same summer of 1742), is indeed a

---

[1] *A Criticism on the Elegy written in a Country Church Yard* (1783), p. 11.

recurring theme in Pope's verse. (The word *pride* occurs twenty-three times in the *Essay on Man* alone.) The trouble with Timon, the incarnation of aristocratic pride in the *Epistle to Burlington*, was his uselessness, and Gray points the same contrast between the 'useful toil' of the villagers and the 'pomp of pow'r'. With Gray's

> Oft did the harvest to their sickle yield,
> Their furrow oft the stubborn glebe has broke,

one can compare Pope's lines foretelling the disappearance of Timon's pretentious villa and purely ornamental gardens:

> Another age shall see the golden Ear
> Imbrown the Slope, and nod on the Parterre,
> Deep Harvests bury all his pride has plann'd,
> And laughing Ceres re-assume the land.

Of course, neither Pope nor Gray was a revolutionary. They had no wish to overthrow the squirearchy. Their satire was aimed essentially at shaming the arrogant oligarchy into a recognition of the original egalitarian basis of the régime. They would, no doubt, have been perfectly satisfied with a return to the less rigidly stratified class-system of the Restoration, when a statistician like John Graunt, a shopkeeper's son like themselves, was proposed for the Royal Society by no less a person than the King.[1]

If the 'proud' have this dual significance for Gray, as both public and private symbols, so have the 'rude Forefathers of the hamlet'. Their home is not Stoke Poges, or indeed any real recognizable place. Whatever Gray was doing he was not writing with his eye on a phenomenal object. The descriptive inaccuracies therefore do not matter. It is true that cattle do not normally 'low' or 'wind' their way at sunset, and that 'drowsy tinklings lull the distant folds' is a confusion of two sheep-farming systems (if the sheep are folded there is no need for a bell-wether). It is also true that owls do not really 'mope' or 'complain,' and that elms are not particularly 'rugged'. But literal accuracy would have been inappropriate in a description of a symbolic village, whose essential function was simply to be the opposite of 'polite Company'.[2] Its inhabitants are 'rude', 'lowly',

---

[1] See Sprat's *History of the Royal Society* (1667), p. 67. Sprat also contrasts (p. 407) the snobbery of the previous generation with the country gentlemen of his own time; 'The course of their *Ancestors* lives was grave and reserv'd . . . now they are engag'd in freer modes of *Education*; now the vast distance between them and other orders of men is no more observ'd . . .'

[2] Cp. Voltaire's comment on Congreve's comedies; 'The Language is everywhere that of Men of Honour, but their Actions are those of Knaves: a proof that he was perfectly well acquainted with human Nature, and frequented what we call polite Company' (*Letters concerning the English Nation* (1733), p. 188).

'busy', 'jocund', 'sturdy', 'useful', 'homely', and 'obscure', primarily as a foil to 'Ambition', 'Grandeur', 'pow'r', and their attendants 'Honour', 'Flatt'ry', 'Knowledge' and 'Luxury'. The idyll of the village is opposed to the satire of 'the Town', not because Gray was under any pastoral illusions, but to give picturesque emphasis to his argument. Indeed, in the central section of the poem he has explicitly recognized that human nature does not change much whatever the environment may be. The village Hampdens, Miltons and Cromwells – 'Cato', 'Tully', and 'Cæsar' in the *Stanzas* – have the same virtues and vices as their national counterparts; it is only their range that is circumscribed.

The country hamlet is not the only recurrent symbol in the poem. More interesting, because it is probably unconscious, is an apparent identification of the 'thoughtless World' with noise and of the 'Innocence' of the village with silence. Thus the initial landscape is characterized by 'a solemn stillness', which the occasional natural sounds only emphasize, and the *Stanzas* conclude in a 'sacred Calm' punctuated by 'still small Accents'. Opposed to it are the 'pealing anthem' of the proud man's funeral, the loud flattery of 'Honor's voice', the lyre 'wak'd to escctasy' by a Milton who is *not* mute, and the 'list'ning senates' intent on a Cromwell's oratory. In the light of this symbolism Gray's final decision in the *Stanzas* to 'Pursue the silent Tenour' of his doom takes on a further meaning. The fine Alcaics written at the Grande Chartreuse in August 1741 on his journey home after the quarrel with Walpole had already recorded his regret that his lot forbade him to enjoy the monks' sacred rule of silence:

> invidendis sedibus et frui
> Fortuna sacra lege silentii
> Vetat volentem.

In this concept of a Sacred Silence, positive and rational, both the public and the private conflicts of the *Elegy* find their solution. It is not the silence of death, though it resembles death (hence the appropriateness of the churchyard setting), but of 'eternal Peace'. The Christian humility that is to provide the solvent of his personal difficulties is paralleled by the Christian charity that is the implied prescription for the social ills of Augustan England.

The presence of symbolism, though Gray's differs from Romantic symbolism both in the mode of action and in the choice of symbols (Gray shows little interest in wild nature), is a reminder that the *Elegy* came some twenty-five years after the classic moment of the Augustan tradition. The Polished Craftsman was feeling his way towards a variation of the Augustan formula. The personal note in the four cancelled verses was also new. They should be compared with the parallel passage in the *Elegy to the Memory of an Unfortunate Lady* (which was written about 1717):

> Poets themselves must fall, like those they sung;
> Deaf the prais'd ear, and mute the tuneful tongue.
> Ev'n he, whose soul now melts in mournful lays,
> Shall shortly want the gen'rous tear he pays;
> Then from his closing eyes thy form shall part,
> And the last pang shall tear thee from his heart.
> Life's idle business at one gasp be o'er,
> The Muse forgot, and thou belov'd no more!

Here Pope is merely striking a series of rhetorical attitudes. As I. A. Richards has said in commenting on this poem, 'the poet's eye is very plainly on himself and on his reader rather than on the imaginary object'.[1] In Gray, on the other hand, the imaginary object is himself. Here, as occasionally in Shenstone, Cowper and Frances Greville[2] – all contemporaries of Gray's – is authentically introspective poetry. Quantitatively, though, the personal element does not bulk large in Gray's verse. The autobiographical conclusion of 'The Progress of Poesy' is so inconspicuous that many readers have failed to realize that it is Gray who is 'Beneath the Good how far – but far above the Great'. And perhaps the most important thing about the cancelled stanzas in the *Elegy* is that they *were* cancelled. In spite of the occasional deviations Gray is primarily an Augustan poet. Unlike Collins (who is most successful when he is least Augustan – and was absurdly over-rated by the Romantics in consequence),[3] Gray writes best when he keeps to the central literary tradition of Dryden and Pope. It is significant that there are no paradoxes in the last fifty-two lines of the *Elegy*, whereas the first seventy-two lines are full of them, or of related

---

[1] *Practical Criticism* (1929), p. 356.

[2] 'A Prayer for Indifference' is the one great poem written by an Englishwoman in the eighteenth century. Its first appearance in print was in the *Edinburgh Chronicle* 1759, pp. 270-3, though it was probably written some years before, *c.* 1756. The text in the *Oxford Book of Eighteenth Century Verse* is inferior to that in I. A. Williams's *Shorter Poems of the Eighteenth Century*.

[3] C. S. Lewis, one of our latter-day Romantics, has recently attributed to *How Sleep the Brave* a 'depth and ambiguity of real experience' not to be found in Donne! (See *Seventeenth Century Studies presented to Sir Herbert Grierson* [1938], p. 80.) This 'Ode, Written in the beginning of the year 1746' is merely a deft medley of Collins's own poem on the death of Colonel Ross (killed at Fontenoy, 11 May 1745) and a passage from Pope's *Unfortunate Lady*. Saintsbury thought it 'faultless' (*C.H.E.L.*, vol. x, p. 144), but the repetion of *their* and *there* eight times in twelve lines is clumsy, and 'Choirs unseen' would have been better than 'Forms unseen' in l. 8.

figures.[1] The central section on the village Hampdens, Miltons and Cromwells – in my own opinion the best passage in the poem – is a continuous expanded paradox. The concept of a 'village-Hampden' appears to be a contradiction in terms. (How can you be a national hero *and* unknown outside your own village?) Its resolution, carrying with it the implication that the smaller unit is at least as favourable a soil for the display of moral grandeur, shows Gray equally in the central social tradition of his time. The *Elegy*, in addition to all the other things that it is, was a tract for the times. It was a plea for decentralization, recalling the over-urbanized ruling class to its roots in a rural society based upon the benevolent despotism of the manor-house.[2]

[1] E.g., 'short and simple annals' (l. 23). 'The paths of glory lead but to the grave' (l. 36), the 'gem of purest ray' in 'The dark unfathom'd caves' (ll. 53-4), etc. The zeugmas of 'leave the world to darkness and to me' (l. 4) and 'By Night and lonely contemplation led' (l. 7 of the cancelled stanzas) are a kind of paradox.

[2] The change from Cato to Hampden and from Cæsar to Cromwell clinched the argument. The historical Hampden and Cromwell had in fact owed their later success to the training they had acquired in the 'village'.

# 11

# The Quickest Way Out of Manchester:
# Four Romantic Odes

I

DRINK was only one of the ways of getting out of the Manchesters of the nineteenth century. The worship of the Gin-Juggernath that Cruickshank portrayed in 1834 in an effective print was confined to all intents and purposes to the working classes. But the middle classes, especially the self-styled 'upper middle class' – which soon after 1800 had become in effect the English ruling class, only retaining the aristocracy as its administrative agents[1] – were able to escape from social realities quite as effectively via Romantic poetry, the historical novel and the Anglo-Catholic religion. The motives for escape were, of course, not the same. The Ancoats mill-hands, the Yorkshire miners and the agricultural chain-gangs of East Anglia drank their gin as an alleviation of sheer physical misery. The Victorian *bourgeois gentilhommes*, on the other hand, *physically* were extremely well off. Food was cheap, servants were plentiful, wives did their duty and property was relatively secure. Their troubles were psychological – a sense of guilt, a consciousness of sin.

> Each with never-ceasing labour,
> Whilst he thinks he cheats his neighbour,
> Cheating his own heart of quiet.[2]

The upper middle class had inherited from their humble seventeenth-century ancestors, along with the energy and the 'horse sense', a Christian conscience. 'Thou shalt love thy neighbour as thyself' was a command impossible to obey under the economic conditions of the nineteenth century. A cut-throat competitiveness is the logical essence of *laissez-faire* capitalism. But the Puritan conscience didn't like it. The left hand refused to acknowledge what the right hand was doing, and a division of labour

[1] Matthew Arnold ('My Countrymen'. *Cornhill Magazine* [Feb. 1856]) quotes Sir Robert Lowe as saying that England was happy in having her middle part strong and her extremes weak, and adds, 'though we are administered by one of our weak extremes, the aristocracy, these managers administer us, as a weak extreme naturally must, with a nervous attention to the wishes of the strong middle part, whose agents they are'. Arnold's whole essay is a brilliant piece of sociological analysis. It is reprinted in the 'Everyman' edition of *On the Study of Celtic Literature*.
[2] Shelley, *Peter Bell the Third*, pt. 3, stanza xi.

began to operate in the individual *psyche*. The Understanding, in Coleridge's terminology, remained in the counting-house, the calculable world of cause and effect; the Reason plunged into the mysterious sea of the subconscious mind, the world of 'imagination'. Nevertheless this process of psychic specialization tended to remain incomplete. Expelled by the economic pitchfork human nature had a way of reasserting itself in its old integrated totality. And it is essentially this conflict, between the personality integrated in a social environment and the anti-social 'split man' (Dr Jekyll and Mr Hyde), that is mirrored in Romantic poetry. In so far as the poetry was in the central tradition of Romanticism the Split Man was its hero and Society was its villain. But in so far as the poetry was *poetry* (by the standards set by the Greek and Latin classics, which the Romantics accepted as fully as the Augustans) the issue of the conflict had to appear to hang in the balance. The hero (the ideal) must not win too easily; the villain (social reality) must be given a chance. And so by a curious paradox to be a good Romantic poet you had to know the case against Romanticism. You had to be a rationalist as well as an irrationalist, a functioning member of society as well as a social revolutionary or a social escapist. There were therefore two dangers to which the Romantic poet as such was exposed. On the one hand, he could be too Romantic – in which case his poetry would degenerate into verse because there was no genuine basic conflict. This is what seems to have happened in Wordsworth's later work as well as in much of Shelley's poetry. On the other hand, he could be too anti-Romantic – in which case he would find it difficult to write any poetry at all. (It was a fundamental thesis of the theoretic argument in Chapter Four that, within broad limits, only one *kind* of poetry can be written successfully at one time.) And this, I suggest, is why Coleridge's later writings are almost all in prose. If Keats had lived to be thirty-five, it is possible, I think, that he too would have abandoned poetry.

It is proposed to attempt to substantiate these propositions by a detailed examination of Wordsworth's 'Intimations of Immortality from Recollections of Early Childhood' (begun March 1802), Coleridge's 'Dejection: An Ode' (April 1802), Shelley's 'Ode to the West Wind' (October or November 1819), and Keats's 'Ode on a Grecian Urn' (early summer 1819).

## II

The peculiar importance that Wordsworth attached to his 'Ode,' as it was originally called (the polysyllabic subtitle was not added until 1815), is shown by its position in the editions of his poems issued in his lifetime. In *Poems in Two Volumes* (1807), where the poem made its first appearance, it comes at the very end of the second volume with a special half-title (it is the only poem to be so distinguished), the verso of which reads *Paulo majora canamus*. It retains the same honourable segregation – *finis coronat opus*, as it were – in the collected *Poems* of 1815 as well as in the later editions of Wordsworth's poetical works. And this splendid isolation is generally maintained in modern editions.

On the whole, the critics have accepted the poem at Wordsworth's implied valuation, though with some reservations. A. C. Bradley, for example, an expert Wordsworthian, has pronounced the Ode '[his] greatest product, but not his best piece of work'.[1] There is certainly some verbal imprecision. A number of the phrases are tautological,[2] and it is clumsy to say 'there hath past away a *glory* from the earth' (l. 18) immediately after calling the sunshine 'a *glorious* birth' (l. 16).[3] Moreover there are rather too many quotations and accidental literary reminiscences. Daniel's 'humorous stage' (l. 104) and Gray's 'meanest floweret' (l. 203) were hardly worth the carriage. And it is decidedly disconcerting to be reminded of the Ghost in *Hamlet* in

> High instincts before which our mortal Nature
> Did tremble like a guilty Thing surprised;[4]

as it is to learn that 'Our noisy years' (l. 155) comes straight out of an anonymous 'Address to Silence' that Dorothy Wordsworth had copied out of the Sherborne *Weekly Entertainer; Or, Agreeable and Instructive Repository*.

The question that this kind of thing must suggest to anybody who is not a Wordsworthian is whether the clumsiness and the derivativeness do not go deeper. Are they perhaps the outward and visible sign of an inner spiritual factitiousness? Is the Ode pretending to be something more than it really is?

It will be advisable before attempting to answer this question to define what exactly the poem is about. A definition can perhaps be best approached by a consideration of its structure.

Structurally the outstanding features of the Ode are the detailed links (*a*) between stanzas I-II and XI, and (*b*) between stanzas III-IV and X. The opening lines of stanza X,

---

[1] *Oxford Lectures on Poetry* (1909), p. 117.

[2] E.g., beautiful and fair' (l. 15), 'young lambs' (l. 20), 'A mourning or a funeral' (l. 95).

[3] There is a similar contradiction between the Youth who is 'Nature's Priest' (l. 73), i.e., the antenatal glory's, and the Earth's yearnings 'in her own *natural* kind' (l. 79).

[4] Cp. *Hamlet*, I, i, 148-9,
> 'And then it started like a guilty thing
> Upon a fearful summons.'

> Then sing, ye Birds, sing, sing a joyous song!
> And let the young Lambs bound
> As to the tabor's sound!

repeat almost verbatim the opening lines of stanza III:

> Now, while the birds thus sing a joyous song,
> And while the young lambs bound
> As to the tabor's sound.

And the reader, having been thus instructed to make the reference back, will note *inter alia* the following connections:

(i) the 'heart of May' (l. 32), with which the countryside is welcoming the spring, on 'This sweet May-morning' (l. 44) and ll. 174-5,

> Ye that through your hearts to-day
> Feel the gladness of the May!

(ii) the 'thought of grief' (l. 22) temporarily relieved ('I again am strong' (l. 24)) and ll. 180-1,

> We will grieve not, rather find
> Strength in what remains behind;

(iii) the 'meadow, grove, and stream' of l. 1, and their echo in the 'Fountains, Meadow, Hills, and Groves' (l. 188) which the last stanza of the poem begins by invoking.

Between the six interconnected opening and closing stanzas, all of which can be described as autobiographical, Wordsworth has inserted five stanzas that are not linked verbally or by the imagery to the rest of the poem. These central stanzas expound the 'myth' (to use the word in the Platonic sense of a parable that is more than mere allegory) of the soul's pre-existence with God. The evolution of the Ode is therefore, at least in intention, (i) a statement of Wordsworth's personal problem (stanzas I-IV), (ii) an exposition of the theoretical solution (stanzas V-IX), and (iii) the application of the solution to Wordsworth's own case (stanzas X, XI). The *problem* may be said to be Wordsworth's distress at discovering that his response to sensuous experience (sights in stanzas I, II, sounds in III, IV) is becoming less keen. The theoretical *solution* – that growing older inevitably dulls the freshness of the senses' reactions – relieves Wordsworth of any personal responsibility for what is in fact inherent in the nature of things. And the application sees Wordsworth resigning himself to a decay of the senses in the consolations of 'thought'[1] and emotion recollected in tranquillity.[2]

Wordsworth's overt intentions are clear enough. The poem is meant to be the record of a process of psychological stocktaking that results in a final mental readjustment. The Wordsworth that is supposed to emerge is a wiser if sadder man than the sentimentalist of the opening stanzas. But is this, in fact, the impression that the poem leaves? Is not the reader finally left with a feeling that the Philosophic Mind of middle age is decidedly a second-best? *Nothing* can bring back the 'splendour in the grass'! The 'glory' has departed! All that is left is 'the light of common day'! Even the sunset clouds now 'take a sober colouring'!

The contradiction between what the Ode is meant to say and what it actually says is acute. And it is implicit in the central myth. If the process of growing up is essentially a growing away from God, what is there for the middle-aged man to live for? In Henry Vaughan's poems – where Wordsworth probably found his myth[3] – there was the ultimate prospect of reunion with God, but Wordsworth had not the same conviction of personal immortality. (For Wordsworth middle age was simply a half-way stage to the final exit

From sunshine to the sunless land.)

And even recollection in tranquillity, though nothing 'Can utterly abolish or destroy' it as long as life lasts, necessarily becomes fainter and feebler as the time-interval increases between the remembering mind and the remembered experience.

But before convicting Wordsworth of mental dishonesty it will be desirable to restore the poem to its contemporary setting. Whom was it written for? When was it written? Why was it written?

An entry in Dorothy Wordsworth's *Journal* establishes that the poem

---

[1] 'We in *thought* will join your throng' (l. 172),
   'the soothing *thoughts* that spring
     Out of human suffering' (l. 185),
   'the philosophic mind' (l. 187),
   '*Thoughts* that do often lie too deep for tears' (l. 204).

[2] This is the prose sense of the imagery of ll. 162-8. Provided there is 'a season of calm weather' (tranquillity), even adults ('Though inland far we be') can recapture in memory ('Our Souls have sight') the mystical ecstasies of childhood ('And see the Children sport upon the shore, And hear the mighty waters rolling evermore').

[3] A copy of Vaughan's *Silex Scintillans* was found in Wordsworth's library after his death. At what date he acquired it is not known, but the parallels between the Ode and 'The Retreat' are so striking that he must at any rate have known Vaughan's poem when he wrote stanzas V-IX. Although many partial parallels have been cited from the Neoplatonists and Christian mystics nowhere but in Vaughan is there to be found the inch-by-inch regression that is the essence of Wordsworth's myth.

was begun on 27 March 1802 ('Wm. wrote part of an Ode'). Years later Wordsworth told Isabella Fenwick that 'two years at least passed between the writing of the four first stanzas and the remaining part', and as the complete poem was certainly in existence in March 1804 (when Coleridge was given a copy to take to Malta) it has been assumed that stanzas I-IV date from March 1802 and stanzas V-XI from March 1804.[1] In fact, however, only the *termini a quo* and *ad quem* and an interval of undefined length between them can be considered certain. The 'myth' and the concluding stanzas are more likely, in my opinion, to have been written in 1803 than in 1804, and it is probable, I think, that the opening stanzas were expanded as early as May 1802.[2] Wordsworth would not have written 'This sweet May-morning' (l. 44) if it had really been a March morning. And the curious reference in ll. 22-3,

> To me alone there came a thought of grief;
> A timely utterance gave that thought relief,

is less likely to be to the lines beginning 'My heart leaps up,' as H. W. Garrod has suggested, than to 'Resolution and Independence'. Both of these poems were in process of composition at the time, the former having been drafted on 26 March and rewritten on 14 May, and the latter having been begun on 3 May and finished on 9 May (some changes were made later). But 'My heart leaps up' cannot have given Wordsworth the relief he describes. His trouble was that his heart would *not* leap up! On the other hand 'Resolution and Independence' is a dramatization of exactly the psychological state described in the Ode. Wordsworth summarized his intentions in 'Resolution and Independence' in a revealing letter to Sara Hutchinson:

I describe myself as having been exalted to the highest pitch of delight by the joyousness and beauty of Nature and then as depressed, even in the midst of those beautiful objects, to the lowest dejection and despair. A young Poet in the midst of the happiness of Nature is described as overwhelmed by the thought of the miserable reverses which have befallen the happiest of all men, viz. Poets – I think of this till I am so deeply impressed by it, that I consider the manner in which I was rescued from my dejection and despair almost as an interposition of Providence.[3]

Here at any rate, whichever the poem was that 'gave that thought relief', is the mood out of which the Ode grew. And here too is a hint of the

---

[1] See *The Poetical Works of Wordsworth*, ed. E. de Selincourt and H. Darbishire, vol. iv (1947), pp. 464-5.

[2] He was still tinkering with the poem in June. Dorothy noted in her *Journal* for 17 June, 'Wm. added a little to the Ode he is writing'.

[3] 14 June 1802.

personal problems of Wordsworth and his circle – the Ode's 'human suffering' productive of 'soothing thoughts' – that were clamouring for a solution in the year 1802. Wordsworth's use of the word 'dejection' was probably without *arrière pensée*, but it is worth noting that the original version of Coleridge's 'Dejection: An Ode' had been addressed to this same Sara Hutchinson as recently as 4 April[1] and had been 'repeated' to the Wordsworths by Coleridge himself on 21 April. Sara and Coleridge were in love (a tragic idyll in Coleridge's career that his early biographers did not know about), and the poet whose 'miserable reverses' Wordsworth's words must at once have turned her mind to would not be Chatterton or Burns, as in the poem, but Coleridge. Unlike Wordsworth, who had been temporarily rescued from his dejection by Providence (he had now become formally engaged to Sara's sister Mary), Coleridge was 'Past Cure, and past Complaint':

> A Grief without a pang, void, dark and drear,
> A stifling, drowsy, unimpassion'd Grief
> That finds no natural outlet, no Relief
> In word, or sigh, or tear –
> This, Sara! well thou know'st,
> Is that sore Evil, which I dread the most,
> And oft'nest suffer!

There could be no question of a 'timely utterance' relieving *this* grief.

But, though Coleridge's case was worse than Wordsworth's, their diseases were really the same, as their accounts of their separate symptoms demonstrate. Wordsworth's case-history is to be found in Book XI of *The Prelude* (Book XII in the 1850 text), which supplements the evidence of the Ode. His first crisis, according to his own diagnosis, had come when he was twenty-one or twenty-two. Before going to Cambridge, he still retained

> The first diviner influence of this world (l. 232),

and this uncritical love of all created things persisted until the last Long Vacation of his university career:

> through the gorgeous Alps
> Roaming, I carried with me the same heart (ll. 22-41).

The change apparently came during his residence in France. He became a rationalist, a perfectibilist and an aesthete. Like Coleridge ('I see, not feel,

---

[1] The MS (which was printed by E. de Selincourt in the English Association's *Essays and Studies* for 1937) is headed 'A Letter to——'. A shorter version that was printed in the *Morning Post* on 4 Oct. 1802 seems to be the first with the familiar title.

how beautiful they are'), Wordsworth then allowed the eye to become 'master of the heart' (l. 272). And if Annette Vallon is to be associated with 'this degradation' (l. 244), as she may have been, her rôle must have been parallel to Mrs Coleridge's.[1] In 1795, under the influence of his sister Dorothy, Wordsworth returned to the nature mysticism of his youth, and it was at this period, according to his own account, that he worked out the technique of an emotional recollection of early childhood. Childish incidents seem to have had a particularly 'vivifying Virtue' (l. 26;), replenishing his 'power' and 'strength'. Coleridge, the lover of living children, laid less emphasis on memories of his own childhood, though in 'Dejection' a recollection of 'sky-gazing' at Christ's Hospital has unconsciously relieved him:

> The Weight was somewhat lifted from my Breast.

That the process was not a purely passive one is made clear by Wordsworth:

> this I feel,
> That from thyself it is that thou must give,
> Else never canst receive (ll. 332-4).

And here the parallel is particularly close with 'Dejection':

> O Sara! we receive but what we give,
> And in *our* life alone does Nature live.

More therefore was involved than an act of memory. According to Coleridge what was primarily required, the 'beauty-making Power', was joy, the spontaneous happiness of the innocent, like Sara. Wordsworth is less clear on this point. 'Joy', 'bliss', 'gladness', 'delight', 'glee', and 'happiness' are words that recur again and again in his poems, but they are apparently the effect of recollection rather than an essential constituent of it. For both, however, their own joylessness ('grief'), or at least the intermittent character of their joy, is the real problem. Coleridge called Wordsworth's trouble 'hypochondria'; 'a hypochondriacal graft in his nature' is the way he put it to Richard Sharp in 1804. And during their Scotch tour of 1803 he complained in a letter to his wife that 'Wordsworth's hypochondriacal feelings keep him silent and self-centred'. But the real name for the disease from which both of them were suffering was

---

[1] It may not be a coincidence that Wordsworth had written to Annette, the first letter for a great many years, on 26 March, the day before he began the Ode. The Peace of Amiens, which temporarily restored normal communication with France, was not formally signed until 27 March. Wordsworth's seizing of the very first opportunity that had occurred to write *finis* to the Annette episode is surely significant.

Romanticism. Wordsworth and Coleridge were among the first victims of that *mal du siècle* which derived from the attempt to prolong adolescence artificially. The interest of their two Odes is the different ways in which the two friends react to what is fundamentally the same phenomenon.

For Coleridge the temptation was always to self-pity. But in 'Dejection' he was able to emerge out of his own self-pity, walk round it and record it objectively:

> For not to think of what I needs must feel,
> But to be still and patient all I can;
> And haply by abstruse Research to steal
> From my own Nature, all the Natural man –
> This was my sole Resource, my wisest plan!
> And that, which suits a part, infects the whole,
> And now is almost grown the Temper of my Soul.

There is a clinical completeness about this poem that is most satisfying. The moon, the larch, the sky with 'its peculiar Tint of Yellow Green', and the suspension of his own 'shaping spirit of Imagination' (the romantic *sine qua non*) are all observed with the same inclusive detachment. Coleridge has made a moving poem out of the failure to prolong his own Golden Age, when

> The Joy within me dallied with Distress;
> And all Misfortunes were but as the Stuff
> Whence Fancy made me Dreams of Happiness.

It had been lovely while it lasted, but it had had no basis in reality. That happiness was only a dream – and not a real dream but one that was the creation of fancy, a dream of a dream.

If 'Dejection' is a confession of failure, Wordsworth's Ode is, superficially at any rate, a claim to success. He has solved the problem of prolonging the excitements of adolescence by his technique of emotional recollection! But the tone of voice in which the claim is advanced at once throws doubt upon its validity. Can what is so clearly felt to be only a second best be considered a success at all? And there is one piece of deliberate falsification. It is contained in ll. 193-4:

> I love the Brooks which down their channels fret,
> Even more than when I tripped lightly as they.

It is quite impossible to accept this statement at its face-value. All the evidence of the other autobiographical poems confirms the account of his development that Wordsworth gave in the 'Lines composed a few miles above Tintern Abbey'. There *was* a time when the cataract had haunted him 'like a passion', but that was from about 1786 to 1793. By 1803 the 'Nature's Priest' had become the 'Man' living in 'the light of common day'. The two lines are in reality the merest wishful thinking. They are almost the first indication of the indifference to fact in the later Wordsworth that was to startle Hazlitt and Shelley.[1]

The explanation of Wordsworth's self-deception is that by 1803 it had become essential to his self-esteem. The whole basis of his life had been that he was to be the Great Poet, the modern Milton. Hitherto, with the help of his sister Dorothy and Coleridge, he had been training himself for the rôle, working out a style, elaborating a philosophy. The *Lyrical Ballads* of 1798 were only 'experiments' (the 'Advertisement' says so), but by 1803 he might be forgiven for thinking that he had 'arrived'. The *Lyrical Ballads* were already in a third edition, his admirers included great men like Charles James Fox, and in John Wilson of Glasgow University, who had written to him on 24 May 1802, he had found the first of the Wordsworthians. It was a pardonable mistake to think he could now marry and 'settle down'; his contemporaries like Crabbe and Scott had done so with apparently beneficial results. The antipathy between respectability and Romantic poetry was then still an undiscovered psychological law. Wordsworth found it out for himself – and then tried to save the situation by bluff. Hence perhaps the special importance that he assigned to the Ode. He was cheering himself up. The rhetoric was so good that he may almost have convinced himself.[2]

Wordsworth's self-esteem also demanded a moral to his Ode different from that of Coleridge's Ode. The two poems were closely associated in the intimate circle who were Wordsworth's real poetic audience at this time, and in elaborating his fragment he can hardly have failed to realize that he was entering into a sort of competition with Coleridge. When Coleridge wrote 'Dejection' he had just seen the embryonic first four stanzas of Wordsworth's Ode (all that was then written), as one or two passages in his own poem make clear. His 'I too will crown me with a Coronal' might even be interpreted as an acceptance of the implied challenge in Wordsworth's 'My head hath its coronal'. As no MS survives of Wordsworth's first draft it is impossible to say whether the metrical irregularity (inherited from Dryden and Cowley) is Coleridge's or

---

[1] A curious example of this petty dishonesty is the section-heading in *Poems in Two Volumes*, 'Poems, composed during a Tour, chiefly on Foot'. Of the five poems in this section three were certainly composed at Grasmere and the other two may have been!

[2] Almost, but not quite. No. IX of the *Evening Voluntaries* (written in 1817) speaks of 'the light! Full early lost, and *fruitlessly* deplored', and a prose note by Wordsworth specifically connects the passage with the Ode.

Wordsworth's contribution; but *a priori* one would expect it to be Coleridge's, as this was Wordsworth's first ode. Wordsworth had certainly read 'Dejection' carefully – one MS version is addressed to him, 'William' taking the place of 'Sara' – and his 'little Actor' (l. 103) and 'Mighty Prophet' (l. 115) may be reminiscences of Coleridge's

> Thou Actor, perfect in all tragic Sounds!
> Thou mighty Poet . . .

In this domestic competition it may be assumed that Wordsworth won (he always did), but Coleridge's Ode is the better poem of the two. The variations of 'tone' are particularly admirable. Instead of the monotone of Wordsworth's 'egotistical sublime', as Keats called it, Coleridge is in turn conversational, pathetic, rhetorical, analytic and descriptive. It is a human being who is speaking. And it is to Coleridge's credit that 'Dejection' was a junction, not a terminus. There were to be no more *Kubla Khans*, but on the wreckage of his youth Coleridge managed to build a second career as critic, philosopher and theologian. If he did not achieve the return to Manchester it was something to have been able to hold London spellbound with the eloquence of his table talk. Wordsworth's Ode, on the other hand, *was* a terminus – or very nearly. After 1803 the man hardens and the style becomes clumsily Miltonic ('thick-ankled' was Tennyson's term for it). The lie had entered into the soul. Instead of the actuality and veracity of the early poems, the eye on the object, we get sermons in stones and sonnet sequences in the running brooks. Their Grasmere neighbours would soon be able to watch the Wordsworth family taking its daily walk, with William striding ahead, 'sayin' nowt to noan of 'em'. He had nothing left worth saying perhaps.

Wordsworth's case is a complicated one. He *was* a Lost Leader, but not in the vulgar sense imputed by Browning. It was rather that he had lost any sense of social direction. The good intentions of the *Lyrical Ballads* must be commended. They were intended, he says, to counteract the psychological effects of the Industrial Revolution:

For a multitude of causes, unknown to former times, are now acting with a combined force to blunt the discriminating powers of the mind, and, unfitting it for all voluntary exertion, to reduce it to a state of almost savage torpor. The most effective of these causes are the great national events which are daily taking place, and the increasing accumulation of men in cities, where the uniformity of their occupations produces a craving for extraordinary incident, which the rapid communication of intelligence barely gratifies.[1]

Instead of the melodramatic excitements of the contemporary street ballads Wordsworth offered 'the middle and lower classes of society' a new

[1] Preface to second edition (1800).

kind of ballad containing 'a *natural* delineation of human passions, human characters, and human incidents.'[1] And it is clear that he had taken a good deal of trouble to learn the language of the popular ballad-writers. Most of the uncouthnesses and *naïvetés* of 'The Idiot Boy' and 'Simon Lee' are attributable to a deliberate attempt to reproduce the ballad manner rather than to any new theory of poetic diction. One of Wordsworth's ballad masters was Robert Anderson of Carlisle, whose song 'Lucy Gray of Allendale' was 'sung by Master Phelps, at Vauxhall, 1794'.[2] But it is only necessary to compare Anderson's Lucy Gray with Wordsworth's to realize why Wordsworth never became the poet of the nineteenth-century proletariat:

> O have you seen the blushing rose,
> The blooming pink, or lily pale;
> Fairer than any flow'r that blows
> Was Lucy Gray of Allendale. . . . .
>
> 'Twas underneath the hawthorn shade
> I told her first the tender tale;
> But now low lays the lovely maid,
> Sweet Lucy Gray of Allendale.
>
> Bleak blows the wind, keen beats the rain,
> Upon my cottage in the vale:
> Long may I mourn a lonely swain,
> For Lucy Gray of Allendale.

This is almost the exact opposite of the psychological realism of the *Lyrical Ballads*. But Anderson, in spite of his sentimentality and his technical incompetence, was writing in the tradition of English folk-poetry. The poet-reader relationship was definite and intimate. Wordsworth, though immensely his superior in natural gifts, was reduced to fabricating, and even *faking*, a poet-reader relationship. And it was the failure of his social mission – for the middle and lower classes consistently refused to read the *Lyrical Ballads* – that drove Wordsworth in on himself. For a year or two the little group at Dove Cottage – Dorothy, Coleridge, the Hutchinsons – provided an audience for his introspective recollections. It was Wordsworth's golden moment, the period of *The Prelude*, the Lucy poems, 'Michael' and 'Resolution and Independence.' But each

---

[1] 'Advertisement' to first edition (1798). The italics are mine.
[2] See Anderson's *Poems on Various Subjects* (Carlisle, 1798), p. 149. Wordsworth's 'Lucy Gray: or Solitude' was written in 1799 and printed in 1800. Anderson's 'Ruth', who went off 'wid a taistrel sowdger lad' (it is a song in the Cumberland dialect) also invites comparison with Wordsworth.

member of the group was too closely attached emotionally to him and to its other members for the group to be able to persist as a harmonious and beneficent social entity. As it breaks up – the rejection of Dorothy implied in the marriage to Mary Hutchinson is the first fissure – the social basis of Wordsworth's poetry disappears. The process was completed by the quarrel with Coleridge in 1810. Wordsworth was only forty in 1810, but he had not the humility or the curiosity to attempt a new relationship with a new audience. Indeed, it would never have crossed his mind that such a thing was necessary. The disadvantage of Romanticism was that it discouraged self-knowledge and self-criticism. Wordsworth had never been certain why he wrote poetry or where it came from. The habit of composition persisted after 1810 and for him the fact of persistence guaranteed the quality of the products. It is true the emotions still overflowed spontaneously into words, but because they were not addressed to anybody in particular the result was no longer poetry.

### III

Shelley seems to have been the first critic to mark the stages of Wordsworth's poetic decay. 'He was at first sublime, pathetic, impressive, profound; then dull; then prosy and dull; and now dull – O, so very dull! it is an ultra-legitimate dulness.'[1] It is an admirably accurate division, the first stage presumably ending in 1802 or 1803, the second in or about 1810, while the third is that of *The Excursion* (1814) and its successors. And what was right in the early Wordsworth (his 'Wakening a sort of thought in sense') and what was wrong in the later Wordsworth, 'A solemn and unsexual man,' are distinguished with equal felicity. Could anything be better than this summary of the second volume of *Lyrical Ballads*?

> Of lakes he had intelligence,
>     He knew something of heath, and fell.
>
> He had also dim recollections
>     Of pedlars tramping on their rounds;
> Milk-pans and pails; and odd collections
> Of saws, and proverbs; and reflections
>     Old parsons make in burying-grounds.

Unfortunately Shelley's faculties of self-criticism were less acute. The accident of his place in the Romantic succession, the fact that he was twenty-two years younger than Wordsworth – an Assured Master rather than the Leader of a New Movement – saved him from the lapses of diction that are so frequent in Wordsworth and Coleridge. And his

---

[1] *Peter Bell the Third* (Oct. 1819), 'Dedication'.

control of symbolic technique is more certain. The failure of the 'myth' in Wordsworth's Ode is largely attributable to the injudicious choice of symbols. It was foolish of the still semi-republican Wordsworth to equate the pre-natal glory with an 'imperial palace', and it was equally rash to compare the corrupting influence of the world to the 'Yearnings . . . of a Mother's Mind'. In both cases the associations derived from Wordsworth's earlier poetry work *against* the intended meaning, the connotations cancelling out the denotations. This kind of mistake, the consequence of a failure to appreciate that the symbol is the basic unit of Romantic poetry, is hardly ever found in Shelley's poetry. Without being systematic (Yeats's attempt to unravel a symbolic system in Shelley's poems doesn't get very far[1]), Shelley's symbolism is remarkably self-consistent. But the internal contradiction that was a mark, as we have seen, of Wordsworth's declining power is discernible in even the best of Shelley's poems.

The 'Ode to the West Wind' is said to be 'the most symmetrically perfect as well as the most impassioned'[2] of Shelley's shorter poems. E. M. W. Tillyard has called it 'the most powerful' of all Shelley's lyrics because the most 'masterfully shaped'.[3] And N. I. White, Shelley's last and best biographer, thinks 'few poems, if any, have ever been written with a finer sense of structure than the "Ode to the West Wind"'.[4] This emphasis upon the structural perfection of the Ode suggests that the fairest line of critical approach will be, as with Wordsworth's Ode, by a process of structural analysis.[5]

Structurally, then, Shelley's poem consists of three parallel invocations of the West Wind in its three fields of operation, on the land, in the sky and on the sea. The invocations are followed by a prayer to the Wind:

[1] See 'The Philosophy of Shelley's Poetry' in Yeats's *Essays* (1924).
[2] J. A. Symonds, *Shelley*, 'English Men of Letters' series, pp. 119-20.
[3] *Milton* (1934), p. 241.          [4] *Shelley* (1947), vol. ii, p. 453.
[5] In the remarkable depreciation of Shelley in *Revaluation* (1936), pp. 204 ff., F. R. Leavis has approached the Ode by way of the imagery. The confusions that he finds in stanza II – 'the tangled boughs of Heaven and Ocean', he says, 'stand for nothing that Shelley could have pointed to in the scene before him' – can be paralleled in stanza I. L. 4, 'Yellow, and black, and pale, and hectic red' *following* 'like ghosts from an enchanter fleeing' suggests that the ghosts have not been visualized. Ghosts are essentially colourless. In ll. 5-6 the metaphors are hopelessly mixed: a *chariot* containing *winged seeds* is proceeding to a *bed*. L. 11 ('Driving sweet buds like flocks to feed in air') compares the shoots of the spring flora to a shepherd driving his sheep, i.e., a vertical to a horizontal process. And so on. The significant thing, however, is that such defects are not noticed until one's attention is drawn to them. Shelley's images are not meant to build up a landscape or effect a comparison. Their function is simply to add to the kaleidoscope of associations which surrounds the central symbol. The ghosts, the enchanter and the bright colours are merely intended to enrich the *idea* of the West Wind rather than to illustrate one of its spheres of action.

> If I were a dead leaf thou mightest bear;
> If I were a swift cloud to fly with thee;
> A wave to pant beneath thy power. . . .

which resumes the invocations of stanzas I-III. The autumn leaf typifies the objects of the Wind's impact on land (stanza I); the cloud (conceived as the leaf of a sky forest, 'Shook from the tangled boughs of Heaven and Ocean') typifies the sky (stanza II); the wave typifies the sea, with its submarine 'oozy woods' and their 'sapless foliage' (stanza III). Shelley's prayer is for a similar impact of the Wind upon himself:

> Oh, lift me as a wave, a leaf, a cloud!
> I fall upon the thorns of life! I bleed!

The Wind, in other words, is to provide Shelley with a means of escape from the difficulties of everyday life. So far (stanza IV) his prayer is self-regarding only. In stanza V it becomes altruistic and there is a slight extension of the symbolism. The Wind is no longer conceived simply as the force that whirls leaves about; it is also, as it lashes the forest, the creator of a wild music. Shelley is now praying for a resurgence of poetic inspiration. With the Wind's help his poems will be whirled 'over the universe' and serve as 'The trumpet of a prophecy'. And there is a final return here to a theme originally broached in stanza I – the West Wind of autumn is only the precursor of the creative West Wind of spring.

Shelley's structural intentions are clear enough. In so far as they are carried out they are, of course, to his poetic credit. But a close examination raises one central difficulty. In stanza I the Wind is invoked as 'Destroyer and preserver' (it destroys the leaves and preserves the seeds), and Shelley appears to assign a similar dual function to his poetry in stanza V (as 'Ashes and sparks' it will destroy the dead heritage of the past; as 'withered leaves' it will fertilize the Utopia of the future). The connection is not altogether clear, but there can at any rate be no doubt that a socio-political implication is intended. Shelley wants his reader to see the West Wind as a symbol of the forces of progress. That is what the poem ought to be about.

But is it? Is not the real subject of the poem (i) Shelley's delight in natural violence, (ii) Shelley's self-pity, (iii) Shelley's consciousness of failing inspiration? It is surely extremely significant that the Wind's destroyer-preserver rôle, so essential to the political argument, is lost sight of entirely in stanzas II and III. The minute structural parallelism of stanzas I-III presumes an identity of content in them. But in fact in stanzas II and III the Wind is conceived simply as an irresistible natural force. What it symbolizes is not political reform but the instinctive energies of the subconscious mind. Its contemplation restores Shelley to his boyhood (the typical Romantic reversion);

> If even
> I were as in my boyhood, and could be
> The comrade of thy wanderings over Heaven,
> As then, when to outstrip thy skiey speed
> Scarce seemed a vision.

And the altruism of stanza v is only on its surface. Essentially the ageing Shelley ('my leaves are falling') is demanding the restoration of his own adolescent ecstasies:

> Be thou, Spirit fierce,
> My spirit! Be thou me, impetuous one!

So the spring that is not far behind is less a prophecy of the Reform Bill than the personal consolation that a Romantic poet is offering himself. Like Wordsworth in his Ode, Shelley is *primarily* cheering himself up.

This is not to accuse Shelley of conscious insincerity. Shelley's political interests were genuine enough but they were superficial. Their emotional basis was not a rational conviction of the desirability of political reform, but a boy's reaction against domestic tyranny. As he grew up, the interest in politics began to wane. In the 'Ode to the West Wind' it provided an excuse for a poem that is really only concerned with Shelley himself. By June 1822 – over two and a half years after he had written the Ode – Shelley could write to Horace Smith:

England appears to be in a desperate condition, Ireland still worse; and no class of those who subsist on the public labour will be persuaded that *their* claims on it must be diminished. But the government must content itself with less in taxes, the land-holder must submit to receive less rent, and the fundholder a diminished interest, or they will all get nothing. I once thought to study these affairs, and write or act in them – I am glad that my good genius said *refrain* – I see little public virtue, and I foresee that the contest will be one of blood and gold, two elements which how-ever much to my taste in my pockets and my veins, I have an objection to out of them.[1]

The retreat from politics, here explicit, had been implicit in Shelley's poetry almost from the beginning. If he had lived he would no doubt have followed Wordsworth and Coleridge into a non-political con-servatism. Romanticism and politics are inherently incompatible, as even Blake eventually discovered.[2] The political façade that Shelley's poems

---

[1] 29 June 1822. Shelley was drowned ten days later.

[2] Blake told Crabb Robinson that Christ 'should not have attacked the govt. He had no business with such matters', and that Dante was 'wrong' in having 'political objects' (*Blake, Coleridge, Wordsworth, Lamb, etc.*, ed. E. J. Morley (1932), pp. 3, 5).

retain was a form of unconscious hypocrisy – the tribute of the escapist to the social conscience. They are pretending to be more serious than they really are. I am inclined to think Shelley's light verse is his best poetry. *Peter Bell*, *The Witch of Atlas* and the group of lyrics addressed to Jane Williams ('Ariel to Miranda', 'The keen stars are twinkling', 'Best and brightest', etc.), though often carelessly written and always rather 'thin,' are at any rate completely successful in what they set out to be.

## IV

Keats's 'Ode on a Grecian Urn' was written in the early summer of 1819.[1] It therefore antedates the 'Ode to the West Wind' by only three or four months. 1819 was also the year of the Peterloo Massacre. Shelley's poem, as we have seen, though explicitly political, is not really political at all. The interest of Keats's poem is that, though explicitly non-political, it is implicitly political. In spite of the Romantic trappings it is not at bottom a wholly Romantic poem.

The Urn, for one thing, is not a symbol in the sense in which the West Wind and Blake's Tiger and Keats's own Nightingale are symbols. There is no question here of an 'objective correlative'. The Urn really only provides an object lesson. By the use of analogies from the Urn Keats is able to make a number of points about the nature of poetry.

The Urn is introduced as comparable with but superior to poetry:

> Sylvan historian, who canst thus express
> A flowery tale more sweetly than our rhyme.

*Endymion*, it will be remembered, had opened with the claim that poetry provided 'A flowery band to bind us to the earth'. The Urn, then, can beat poetry at its own game. And what that game is is exemplified in the *motionless movement* of l. 9 of stanza I,

> What mad pursuit? What struggle to escape?

Stanza II elaborates the definition with examples of *soundless sound* ('ditties of no tone'), *stationary growth* ('Nor ever can those trees be bare'), and *timeless time* ('For ever wilt thou love, and she be fair'). Stanzas III and IV draw certain pathetic and whimsical corollaries, and stanza V sums up the paradox of poetry. As Coleridge, with whom

---

[1] It is impossible to be more specific. Metrically the 'Grecian Urn' clearly derives from the irregular 'Ode to Psyche' (included in the journal-letter of 30 April): it represents an inter-mediate stage between that poem – and perhaps the 'Ode to a Nightingale' which retains the occasional short lines of 'Psyche' – and *To Autumn* (written at Winchester, 19 and 20 Sept.). Its Stanzas III, IV have the same rhyme scheme as the 'Ode on Indolence', which had been completed before 9 June.

Keats had walked across Hampstead Heath as recently as the previous April, had taught his contemporaries, poetry 'reveals itself in the balance or reconcilement of opposite or discordant qualities'.[1] And Hazlitt, Keats's principal critical mentor, had made the same point even more clearly when he attributed to Shakespeare 'the combination of the greatest extremes.' 'Shakespeare's imagination is rapid and devious. It unites the most opposite extreme'.[2] The Urn, in other words, in the terminology of Part One of this book, exemplifies the Synthetic Function of poetry and the Principle of the Semantic Gap.

The much-debated 'Beauty is truth, truth beauty' must be interpreted in this context. The Urn is a 'Cold Pastoral'; that is to say, like pastoral poetry (the only sense the noun *pastoral* had in the nineteenth century), it is allegorical.[3] Behind the particular unions of opposites depicted on the Urn (motion and immobility, growth and permanence, time and time-lessness, etc.) a general synthetic principle is implied. This is the necessity for uniting Romanticism ('beauty') and realism ('truth'), the subconscious with the conscious mind, the feeling with the concept, poetry and philosophy. It is Keats's protest against the Romantic 'split man'. And the point of particular interest is Keats's *social* motive in propounding this generalization. The Urn is 'a friend to man'. The lesson that it teaches will be consolatory to the next generation as well as to Keats's.[4] Indeed, compared to the need for psychological integration other social problems are of secondary importance:

> that is all
> Ye know on earth, and all ye need to know.

Keats oversimplified, of course, but to say, as Allen Tate has done,[5] that

---

[1] *Biographia Literaria*, chap. xiv. The whole passage is quoted on p. 38 above.

[2] See J. R. Caldwell's admirable discussion of the poem in *Keats's Fancy* (1945), pp. 177, 183. Caldwell lists a number of eighteenth-century anticipations of Keats's 'Beauty is truth, truth beauty', but has missed the closest of all. This is in Shaftesbury's *Sensus Communis* (1709), p. 111; 'For all *Beauty* is TRUTH . . . In Poetry, which is all Fable, Truth still is the Perfection. And whoever is Scholar enough to read the antient Philosopher, or his modern Copists, upon the nature of a Dramatick and Epick Poem, will easily understand this account of *Truth*.'

[3] Hazlitt discusses the English pastoral in the fifth of the *Lectures on the English Poets* (1818), stressing particularly its allegoric elements, e.g. 'Browne, who came after Spenser, and Withers, have left some pleasing allegorical poems of this kind.' Keats had heard Hazlitt deliver this actual lecture (letter to George and Thomas Keats, 14 Feb. 1818).

[4] Note that Keats speaks throughout in a representative capacity. In stanza I it is '*our* rhyme': in stanza v the Urn teases '*us* out of thought', and there is 'other woe Than *ours*'. Shelley would have written in the first person singular throughout. J. Middleton Murry (*Studies in Keats New and Old* (1939), p. 75) assigns 'that is all Ye know on earth and all ye need to know' to the poet. Obviously, however, this is also spoken by the Urn, the 'ye' being the *we* implied in '*ours*'.

[5] 'A Reading of Keats', *New English Review* (Feb. 1946).

stanza v 'is an illicit commentary added by the poet to a "meaning" which was symbolically complete at the end of the preceding stanza' is to miss Keats's point. Stanza IV had been a relapse into Romanticism. The 'green altar', the 'mysterious priest' and the 'little town' were alluring invitations to reverie. But Keats was too honest to leave it at that. The 'Ode to a Nightingale' had ended with the explicit admission that the 'fancy' is a 'cheat', and the 'Grecian Urn' concludes with a similar repudiation. But this time it is a positive instead of a negative conclusion. There *is* no escape from the 'woe' that 'shall this generation waste', but the action of time can be confronted and seen in its proper proportions. To enable its readers to do this is the special function of poetry.

Keats took the argument a stage further in the remarkable dialogue between Moneta and the poet in 'The Fall of Hyperion' (written some two months later):

> 'Art thou not of the dreamer tribe?
> 'The poet and the dreamer are distinct,
> 'Diverse, sheer opposite, antipodes.
> 'The one pours out a balm upon the World,
> 'The other vexes it.' Then shouted I
> Spite of myself, and with a Pythia's spleen
> 'Apollo! faded! O far flown Apollo!
> 'Where is thy misty pestilence to creep
> 'Into the dwellings, through the door crannies
> 'Of all mock lyrists, large self worshippers
> 'And careless Hectorers in proud bad verse.
> 'Though I breathe death with them it will be life
> 'To see them sprawl before me into graves.'[1]

Here is Keats, at the end of his poetic career, repudiating Romantic poetry at least as emphatically as he had repudiated Augustan poetry at its beginning (in 'Sleep and Poetry'). And more specifically. The objects of his attack are, I think, easily identifiable. The 'careless Hectorers' are presumably Byron and Shelley ('be more of an artist'[2]). The 'large self-worshippers' are almost certainly Wordsworth and Coleridge. And the 'mock lyrists' must include Leigh Hunt, Tom Moore, Southey and Rogers, who are grouped together in the journal-letter of March 1819 as poets Keats did *not* admire. The basis of the repudiation of these poets is that they are 'dreamers', who only 'vex' the world. Put into modern terms, Keats's criticism of the Romantic Movement is that it represents

---

[1] At the last moment Keats decided to cancel this passage: not, however, because he disagreed with its doctrine, but because he seems to have felt that it complicated the argument unnecessarily.

[2] Keats to Shelley, 16 Aug. 1820.

a mere exploitation of the subconscious mind without a satisfactory relationship with its audience. The poetry that Keats admired – and that he was hoping to write – was the exact opposite of this. Instead of the irresponsible subliminal excitements of Romanticism Keats wanted poetry to pour 'a balm upon the World', i.e. a soothing and healing influence. Its function was to be social. In the last letter he wrote to Fanny Brawne he gives an example of what he meant:

If my health would bear it, I could write a Poem which I have in my head, which would be a consolation for people in such a situation as mine. I would show some one in Love as I am, with a person living in such Liberty as you do.

The poem – its heroine apparently was to have been the Sabrina of Milton's *Comus* – was never written, and *could* never have been written, even if his health had improved. The only consolation that poetry could provide in the nineteenth century, given the social setting and the contemporary condition of the English language, was the consolation of the daydream. Keats's Sabrina could only have been 'La Belle Dame Sans Merci' over again. In turning his back on that kind of thing – the 'vision' of the 'Ode to a Nightingale' *was*, he had decided, only 'a waking dream' – Keats had in fact condemned himself to poetic silence. It was not to be possible to write the sort of poetry that the mature Keats wanted to write for a hundred years. Eventually Wilfred Owen (for whom Keats was the poet of poets) was to take up the torch that Keats had kindled. 'Strange Meeting' (1918) can perhaps be said to carry on where 'The Fall of Hyperion' (1819) had left off.[1]

---

[1] The precocious maturity of Keats is a problem of its own. The turning-point seems to have been the winter of 1817-18. *Endymion* (finished Nov. 1817) is adolescent, *Isabella* (finished April 1818) is adult. I am inclined to connect the change with the moral shock that the syphilis contracted at Oxford in Sept. 1817 had given him. Amy Lowell tried to dispose of the tradition of Keats's syphilis, first recorded by W. M. Rossetti, by showing that the mercury referred to in the letter to Bailey of 8 Oct. 1817 might have been taken for a number of other diseases (*John Keats* (1925), vol. i, pp. 512-15). But she overlooked the information supplied by Keats's medical friend Henry Stephens (who must have known the facts): 'In the autumn of the same year, 1817, he visits a friend, Bailey by name, at Oxford, and in that visit runs loose, and pays a forfeit for his indiscretion, which ever afterwards physically and morally embarrasses him.' See Sir B. W. Richardson, *The Asclepiad* (April 1884), p. 143.

# 12

# Romantic Schizophrenia: Tennyson's 'Tears, Idle Tears'

BY its own utilitarian criterion the Early Victorian Age must be accounted a failure. Never before in English history had so great a number of people been so acutely conscious of their own unhappiness. If the dominant social incentive was self-help, the dominant social fact was the accumulated misery of those who had not succeeded in helping themselves. And its consequence, as Léon Fancher, a Belgian observer who was here in the 1840s, noted, was that 'les diverses classes de la population, vivent non seulement séparées, mais hostiles, et où l'état de guerre semble être l'état naturel'[1] – an analysis that is confirmed by the sequence of riots and prosecutions, strikes and lock-outs, that preceded the Reform Act and accompanied the three Chartist Petitions. In addition to its intensity, there was one other feature that distinguished the class-warfare of the 1830s and 1840s from earlier and later social antagonisms. This was its simplicity. As Marx and Engels pointed out in the *Communist Manifesto* (1848), 'Society as a whole is more and more splitting up into two great hostile camps, into two great classes directly facing each other – bourgeoisie and proletariat'. And, though their terminology is more naïve, the same conclusion had already been reached by such English social reformers as Thomas Arnold, Dickens, Carlyle and Disraeli. In one of his *Sermons Preached in the Chapel of Rugby School* (1832) Dr Arnold accused his boys of thinking that 'the rich and the poor are . . . two distinct castes – I had almost said two distinct races'.[2] And in Disraeli's *Sybil or the Two Nations* (1845), a brilliantly objective social guidebook that only *pretends* to propound a political philosophy, the two nations are specifically defined in the same terms:

'This is a new reign', said Egremont, 'perhaps it is a new era.'

'I think so,' said the younger stranger.

'I hope so,' said the elder one.

'Well, society may be in its infancy,' said Egremont, slightly smiling; 'but, say what you like, our Queen reigns over the greatest nation that ever existed.'

[1] *Etudes sur l'Angleterre* (Brussels 1845), vol. i, p. 166.
[2] Sermon xvi. As a small step in the right direction Arnold suggested that the boys should stop using 'that contemptuous word by which you call the poor'. Although the word itself is not specified by Arnold, *Tom Brown's Schooldays* makes it clear that the 'insulting name' he had in mind was *lout*.

'Which nation?' asked the younger stranger, 'for she reigns over two.'

The stranger paused; Egremont was silent, but looked inquiringly.

'Yes,' resumed the younger stranger after a moment's interval. 'Two nations; between whom there is no intercourse and no sympathy; who are as ignorant of each other's habits, thoughts and feelings, as if they were dwellers in different zones, or inhabitants of different planets; who are formed by a different breeding, are fed by a different food, are ordered by different manners, and are not governed by the same laws.'

'You speak of . . .' said Egremont, hesitatingly.

'THE RICH AND THE POOR.'[1]

The social skeleton in the Victorian cupboard looms behind the poetry of Tennyson. As a young man he is reported to have said that the two great social questions impending in England were 'the housing and education of the poor man before making him our master, and the higher education of women'.[2] And an anecdote confirms his twinges of social conscience. In 1842, when the two-volume edition of his *Poems* had just publicly established his status as a poet, with other members of Edmund Lushington's house-party at Park House, Maidstone, he was in the walled garden, eating the peaches and the apricots. Many years later one of the younger members of the party recalled, in a letter to Tennyson's son, the conversation that took place that August. 'Some one made a remark about the fruit being liable to disagree with himself or others, to which another replied with a jocular remark about the "disturbed districts", alluding, of course, to some disorders apprehended or existing in the centres of industry. I remember being startled by your father's voice and accent, "I can't joke about so grave a question".'[3] But it was Tennyson the earnest citizen who was shocked; Tennyson the poet excluded such questions from his verse, except on the rarest of occasions, for the sufficient reason that he could not make poetry out of them. Between his conscience and his imagination there was a hiatus, a total lack of connection, that parallels the social gulf between the two nations. And the same psychic division is to be found *inside* his poetry. In 'Tears, Idle Tears' it can be shown, I believe, that two elements of his personality coexist without ever coalescing.

'Tears, Idle Tears' was written at Tintern Abbey, no doubt on some unrecorded excursion from Cheltenham, Tennyson's headquarters during the years immediately preceding his marriage. Though it cannot be dated precisely it must have been composed at some time between the publication of *Sybil* (1845) and the commissioning of the *Communist Manifesto*

---

[1] Book II, ch. v.       [2] *A Memoir by his Son* (1897), vol. i, p. 249.

[3] *Ibid.*, vol. i, p. 205.

by the Communist League (November 1847). It was published in the fourth canto of *The Princess* (1847). Unlike the songs added in 1850, 'Tears, Idle Tears' is an integral part of the story of that 'Medley' and strictly speaking it should not be read, as it generally is, out of its dramatic context. There it is a song that is sung at the Princess's request:

> lightlier move
> The minutes fledged with music.

But the song proves less sedative in the poem than the Princess had anticipated, and she dismisses 'with some disdain' this reactionary plea for 'the moulder'd lodges of the Past'. As a progressive feminist her motto is 'let the past be past,' and she asks the disguised Prince to sing instead a song about the republican future,

> Not such as moans about the retrospect.

The significance of these comments is the light they throw on Tennyson's own interpretation of 'the days that are no more', the phrase that provides the poem's theme as well as its refrain. Apparently the days that are no more are the subject-matter of the history books. The unmotivated, incomprehensible tears must be taken, it seems, as a tribute to the glamour of the heroic past. A later comment by Tennyson himself seems to imply a similar interpretation: 'This song came to me on the yellowing autumn-tide at Tintern Abbey, full for me of its bygone memories. It is the sense of the abiding in the transient.'[1] The 'bygone memories', in addition to those suggested by the Cistercian monastery, may also have included memories of Wordsworth's *Lines Composed a Few Miles above Tintern Abbey*. It is at any rate curious that Tennyson characterized Wordsworth's line 'Whose dwelling is the light of setting suns' in almost identical terms as 'almost the grandest in the England language, giving the sense of the abiding in the transient'.[2] Another recorded comment makes it even more certain that the 'days that are no more' do not refer to Tennyson's (or the reader's) past:

It was written at Tintern Abbey, when the woods were yellowing with autumn, seen through the ruined windows. It is what I have always felt as a boy, and what as a boy I called the passion of the past. And it is always with me now; it is the distance that charms me in the landscape, the picture and the past, and not the immediate to-day in which I move.[3]

---

[1] *The Works of Tennyson with Notes by the Author* (1931), p. 931.
[2] *Memoir by his Son*, vol. ii, p. 288.
[3] W. M. Dixon, *A Primer of Tennyson* (1896), p. 134.

Obviously, if the emotion that the poem records was felt by Tennyson as a boy, it cannot reside in the mature Tennyson's recollections of his boyhood. The days that are no more must belong to a public past.

But Tennyson's interpretation is certainly not the natural interpretation of the poem. And, as a matter of fact, most of his commentators have given 'the days that are no more' the personal sense that he consistently excluded. Sir Alfred Lyall has paraphrased the poem's mood as 'the tender melancholy of a feeling that life may be passing without love, of vague regrets and longings'.[1] W. M. Dixon's comment is on the same lines.[2] And more recently Cleanth Brooks, who describes the poem as an exploration of the nature of memory, has confirmed its subjective character.[3] It is almost impossible, indeed, to resist the impression that Tennyson's emotion is connected in some way with his own past. Nevertheless the poem *can* be given the meaning that he indicated. It is not the natural sense, but it is a possible sense. The one thing, in fact, that it is impossible to do is to give the poem both senses at once. *Either* the days that are no more are the objective past of kings and monasteries, *or* they are the subjective past of the poet's and reader's own earlier life. They cannot be both together.

There is a similar contradiction in the separate phrases and images. The clearest case perhaps is the phrase 'Dear as remember'd kisses after death'. This can be read in two ways. The natural sense is to take the person who remembers and the person who has died as one and the same. The meaning then will be that the dead man is remembering the kisses he exchanged when still alive – an effective if uncanny idea rather like the half-life of regret and reminiscence accorded to the Homeric hero after death. But, though this is certainly the sense that the grammar would suggest, the context makes it clear that Tennyson meant the person who remembers to be distinct from the person who is dead. Presumably it is the survivor who remembers the kisses exchanged with a loved one who is now dead.

An even more interesting example of this conflict between the natural interpretation and the intended meaning is provided by the lines,

> Fresh as the first beam glittering on a sail,
> That brings our friends up from the underworld.

Overtly Tennyson is here defining the retrospective vividness that attaches to episodes of the historic past. This 'freshness', which derives from the

[1] *Tennyson*, 'English Men of Letters' series (1902), p. 57.
[2] Op. cit., p. 61.
[3] *The Well Wrought Urn* (New York, 1947), ch. ix.

absence of commonplace associations, Tennyson compares to a visual sensation that must have been equally rare to the middle-class Victorian reader – the shimmer of sunrise on the sails of an East Indiaman on the horizon. But the comparison does not stop, as it ought to logically, at the visual image. This is not just a large sailing ship; the boat has passengers on board and the passengers are 'our friends' (yours, Gentle Reader, and mine!), who have returned from the antipodes. And with the addition the vividness of the image ('glittering' surely implies that the early morning dew is still on the sails?) is blurred by the emotional exaltation that the prospect of this reunion imposes. It is difficult to find anything especially 'fresh' in the sentimental excitements of such an occasion. It looks as if, when he added the second line, Tennyson had forgotten about his simile and was simply surrendering to the subconscious suggestions of the imagery. Was he, in the depths of his mind, expecting to find Arthur Hallam – buried at Clevedon only twenty miles or so, as the crow flies, from Tintern – on board the incoming boat? The use of the word 'underworld' invites some such interpretation. Its overt sense here is certainly not its natural sense or its ordinary sense. Indeed, according to the Oxford Dictionary, Tennyson's use of 'underworld' as a synonym either for the antipodes or for 'the part of the earth beyond the horizon', is the first occurrence of either sense in English. The *natural* sense of 'underworld' in this context is of Hades, a world of departed spirits under the earth – a sense that goes back to the Elizabethans; and the natural interpretation of the line is to read it as a sort of nineteenth-century version of Charon's boat. The East Indiaman, in other words, is bringing back Hallam, a modern Eurydice, alive from the grave!

The poem's third stanza is also ostensibly a prolonged simile – one by means of which the peculiar combination of strangeness and sadness that the contemplation of the heroic past evokes is to be defined. But in fact, in a natural reading of the lines, is not the analogy – a somewhat forced one, in any case – almost immediately lost sight of and the whole of the reader's attention concentrated on the brilliantly recorded sense-reactions of the dying man?

> Ah, sad and strange as in dark summer dawns
> The earliest pipe of half-awaken'd birds
> To dying ears, when unto dying eyes
> The casement slowly grows a glimmering square;
> So sad, so strange, the days that are no more.

The dying man in this stanza is not, of course, in any literal sense Arthur Hallam, who died at midday on 15 September (not on a summer dawn) and in any case had no idea that he was dying (a blood-vessel near the brain suddenly burst). But the selection of this particular image, with its close connection both with the 'underworld' immediately preceding it and with the kisses 'after death' that follow it, is surely significant.

The last stanza of the poem seems to *demand* a personal interpretation:

> Dear as remember'd kisses after death,
> And sweet as those by hopeless fancy feign'd
> On lips that are for others; deep as love,
> Deep as first love, and wild with all regret;
> O Death in Life, the days that are no more.

The kisses are obviously not mere abstract poetic properties. And if they are not – and their strict relevance in this summing up of 'the passion of the past' is far from clear – may they not be the kisses that Hallam and Tennyson (and Emily Tennyson, Alfred's sister who was also Hallam's fiancée) did or did not exchange? It is at least *possible* that the 'first love' is Tennyson's for Hallam ('deep' because frustrated and repressed), and that the 'lips that are for others' are Hallam's lips – which were presumably reserved for Emily, with whom Hallam had fallen in love almost as soon as he and Tennyson had got to know each other.[1]

If the preceding analysis is not wholly misguided, it looks as if 'Tears, Idle Tears' was not really one poem but two. On the conscious level it is a poem about that feeling for the past that had been discovered by Carlyle and Froude, among the historians, in Tennyson's own generation, and by Scott in the previous generation. On the subconscious level, on the other hand, it is a poem about the relations between the living and the dead – and specifically perhaps those between the living Tennyson and the dead Hallam. It is possible, of course, that Tennyson was aware of the auto-biographical elements in the poem, and that its incorporation in *The Princess* and his various expository comments upon it represent an elaborate attempt to put the reader off the scent. Or the censorship may have been subconscious – in which case we must envisage one subliminal layer in his mind covering up the indiscretions of an even deeper layer. But either hypothesis presupposes a purposiveness and a degree of integration of the psychic material that I cannot find reflected in the poem. Within the limits of his self-knowledge Tennyson's comments ring true to me. I doubt if there was any intention to deceive. And the poem too is, in its way, sincere – the authentic expression of an unintegrated personality. The morbidity lies in the absence of any effective connection between the two levels of statement. The days that are no more are at one and the same time

[1] I would like to know more about Emily Tennyson and her brother's attitude towards her. She married Richard Jesse in 1842.

the historic past and Tennyson's passionate, unhappy twenties. And between the two meanings no real link whatever is provided or apparently even felt necessary.

Tennyson was not the only Victorian poet who suffered from schizophrenia. It was the occupational disease of the period. The case of Browning is notorious. Henry James wrote a short story about it ('The Private Life'): Clare Vawdrey – 'the greatest (in the opinion of many) of our literary glories' – has a Mr Hyde, a copiously commonplace talker, and a Dr Jekyll, a lonely genius who sits up in his room and is never seen. James's preface explains that Vawdrey is Browning (whom he knew quite well): 'I have never ceased to ask myself, in this particular loud, sound, normal, hearty presence, all so assertive and so whole, all bristling with prompt responses and expected opinions and usual views . . . what lodgement, on such premises, the rich proud genius one adored could ever have contrived, what domestic commerce the subtlety that was its prime ornament and the world's wonder have enjoyed, under what shelter the obscurity that was its luckless drawback and the world's despair have flourished.'

James noted the contradiction, but was not able to explain it, or even to define it, except in terms of a fairy story. But the Victorian 'split personality' is clearly a reflection in some sense of the split in Victorian society. It would be to oversimplify to suggest that the psychic division that is revealed in 'Tears, Idle Tears' is the direct consequence of the coexistence of the two nations in the 1840s. But the two traumata are almost certainly related. They can, I believe, both be attributed to the *inhuman specialization* (a specialization that repressed the full development of the human being, reducing, for example, the man to the 'hand') that the economic system encouraged. Physically it was the poor who suffered most, but the worst psychological victims were among the rich. The system, which assumed as its basic premise that the prosperity of society depends upon the selfishness of its constituent individuals, discouraged at one and the same time social planning and individual integration. 'Each for himself' became as true of the separate elements in the personality as of the various competitors in the market. That was the Spirit of the Age. Its recognition should make for a fairer assessment of Victorian poetry than it has hitherto received.

# 13

# From Escapism to Social Realism: Two Poems about Oxford

THE poetry of consolation that Keats projected and Wilfred Owen consolidated received its most memorable definition in the fragmentary Preface that was found among Owen's papers after his death. Familiar though it is, it is worth reproducing once more:

This book is not about heroes. English Poetry is not yet fit to speak of them.

Nor is it about deeds, or lands, nor anything about glory, honour, might, majesty, dominion, or power, except War.

Above all I am not concerned with Poetry.

My subject is War, and the pity of War.

The Poetry is in the pity.

Yet these elegies are to this generation in no sense consolatory. They may be to the next. All a poet can do to-day is warn. That is why the true Poets must be truthful.

*The true poets must be truthful.* Owen's variation on Keats's 'Beauty is truth, truth beauty' might be taken as the battle cry of modern English and American poetry. Its application provides the acid test at any rate between modern poetry and modern pseudo-poetry, such as that of Edith Sitwell. Their failure by its standards is what consigns most of the later Romantic poets to unreadability today. Once the singing robes were on, the Pre-Raphaelites and their successors could not or would not tell the truth about themselves and their society.

Lionel Johnson's 'Oxford' is a typical specimen of Romantic poetry in its Polished Craftsman and Decadent phases.[1] (Its representativeness is guaranteed by its inclusion in *The Oxford Book of Victorian Verse*.) Here is the kind of thing that modern poetry was in reaction against:

### Oxford

Over, the four long years! And now there rings
One voice of freedom and regret: *Farewell!*
Now old remembrance sorrows, and now sings:
But song from sorrow, now, I cannot tell.

City of weather'd cloister and worn court;
Grey city of strong towers and clustering spires:
Where art's fresh loveliness would first resort;
Where lingering art kindled her latest fires!

[1] From *Collected Poems* (1915)

Where on all hands, wondrous with ancient grace,
Grace touch'd with age, rise works of goodliest men:
Next Wykeham's art obtain their splendid place
The zeal of Inigo, the strength of Wren.

Where at each coign of every antique street,
A memory hath taken root in stone:
There, Raleigh shone; there, toil'd Franciscan feet;
There, Johnson flinch'd not, but endured alone.

There, Shelley dream'd his white Platonic dreams;
There, classic Landor throve on Roman thought;
There, Addison pursued his quiet themes;
There, smiled Erasmus, and there, Colet taught.

And there, O memory more sweet than all!
Lived he, whose eyes keep yet our passing light;
Whose crystal lips Athenian speech recall;
Who wears Rome's purple with least pride, most right.

That is the Oxford strong to charm us yet:
Eternal in her beauty and her past.
What though her soul be vex'd? She can forget
Cares of an hour: only the great things last.

Only the gracious air, only the charm,
And ancient might of true humanities,
These nor assault of man, nor time, can harm:
Not these, nor Oxford with her memories.

Together have we walk'd with willing feet
Gardens of plenteous trees, bowering soft lawn;
Hills whither Arnold wander'd; and all sweet
June meadows, from the troubling world withdrawn;

Chapels of cedarn fragrance, and rich gloom
Pour'd from empurpled panes on either hand;
Cool pavements, carved with legends of the tomb;
Grave haunts, where we might dream, and understand.

Over, the four long years! And unknown powers
Call to us, going forth upon our way:
Ah! Turn we, and look back upon the towers
That rose above our lives, and cheer'd the day.

Proud and serene, against the sky they gleam:
Proud and secure, upon the earth they stand.
Our city hath the air of a pure dream,
And hers indeed is a Hesperian land.

> Think of her so! The wonderful, the fair,
> The immemorial, and the ever young:
> The city sweet with our forefathers' care:
> The city where the Muses all have sung.
>
> Ill times may be; she hath no thought of time:
> She reigns beside the waters yet in pride.
> Rude voices cry: but in her ears the chime
> Of full sad bells brings back her old springtide.
>
> Like to a queen in pride of place, she wears
> The splendour of a crown in Radcliffe's dome.
> Well fare she—well! As perfect beauty fares,
> And those high places that are beauty's home.

The first reflection that a reading of Johnson's poem suggests is how easily they got away with it in Good Victoria's Golden Reign! No modern poet would dare to risk such slovenly writing as

> Chapels of cedarn fragrance, and rich gloom
> Pour'd from empurpled panes on either hand;
> Cool pavements, carved with legends of the tomb;
> Grave haunts, where we might dream, and understand.

The reader should surely not have been allowed to think, even momentarily, that the gloom is *poured on* the visitor's hands. And the use of the adjective *grave* immediately after *tomb* is unfortunate.[1]

A more serious matter is the metaphoric incompetence. The trope 'There, Raleigh *shone*' is obviously meant to be 'poetic'. That Johnson could have imagined anybody would think it poetic is a measure of his verbal *naïveté*. The 'crystal lips' he assigns to Newman (who is apparently the answer to the conundrum in the sixth verse) are another example of the same defect. And the metaphoric poverty is not compensated, as in Augustan poems, by solidity of structure. Johnson has only two devices by which to achieve poetic progression (i.e. the linking of line with line and verse with verse). The first is verbal repetition. (In the first verse *now*; in the second *city*, *where*, *art*; in the third *when*, *grace*, etc.) The second is verbal antithesis. The antitheses are most of them *merely* verbal, as

> The city sweet with our forefathers' care:
> The city where the Muses all have sung.

(No contrast is intended between the poets' Oxford and the Oxford the forefathers had cared for.) Occasionally, however, as in the following

---

[1] Equally unfortunate are the city's 'pure dream' (as opposed to an impure dream?), the 'Rude voices' of Oxford's critics, and the identification of the Thames valley with 'those *high* places that are beauty's home'. The sublime should not be quite so near the ridiculous.

lines, a real antithesis seems to be intended, though on inspection it is not clear what the point of the opposition is:

> Proud and serene, against the sky they gleam:
> Proud and secure, upon the earth they stand.

*Sky* is opposed to *earth*, and the *gleaming* of the towers is opposed to their *standing*. But why? There is no incompatibility in the towers simultaneously gleaming in the sky and standing on the earth. The reader, slightly irritated, realizes at this point that the antithesis is a mere literary gesture, and that Johnson is only using it to diversify his descriptive catalogue.

Such technical dishonesty is the appropriate accompaniment of the mental dishonesty of the poem. It is intended to be a tribute to the University by a literary undergraduate who is 'going down' for the last time. The tribute is a *personal* one. Johnson begins by referring to the mixed pleasures and pain of the four years' residence. Later he describes the walks he and his friends had taken in and around Oxford. Now 'unknown powers' are calling him to a career of free-lance journalism in London. But as soon as one asks what Oxford had done for Johnson, as a human being, to deserve the tribute doubts begin to intrude themselves. Instead of the truth – the thrill of having Walter Pater as a tutor, the charms of alcohol and Catholicism, the titillation of literary vanity – we get a versified extract from the Oxford guidebook. Apart from a single reference ('Together have we walk'd') to the friend to whom the poem is dedicated, the only people who come into the poem are the architects and writers of the past. One would imagine that Johnson's time in Oxford had been passed in cloistered solitude, whereas in fact he was a popular figure with many intimate friends. And this misrepresentation of his own debt to the University is accompanied by an equally gross caricature of Oxford's place in the national life. Johnson's case for Oxford against the crying of the 'Rude voices' is based entirely on 'her beauty and her past'. Oxford is the escapist's paradise – 'from the troubling world withdrawn'. This was written in 1890, when Oxford University's grip on the governmental, educational and religious machine was perhaps more complete than at any time before or since.[1]

Like most of his Oxford contemporaries Lionel Johnson professed a profound admiration for Matthew Arnold. The year before 'Oxford' he had written a long elegiac poem on Arnold's grave ('Laleham'), and in 'Winchester' there is an earlier tribute. But the object of this admiration

---

[1] It is true Johnson was only twenty-three in 1890, but he was as mature then as he was ever to be. His best and most familiar poem 'By the Statue of King Charles at Charing Cross' was written in 1889. There is an amusing account of Johnson at Oxford in Arthur Waugh's *Tradition and Change* (1919).

was Arnold the poet, the 'Prince of Song', whose Romantic *juvenilia*, such as 'Empedocles on Etna' and 'The New Sirens', the mature Arnold did his best to disavow. Johnson can have had little sympathy with the prose Arnold with his constant harping on the importance of seeing the thing as in itself it really is. To the aesthetes of the 1890s the thing was to be seen as it wasn't. Oscar Wilde deplored 'The Decay of Lying'. And in his private life, according to his friends, Johnson himself excelled in the gratuitous and unmitigated fib.

W. H. Auden's 'Oxford' is the fifth poem in the collection *Another Time* (1940). It was written in 1937, perhaps when Auden judged a verse-speaking contest in Oxford. Like Johnson's poem it is essentially a report on the University where the poet had been educated, and both poems contain many of the same 'properties' (e.g. the rivers, the architecture, the college gardens, and the neighbouring countryside). But the differences in poetic matter are at least as striking as the differences in poetic method.

An analysis of some of these differences will provide a more satisfactory approach to the assessment of modern poetry than the usual generalizations.

### Oxford

Nature is so near: the rooks in the college garden
Like agile babies still speak the language of feeling;
By the tower the river still runs to the sea and will run,
    And the stones in that tower are utterly
    Satisfied still with their weight.

And the minerals and creatures, so deeply in love with their lives
Their sin of accidie excludes all others,
Challenge the nervous students with a careless beauty,
    Setting a single error
    Against their countless faults.

O in these quadrangles where Wisdom honours herself
Does the original stone merely echo that praise
Shallowly, or utter a bland hymn of comfort,
    The founder's equivocal blessing
    On all who worship Success?

Promising to the sharp sword all the glittering prizes,
The cars, the hotels, the service, the boisterous bed,
Then power to silence outrage with a testament,
    The widow's tears forgotten,
    The fatherless unheard.

Whispering to chauffeurs and little girls, to tourists and dons,
That Knowledge is conceived in the hot womb of Violence
Who in a late hour of apprehension and exhaustion
    Strains to her weeping breast
    That blue-eyed darling head.

And is that child happy with his box of lucky books
And all the jokes of learning? Birds cannot grieve:
Wisdom is a beautiful bird; but to the wise
    Often, often is it denied
    To be beautiful or good.

Without are the shops, the works, the whole green county
Where a cigarette comforts the guilty and a kiss the weak;
There thousands fidget and poke and spend their money:
    Eros Paidagogos
    Weeps on his virginal bed.

Ah, if that thoughtless almost natural world
Would snatch his sorrow to her loving sensual heart!
But he is Eros and must hate what most he loves;
    And she is of Nature; Nature
    Can only love herself.

And over the talkative city like any other
Weep the non-attached angels. Here too the knowledge of death
Is a consuming love. And the natural heart refuses
    The low unflattering voice
    That rests not till it find a hearing.

Auden's poem is much better written than Johnson's. Instead of the stock epithets like *weather'd* cloister, *worn* court, *grey* city, *strong* towers, *clustering* spires, Auden provides the unexpected word – *agile* babies, *nervous* students, the *boisterous* bed, the *talkative* city. The range of the diction is also much wider. Johnson confines himself to the 'poetic diction' of the Decadent Romantics. Periphrases and elegant variations provide him with cushions against reality. (He has written sixty lines on Oxford without once introducing the words *undergraduate, student, don, fellow, university, college, quadrangle, hall* or *library*.) Auden, on the other hand, has no verbal inhibitions, and technical terms like *accidie* (Chaucerian English for *sloth*), *the original stone*, *Eros Paidagogos* (a 'joke of learning' on the analogy of Hermes Psychagogos) and *non-attached* jostle with the colloquialisms.

There is a similar inclusiveness in Auden's range of social reference. Instead of reducing Oxford to its architecture and the Illustrious Dead, as Johnson had done, Auden brings in the townspeople, the tourists and the employees of Morris Motors as well as the undergraduates, the dons and the founders of the colleges. Instead of Johnson's uncritical adulation of the University, Auden sees it as an anomalous, because uncoordinated, part of the modern world. The poem is the dramatization of a general problem, a particular application of E. M. Forster's golden rule 'Only connect'.

Where Johnson was personal (in 'Oxford' he is deliberately running away from his own private experiences at the University),[1] Auden generalizes. (Auden's poem is on the edge of being a miniature sociological treatise.) The difference is one that distinguishes the characteristically Romantic poem from the characteristically modern poem. For the Romantics the direction of interest is always away *from* the generalization *to* the personal statement. This is not to suggest that Romantic poetry is primarily autobiographical, in the ordinary sense of the word. Although there is much only slightly disguised autobiography in English Romantic poetry – in Shelley's *Epipsychidion*, for example – the personal element more generally finds its expression in the objective correlatives of wild nature and other related symbols. The towers and spires of Oxford were perhaps intended to have some such function in Johnson's poem. Auden's poem, on the other hand, is typical of the modern trend to poetic generalization. Not one detail in it leads back to Auden himself. It is significant that the Oxford college suggested by his opening lines is Magdalen, whereas Auden's own college was Christ Church. The image of the tower is an example of the conscious symbolism – made and not found – that seems to provide the basic poetic unit of the modern school. In contrast with Johnson, who tries to dissolve Oxford into 'a pure dream' and 'a Hesperian land', Auden insists on the solidity of his self-conscious tower:

> And the stones in that tower are utterly
> Satisfied still with their weight.

Until Hardy's and Hopkins's experiments this particular extension of the 'pathetic fallacy' was a device not often used by the English poets. Its characteristic flavour is a cool unpretentiousness. There is no suggestion here that the poet is tapping the deepest terrors and desires. All that he is doing is providing the reader with an analogy which will vivify and enlarge the stock response to the object of the comparison. 'Let's pretend', Auden is saying in effect in this passage, 'that Magdalen tower is a big fat man. It's not true, of course, but it will help you to appreciate the impression of complacent solidity that the tower leaves.' The device relieves the underlying symbolism – the tower is clearly a symbol of the University –

---

[1] Ezra Pound who edited Johnson's *Poetical Works* (1915), notes in the Preface the omnipresent 'fear of life, a fear that he was not afraid of, but which he openly acknowledged'.

of portentousness. The symbolism too, it is implied, is a conscious convention, a way of saying something that could not be said in any other way.

Whom was Auden writing for? Or, putting the point more generally, who is the ideal reader in the particular poet-reader relationship that constitutes modern poetry?

The attitudes that Auden has taken for granted in contemporary readers of his 'Oxford' can be divided into the political, the intellectual, and the emotional. Politically Auden assumes an anti-capitalist bias. Unless you can join him in detesting the kind of success that money brings – 'The cars, the hotels, the service, the boisterous bed' – you will not be able to make much of his poems. And this detestation of the rich and the powerful must be accompanied by the ability to identify oneself with the poor and the unsuccessful. You must be able to see the point of view at least of the thousands who 'fidget and poke'. Intellectually Auden assumes an interest in psycho-analysis, a religious scepticism, and a wide range of historical and literary information. ('Eros Paidagogos' would stump most readers.) There is no pretence that his poetry is easy, and he demands the complete intellectual co-operation of his reader. 'Oxford' must be read slowly, carefully and several times. It cannot be rushed. Emotionally the presuppositions are anti-sentimental. Auden's readers must be at once hard-boiled and emotionally adventurous.

If Auden is indeed an Assured Master of modern poetry, our Keats, our Pope or our Donne, there should be a close relationship between his ideal readers and the socially dominant class today. It should be possible indeed to identify the latter by reference to the former. A reading of him seems to me to confirm the tentative conclusion reached at the end of Part One that the socially dominant class in England today is that of the 'managers' or 'planners', i.e. the men and women, of varying social origins, who sit on commissions and committees, the compilers of reports, with their allies in Parliament and the Civil Service, local government and the trade unions. Auden's 'difficulty' and the undeniable obscurity of modern poetry generally are partly explicable in terms of this poet-reader relationship. A society run by a minority of 'managers' presupposes a majority who are 'managed', the non-ruling classes who are more planned against than planning. The success of such a system must depend on the extent to which the Managed are prepared to 'trust' the Managers. For the mass of the people to retain their confidence in the new *élite* they must look up to them as more intelligent and better informed than themselves. *Omne ignotum pro magnifico*, and the consciousness that the *élite* speak a different kind of English from theirs, more condensed, more allusive and with a much larger vocabulary, may act as a political reassurance. The danger, of course, is that the obscurity will come to acquire a value of its own. Some modern poetry, Dylan Thomas's, for example (a compound at times of genius and perversity), sometimes seems to be putting on an 'act' simply to impress the crowd. There is a parallel here, socially and poetically, with the Pindaric Odes of the eighteenth century.

But the Managerial Revolution which Auden is the prophet of goes deeper than that of James Burnham. Burnham's Managers qualified as the new ruling class by virtue of their *expertise*. But what the quality or combination of qualities was that was responsible for their managerial efficiency Burnham did not inquire. His social order is without any dominant incentive. Although he has a chapter on 'The Managerial Ideologies', he seems to regard such terms as 'the people', 'collectivism' and 'planning' as a psychological smokescreen behind which the new rulers are imposing themselves on the community. The motive force in his Managers is apparently just the love of power for its own sake. But this cynicism is an oversimplification of the human factors involved. People only become managers because they are good at managing other human beings, and the essential qualification for this is not a lust for power but an intense interest in human nature, an ability to see things through other people's eyes, and a power of convincing people of one's own personal disinterestedness. Auden calls it 'love'. The word has always been a favourite of his. The most brilliant of his specifically political poems, the Prologue to *Look, Stranger*, began,

> O love, the interest itself in thoughtless Heaven,

and the penultimate stanza of the profound 'September 1, 1939' (in *Another Time*) ended,

> We must love one another or die.

'Love', the supreme value for Auden, is social love, not sexual love. It is nearer to the 'friendship' of Pope than to the egocentric 'love' of the Renaissance poets or the Romantics.[1] To the extent that 'love' is at the creative centre of such measures of social reorganization as the Labour Party's nationalization programme, the Managerial Revolution receives Auden's qualified blessing. But 'All a poet can do to-day is warn', and,

[1] According to Josephine Miles (see p. 21 above), *love* is the major word that recurs most often in Shakespeare, Donne, Herrick, Collins, Coleridge and Tennyson. It comes second in order of frequency in Wyatt, Spenser, Wordsworth and Keats. The most frequently recurring word in Chaucer, Pope, Goldsmith and Cowper is *man*. These findings – which are limited to the poets for whom concordances exist – provide additional confirmation of the links between Chaucer and the Augustans, and the Renaissance and the Romantics. Pope uses *friend* more often than any of the poets examined by Miss Miles.

as one lays the poems down, it is the warnings against managerial indifference to or oversimplifying of the human elements that remain and reverberate in the memory. 'In the end, human integration and social integration are complementary processes.' That is perhaps Auden's final message to us. The parallel with Pope and Gray is interesting. Their warnings were against the 'pride' that was corrupting the English aristocracy of the eighteenth century. Their society, like ours, was basically egalitarian because it was built upon a co-operative rationalism. But by the time it received its classic expression in such a poem as *The Rape of the Lock*, a process of social stratification had set in. Instead of the entry into the ruling class being determined by exceptional 'common sense' it was more and more being determined solely by birth. As Auden has seen, this is our danger too. The qualities required in a Manager are, I suppose, a scientific outlook and 'love'. The exceptional man or woman who possesses both these qualities in an unusual degree may come of any class, and complete equality of opportunity must therefore be the condition of survival of a Managerial Society. But, commendable though the progress has been since the Victorian Age, there is still not as much social equality in England as in most countries today, and as the inevitable consequence too few of our Managers possess more than the rudiments of the scientific point of view or of a social conscience.

# CONCLUSION

# 14

# The Function of Criticism at the Present Time

I

THE title of this chapter repeats that of a well-known essay of Matthew Arnold's. At the end of the introduction to *The Sacred Wood* – an introduction largely devoted to placating the shade of Arnold by quotations from this very essay – Eliot originally printed an excerpt from Johnson's 'Life of Cowley', which he recommended as 'a model to critics who desire to correct some of the poetical vagaries of the present age'. But that was in 1920. In 1920 the right model for us may well have been Johnson's *Lives of the Poets*. Today we have, I think, exhausted the critical edification that is to be obtained by the study of Dr Johnson. The modern Johnsonian tends only too often to be that glossiest of the pseudo-critics – the Academic Playboy. And Johnson, after all, was a fairly representative product of the older Oxford, the 'home of lost causes, and forsaken beliefs, and unpopular names, and impossible loyalties', whose partial demise is attributable, as much as to anyone, to the influence of Arnold. If Oxford is to play a rôle in the second half of the twentieth century in any way comparable with that it performed in the second half of the nineteenth century, it seems rather that it will be by giving the harassed modern world an example of three virtues that are especially associated with Matthew Arnold's literary critcism – intellectual clarity, spiritual integrity, social conscience.

As the critical revolution of the 1920s and the 1930s recedes into the perspective of history, it is becoming possible to count up the gains and the losses. In general, of course, it was a glorious victory. In the long run there can be little doubt, I imagine, that the losses, such as they were, have been out-weighed many times over by the gains. Between the death of Arnold and the emergence of Eliot literary criticism in England and America had reached almost its lowest ebb. A short reign of terror was needed to discredit once and for all the Watts-Duntons and the Stopford Brookes, the Gosses and the Clutton-Brocks, the Herbert Warrens and the Sidney Lees, *et hoc genus omne*. Unfortunately those eminent bores and charlatans were not the only casualties. As is usual in revolutions, some of the innocent and inoffensive perished with the guilty, and the critical losses included here and there such solid literary virtues as factual accuracy, awareness of the historical background, linguistic *expertise*, and even sometimes the ability to write lucid English. It is no longer desirable, or indeed possible, to continue to turn a blind eye to certain deficiencies that characterize, in greater or less degree, the critical writings of such men as T. S. Eliot, J. Middleton Murry, I. A. Richards, John Crowe Ransom, Kenneth Burke, F. R. Leavis, C. S. Lewis, G. Wilson Knight, William Empson and Yvor Winters. And these are probably the best of the older contemporary critics (with the exception of Empson they were all born in the nineteenth century). With their lesser coadjutors and the *epigoni* the wildness and the woolliness have sometimes attained painful, almost spectacular proportions.

A measure of eventual disillusionment was, I suppose, always inevitable. As we have gradually got used to the splendid qualities of the new critical movement, the defects of its qualities have naturally acquired a greater prominence. They do not, in my opinion, seriously affect the ultimate value of what has already been written. Probably no other period in the whole of history of literary criticism could show ten names comparable with those of the English and American critics whom I have just cited. But the question does arise of the respective influence that these qualities and these defects are exercising on the younger writers. It was not a good thing for a critic to be born under the shadow of Coleridge or Sainte-Beuve, or of Matthew Arnold either for that matter. The possibility must at least be faced that Mr Eliot – who is certainly a critical personality of similar stature – may be unconsciously exerting an equally restricting, or even corrupting, influence on the criticism of the younger generation today. And what may be true of Mr Eliot may also be true of Dr Leavis and Mr Empson and their opposite numbers in the United States.

The critical defects that I have in mind can be summed up in the one word *irresponsibility*.[1] The irresponsibility is, of course, the complement of the originality of this criticism. But it is that precisely which makes it dangerous – *corruptio optimi pessima*. At the risk of being thought presumptuous it seems important, as a first step in this Conclusion, to show how reckless and insidious the irresponsibility often is. I shall confine myself to some representative pronouncements by four of our best living critics on some familiar English poems. My specimens have been carefully selected and are, I believe, typical of the kind of amiable nonsense into which even the ablest and the best-informed of modern critics is at any

---

[1] The word is used by R. S. Crane in his remarkable 'Introduction' to *Critics and Criticism* (Chicago, 1952), a collection of critical and literary-historical essays by seven American 'Aristotelians'. According to Mr Crane modern criticism suffers from (i) a proliferation of theories 'developed only slightly beyond the simple distinctions on which they are based', (ii) 'an alarming kind of *irresponsibility* in the interpretation of individual works' (my italics).

time liable to fall. The more theoretical irresponsibilities receive some treatment in later sections of this chapter. I am not proposing to include among these initial *corpora vilia* passages from Eliot's criticism. Many years ago I submitted two characteristic sentences from 'Some Notes on the Blank Verse of Christopher Marlowe' to an unkind and perhaps rather pedantic analysis.[1]

Since examples were provided on that occasion and the list can easily be extended, I shall start instead with I. A. Richards, who was Eliot's principal academic ally in the 1920s and must also be regarded, I suppose, as the founder of the Cambridge school of criticism now popularly identified with Leavis.

Richards has always been more interested in critical theory than in criticism proper, and it is surprisingly difficult to find an extended comment in his writings on a particular literary work or author. But where one does find such a passage the irresponsibility is sometimes positively breathtaking. A notorious early example is the characterization of *The Waste Land* as a poem 'effecting a complete severance between his [Eliot's] poetry and *all* beliefs'.[2] An even odder case, however, is the Richards discovery that Pipit in Eliot's 'A Cooking Egg' was the latter's old nurse.[3] It will be remembered that there is an epigraph to the poem of two lines from Villon:

> En l'an trentiesme de mon aage
> Que toutes mes hontes j'ay beues . . .

Richards deduces from this that the 'I' of the poem is about thirty years old. The deduction, a not unreasonable one, produces the most surprising consequences. 'To whom', Richards demands, 'does one send "Views of the Oxford Colleges" during one's first term up? And who alone would keep the volume on the table after twelve years?' The only possible answer apparently is one's nurse! The alternative that Pipit might have bought the book herself does not occur to him, though the rest of the poem makes it pretty clear that Pipit is a sort of Bloomsbury *demi-vierge*, dull but decidedly upper-middle-class. She had presumably acquired the 'Views' on a recent cultural pilgrimage to Oxford. What is so staggering about the Richards interpretation is the complete inability it betrays to read the poem in a straightforward way. I need only quote one verse:

---

[1] The comments on 'Some Notes on the Blank Verse of Christopher Marlowe' will be found at the end of a letter in *Scrutiny*, March 1935. The letter, with the review by Dr Leavis that provoked it and his reply, are reprinted in *The Importance of Scrutiny*, ed. Eric Bentley (New York, 1948), pp. 16-20.   [2] *Science and Poetry* (1926), pp. 64-5.
[3] *Principles of Literary Criticism*, 2nd ed. (1926), Appendix B.

> I shall not want Society in Heaven,
>     Lucretia Borgia shall be my Bride;
> Her anecdotes will be more amusing
>     Than Pipit's experience could provide.

If the poem is not to be spoilt Pipit *must* have some bathetic relationship to 'Society' and to marriage. One imagines she had attempted to diversify their tepid flirtation, so different from the advances of a Borgia, with a little second-hand gossip about Mayfair. And in that case she cannot possibily have been the narrator's nurse. Every verse of the poem, except the first, immediately refutes the fantastic suggestion. Mr Richards is obviously wrong. And if one asks how so intelligent a man can have made so silly a mistake, the answer, I suppose, must be that he has allowed his ingenuity to get the better of his common sense.

C. S. Lewis's besetting sin was not over-ingenuity so much as perversity. He cannot resist shocking us and surprising us. The jokes and the para-doxes are so good and play so important a part in his critical mission of bringing everyday reality into our appraisals of the literary classics that it must seem churlish to protest against them. But a joke should not only be funny, it should also be relevant. I am afraid that a lot of Lewis's jokes are irrelevant to the point of being seriously misleading. Consider, for example, his comment on the two naked damsels whom Spenser's Sir Guyon found bathing in the garden of the Bower of Bliss. The damsels' names – they are anonymous in *The Faerie Queene* – were, Lewis tells us, 'obviously Cissie and Flossie'.[1] The laugh is obtained all right. The outrageous suggestion *is* funny. But it is an outrageous suggestion all the same, because it imports an irrelevant class concept into Spenser's allegory. The one thing that is certain about girls who are called Cissie and Flossie is that they are vulgarians. And the one thing that is certain about nudity in Spenser is that it is classless. As a matter of historical fact the two damsels come straight out of the garden of Armida in Tasso's *Gerusalemme Liberata*, and to suggest a parallel between two Cockney trollops and these sisters of Circe and the Sirens is to misread Spenser as grossly as Mr Richards misread Eliot.

I may seem in this case to be making a mountain out of a critical mole-hill. My excuse for taking Cissie and Flossie so solemnly is that they are symptomatic of a certain central irresponsibility in *The Allegory of Love*. Lewis can never resist saying a good deal more than he really means. Let me give another example from his discussion of Spenser. The chapter

---

[1] 'Acrasia's two young women (their names are obviously Cissie and Flossie) are ducking and giggling in a bathing-pool for the benefit of a passer-by; a man does not need to go to fairie land to meet them' (*The Allegory of Love*, Oxford, 1936, rev. 1938, p. 331).

ends, it will be remembered, in a sort of deification of Spenser. The history of Spenser-criticism has been 'a history of gross underestimation'. Homer, Milton, Dante and Shakespeare 'indicate the level on which Spenser stands, the poets with whom he is to be compared'. And so on. The view is, I suppose, a tenable one, though I cannot say I share it. What disturbs me, however, is not the implausibility of the contention *per se*, but the incompatibility of Lewis's conclusions with the absolutely devastating criticisms of Spenser's style and subject-matter that precede them. In one passage we had been told, in effect, that if poetry consists of the best words in the best order Spenser was not much of a poet:

So far from being a poet whose excellent and sustained mastery of language is his only merit, he is a poet whose chief fault is the uncertainty of his style. He can be as prosaic as Wordsworth: he can be clumsy, unmusical and flat. On this side, and on this side only, his work requires historical extenuation (p. 318).

A few pages later the whole of the political allegory, which accounts in one form or another for about half the structural and narrative elements in *The Faerie Queene*, is thrown overboard without the blinking of an eye:

By his political allegory Spenser doubtless intended to give his poem a certain topical attraction. Time never forgives such concessions to 'the glistering of this present', and what acted as a bait to unpoetic readers for some decades has become a stumbling-block to poetic readers ever since (p. 321).

Again, in isolation and considered simply on their own merits, the views are no doubt tenable, though I should describe both judgments as over-statements. But to proceed, as Lewis does, from these concessions to hostile criticism, which give away far more than the most virulent denigrator of Spenser has ever demanded, to the final implication that Spenser is one of the five great poets of the world simply does not make sense. If Spenser really wrote as badly as all that, and if he was so incompetent an allegorist that the reader has to skip one half of his dark conceits, the level on which he stands is not that of Homer, Dante, Milton and Shakespeare, but at the very best of people like Empedocles and Langland, or the Blake of the Prophetic Books.

William Empson's critical technique is very different from Lewis's, but they share some of the same fundamental virtues and defects. *Seven Types of Ambiguity* is like *The Allegory of Love* in that they are both books that, when read at the right age, can completely transform one's way of looking at poetry. I owe so much to Empson's book personally that I am perhaps being a little ungrateful in emphasizing its deficiences.

A characteristic specimen of Empsonian irresponsibility is to be found

on the second page of *Seven Types*. It is the by now almost notorious list
of reasons, ten in all, why 'the comparison holds' in

> Bare ruined choirs, where late the sweet birds sang.

Perhaps because of its early occurrence in the book no specific comment of
Empson's has been more often dismissed as over-ingenious. But I am not
sure that the real point has not been missed. The grosser irresponsibility
does not lie in thinking the choirs must have been monastery choirs
(though the reference is more likely to be to the parish churches of the
deserted villages of the period), or that the choirs were made of wood
(choirs are not choir-stalls, and in any case the latter would be the first
thing to disappear from an abandoned church), or that 'the cold and
Narcissistic charm suggested by choir-boys suits well with Shakespeare's
feeling for the object of the Sonnets' (but the ultimate object of the
comparison is not Mr W. H., but the rapidly ageing poet, and anyhow
there were no choirboys in most Tudor churches). These are details that
could be corrected without Empson's essential point about ambiguity
being affected, though it may be significant in a general way that he has
not in fact made any of these corrections in the revised edition of *Seven
Types*. The real critical error is more fundamental. It is simply that the
line on which Empson expatiates is not a separate sentence or even a
separate subordinate clause. It is a verbal fragment that is, strictly speaking,
*unintelligible* when lifted like this out of its syntactic context. And, as it
happens, when the line is restored to its context the choirs assume a new
significance, which is different from any of the paraphrases provided by
Empson. I had better quote the whole of Shakespeare's original sentence:

> That time of year thou may'st in me behold
> When yellow leaves, or none, or few, do hang
> Upon those boughs which shake against the cold,
> Bare ruin'd choirs, where late the sweet birds sang.

It will be seen that the choirs provide a comparison within a comparison.
In the outer comparison the poet, feeling himself so much older than his
friend, compares himself to those days at the end of autumn when the last
leaves are falling from the trees. In the inner comparison, on the other
hand, the trees of the outer comparison are compared to church choirs that
have been abandoned and are now falling into ruin. Syntactically, therefore
the function of the inner comparison is to *qualify* the outer comparison.
Instead of adding an ambiguity, as Empson would have us believe, it
actually protects us against a possible misunderstanding. The reader, who
might be tempted to doubt the finality of a decay merely associated with
boughs in winter (which, after all, are not dead but only leafless), is

reassured. For the purpose of this sonnet, he realizes, the boughs are to be taken at their face value. These boughs are *virtually* dead, like the abandoned church which has already lost its *raison d'être* and will soon disintegrate physically. This, or something not very different from this, is the immediate context in which the possible interpretations of the fourth line must be considered. And within the line the important ambiguity will now be seen to hinge on the word 'where'. The logic of the passage demands an equation of 'where' with the boughs, whereas the word order makes it impossible not to connect the place where the birds sang with the choirs. The total effect, as one reads, is of birds *in* the ruined church as well as *on* leaf-covered trees round about it – and, as a result, the image becomes a symbol not so much of the ageing poet as of a universal process of mutability.

I shall conclude this critical *sottisier* with an American example. John Crowe Ransom's 'A Poem Nearly Anonymous' is one of the best-known exhibits of the so-called New Criticism, but though it has some excellent things to say about poetry *en passant* the treatment of its nominal subject is at least as irresponsible as anything achieved on this side of the Atlantic.[1] The poem in question is 'Lycidas', its near-anonymity (it appeared with Milton's initials only in the memorial volume to Edward King) symbolizing for Ransom a falling-short on Milton's part of the complete depersonalization of the greatest poetry. Nearly half the essay is devoted to the poem's metrical irregularities – the varying number of lines in the stanzas and the irregular incidence of the ten unrhymed lines – in which Ransom finds something peculiarly sinister. Milton had set out to write an English equivalent of the canzone, but instead of sticking to a more or less regular metrical formula (as Spenser had done in 'Epithalamion') he insists, according to Ransom, on being 'different':

In the irregular stanzas and the rhymeless lines is registered the ravage of his modernity; it has bit into him as it never did into Spenser. And we imagine him thinking to himself, precisely like some modern poets we know, that he could no longer endure the look of perfect regimentation which sat upon the poor ideas objectified before him upon the page of poetry, as if that carried with it a reflection upon their sincerity. I will go further. It is not merely easy for a technician to write in smooth metres; it is perhaps easier than to write in rough ones, after he has once started; but when he has written smoothly, and contemplates his work, he is capable actually, if he is a modern poet, of going over it laboriously and roughening it. I venture to think that just such a practice, speaking very broadly, obtained in the

---

[1] *The World's Body* (New York, 1938), pp. 1–28. It is the only essay by Mr Ransom reprinted in *Criticism*, the excellent omnibus anthology of modern criticism edited by Mark Spencer, Josephine Miles and Gordon McKenzie (New York, 1948).

composition of *Lycidas;* that it was written smooth and rewritten rough; which was treason (p. 12).

It is all most ingenious. And it is true that as compared with the approximate regularity of Spenser's 'Epithalamion' Milton's poem *is* metrically irregular. As compared with Dante or Petrarch it is irregular to the point of licentiousness. The metrical innovations, however, are not an overflow of Miltonic egotism, as Ransom argues, but a faithful imitation of Tasso and his successors.[1] It was Tasso, not Milton, who monkeyed with the canzone, making the stanzas of different lengths and working in unrhymed lines almost anywhere. All that Milton did in 'Lycidas' was to anglicize Tasso's metrical innovations in much the same way that he had anglicized della Casa's abrogation of the Petrarcan pause between a sonnet's octave and sestet. The only critical signficance the metrics of 'Lycidas' possess is the evidence they provide of the young Milton's awareness of technical developments on the Continent. It might be possible to argue that this 'uncouth Swain', this poetic apprentice in the pastoral tradition, was devoting rather too much 'eager thought' to 'warbling his *Dorick* lay'. There is a preoccupation with the latest technical gadgets from Italy that suggests a certain lack of poetic proportion. But this is not the point that Ransom was trying to establish. A fair criticism of his point, as of so many of Empson's, would be that it only retains its validity so long as the larger poetic context is excluded. It may be called Desert Island criticism. If Ransom had evolved his theory alone in the Pacific, with nothing to refer to except a copy of *The Oxford Book of English Verse*, he would deserve our heartiest congratulations. A minute poring over the text and a comparison of 'Lycidas' with the other poems in the *Oxford Book*, including 'Epithalamion', might justifiably lead to some such conclusion as his. In the Pacific one might even concede that Ransom was *right* (just as Ptolemy was right until Copernicus came along), but to reach such a conclusion in the United States, a land flowing with libraries and works of reference, can only be described as critical innocence bordering on deliberate nescience. No modern critic, even if he is as acute as Ransom – and at his quasi-metaphysical best Ransom can be very good indeed – has the right, surely, to be as ignorant as all that.

[1] The metrics of 'Lycidas', essentially an English Virgilian pastoral elegy, derive from Renaissance attempts to domesticate the eclogue in Italy. The choruses in Tasso's *Aminta* and Guarini's *Il Pastor Fido*, a loose form of the canzone, were the point of departure. Their success led Tasso and later Marino to use irregular stanzas and occasional unrhymed lines in detached inscriptions, idylls and ecologues, though the basic pattern in these experiments remained the canzone. See F. T. Prince, 'Lycidas and the Tradition of the Italian Eclogue', *English Miscellany*, ed. M. Praz, II (Rome, 1951). I am grateful to Professor Prince for advice on this point.

## II

So far the object of this chapter has been to build up a *prima facie* case for the contention that modern criticism, brilliant and indispensable though its achievements have been, is continuously liable to lapse into irresponsibility. The next stage must be to attempt a definition of irressponsibility.

The word's underlying implication, it is to be noted, is of the evasion of a social duty. The literary critic, in virtue of his profession, *ought* to be responsible. As the accredited reporter on the contemporary literary scene he is under an unspoken obligation not to mislead his readers. And this is not just a matter of eschewing literary mendacity – the deliberate falsification of evidence, the knowing promulgation of an unjust verdict. There is also, and more usually, the critic who is unintentionally misleading, whose factual errors are excused as slips of the pen, who is one-sided because of pardonable excesses of enthusiasm, whose accounts are incomplete because of unsuspected ignorances. This is the Irresponsible Critic. In so far as Richards, Lewis, Empson and Ransom are chargeable with irresponsibility, it follows that they are, as professing critics, implicitly abusing their social function. Their neighbours have come to them asking for bread and they have fobbed them off with stones. For the ultimate *raison d'être* of criticism within a modern mass society – it is significant that small communities seem to manage without literary critics – is to be demonstrably *right* (accurate, just, helpful, relevant, comprehensive).

The failure of critical responsibility takes different forms at different times. To Arnold, confronted with the sentimentalities of Ruskin and the oddities of Francis Newman (and their extra-literary equivalents), the principal dangers seemed to be 'fancifulness', 'arbitrariness' and 'eccentricity'. The words and their synonyms recur again and again in Arnold's earlier critical essays, and the kind of irresponsibility that they represent undoubtedly explains the familiar initial injunction in 'The Function of Criticism at the Present Time'. Seeing the object as in itself it really is was a plea for objectivity amid the subjectivism of Victorian criticism. Arnold's emphasis on 'knowledge' – which Eliot has vulgarized as the 'sense of fact' in *his* essay on 'The Function of Criticism' (which was clearly intended as a corrective to Arnold's[1]) – was directed against the Victorians'

---

[1] Eliot's essay (*Selected Essays*, 1932, pp. 23-34) reduces criticism to fact-finding; 'any book, any essay, any note in *Notes and Queries*, which produces a fact even of the lowest order about a work of art is a better piece of work than nine-tenths of the most pretentious critical journalism, in journals or in books' (p. 33). Opposed to 'fact', e.g. 'Shakespeare's laundry bills', is 'opinion or fancy', which apparently invariably corrupts taste, even when provided by Goethe or Coleridge (ibid.). Arnold's 'knowledge', on the other hand, was always directed towards the creation of 'currents of ideas'.

habit of looking exclusively into their hearts when they wrote. Emotional subjectivism is not, however, a defect from which modern criticism conspicuously suffers. The irresponsibilities are intellectual now rather than emotional. If the literary response is sometimes perverse or absurd, it is not often because it has been distorted by an uprush of irrelevant feelings, but because the particular literary work under discussion has been misunderstood. The nature of this modern incomprehension is the problem to which this chapter may perhaps be considered a prolegomenon. Briefly, the clue proposed here is that modern criticism has lost the sense of literary context. No doubt the actual words on the page are read as closely as ever before, but all that lies behind the words and the word order – the forces, conventions and precedents that have made and modified them – is too often taken for granted.

That the concept of literary context is in special need of reaffirmation today will have been evident from the critical specimens castigated in the first section of this chapter. Richards's indifference to the context of what he was discussing apparently prevented him from even reading, except perhaps in the most cursory way, the whole of Eliot's poem. What he has done has been to apply a critical microscope to the epigraph and the first verse of 'A Cooking Egg', as though they were a self-contained poem, while excluding the remaining seven verses, and even the poem's title, from any consideration whatever.[1] A similar objection on a smaller scale, that of the sentence, applies to most of Empson's interpretations of 'Bare ruin'd choirs'. The ingenuity is merely perverse, because phrases like verses cannot be detached in this way from their verbal context. Ransom's error was the failure to realize that Milton's metrics are part of the European literary tradition, whereas the context within which he discusses them is purely English (Spenser's development of the canzone). The omission of Tasso and his successors from the relevant 'current of ideas' may not have been deliberate, a matter of critical conviction, but it has resulted in a view of 'Lycidas' at least as wrong-headed as Richards's and Empson's verbal atomizations. C. S. Lewis's errors, though not quite in the same category, could also be described as contextual. Thus his concessions to the anti-Spenserians, while acceptable enough in their own context, do not seem to make sense in the larger context of his general critical argument.

A literary context must be distinguished, of course, from a literary background. The latter is best limited, I think, to the constituents of a

[1] The second verse completely disposes of Richards's hypothesis. The daguerreotypes and silhouettes establish Pipit's gentility, and the dance invitation shows that she is still relatively young.

literary work before and after their momentary synthesis in it. An author's biography, the social history of his age, an account of earlier treatments of his subject-matter – these are all background topics and have only, on this basis, a limited critical relevance. Context, however, is the framework of reference within which the work achieves meaning. To read a poem and ignore its context is, in fact, to misread it. A similar ignorance of its background may make a poem a little more difficult to understand but can do no positive harm. Background, in short, is extrinsic, context is intrinsic.

The implications and ramifications of context can be best demonstrated by a concrete example. A good one can be found on page 74 of *Revaluation*, where Leavis has printed side by side four lines by Marvell (from 'A Dialogue between the Soul and Body'):

> A Soul hung up, as 'twere, in Chains
> Of Nerves, and Arteries, and Veins.
> Tortur'd, besides each other part,
> In a vain Head, and double Heart.

and four lines by Pope (*Dunciad* iv, 501-4):

> First slave to Words, then vassal to a Name,
> Then dupe to Party; child and man the same;
> Bounded by Nature, narrow'd still by Art,
> A trifling head, and a contracted heart.

Leavis's point is the 'affinities' between the two passages. It is part of his case that Pope's 'wit' represents a continuation of the Metaphysical tradition. Whatever the merits of the general thesis, it receives no support from these lines, since the 'affinities' only exist within a verbal context of meaning. The verbal similarity between the last line of each passage is, of course, striking and obvious. But Leavis makes the collocation in order to establish a resemblance between Marvell's and Pope's poetic styles, and once the matter is raised to a stylistic context the 'affinities' disappear. In terms of literary tradition the meanings of 'head' and 'heart' are demonstrably quite different in the two passages. In Marvell's lines the vivid images of the first couplet almost compel the reader to visualize the torture-chambers of the 'vain Head, and double Heart'. It is the kind of allegory that was popularized in the early seventeenth century by the Emblem Books, in which a more or less conventional concept is dressed up in some striking new clothes, the new clothes being the real *raison d'être*. In Pope's last line, however, the abstract or quasi-abstract words which lead up to it make it almost impossible to *see* either the 'trifling head' or the 'contracted heart'. Obviously Pope's 'head' and 'heart' belong to the same order of reality as his 'Nature' and 'Art'. They are simply items in his psychological terminology, one the antithetical opposite of the other, and their modern equivalents would, I suppose, be the intellect and the emotions. Nothing could be further removed than these grey abstractions from Marvell's picture-language.

So far the analysis of the two passages has been verbal and stylistic. The apparent verbal identity is, as I have shown, contradicted by the very different figures of speech and stylistic conventions employed by the two poets. In Marvell's lines the image has run away with the antithesis (it doesn't really matter whether the torture chamber is in the head or the heart or some other part of the body), whereas in Pope's lines the concept has almost killed the imagery, the progress being towards a mathematical purity with the sensuous elements segregated into a separate compartment of their own. And there is a still further contradiction. The most interesting feature in the lines is that the Metaphysical style in which he was writing has *forced* Marvell to say what he cannot have wanted to say. And Pope's Augustan style has forced his hand in the same way.

Marvell's poem is a thoroughly serious affair, but the vividness of the imagery has resulted in a blurring of the argument by making it impossible for the reader not to equate – or, indeed, in terms of the poetic impact, *subordinate* – the immoral head and heart with such relatively innocent and secondary members as the nerves, arteries and veins. So gross a breach of the poem's logic cannot possibly have been intended by Marvell. The passage from the *Dunciad* raises a similar problem. How is it Pope, a master of language if ever there was one, has used his concrete terms with so little precision? In these lines 'slave', 'vassal' and 'dupe' are virtually interchangeable. And so are 'Bounded', 'narrow'd' and 'contracted'. These tautologies can't have been *meant* by Pope.

To understand what lies behind these contradictions between what Marvell and Pope would like to have written and what they actually wrote it is necessary to invoke a wider context – that of the 'climate of opinion', or the thought patterns current in their time. There is an obvious connection between Marvell's metaphors and the analogical thinking of the Tudor and Stuart divines. (Hooker, for example, uses the regularity of the motions of the heavenly bodies as an argument for imposing ecclesiastical law upon the Puritans.) And the abstract character of Pope's diction can be related without difficulty to the philosophies of Hobbes, Locke, Berkeley and Hume. But this intellectual context, important though it certainly is for understanding Marvell and Pope, does not seem to provide the ultimate framework of reference within which their poems need to be read. Behind the intellectual context lies a complex of religious, political and economic factors that can be called the social context. As this level of meaning seems to be the final context of which the critical reader of literature must retain an awareness, it will be worth while trying to summarize, however baldly, the social contexts implicit in these two passages.

Marvell's 'A Dialogue between the Soul and Body' seems to have been written in the late 1640s, when he was still a Royalist, if a Puritan Royalist. The language and ideas used in the poem were the expression of a way of life shared by most cultivated Englishmen who had grown up in the half-century preceding the Civil War. The basis of that way of life was a confidence in physical appearances, which were held to be symbolic or anagrammatic of the ultimate realities. With the partial discrediting of medieval hierarchies and values in the transition to a money economy, physical appearances had come to assume a new importance in the sixteenth century. (The wealth that now conferred status, instead of birth or office, was invisible and could only be inferred, therefore, from a 'brave' appearance.)[1] It is perhaps significant that this was the period when portrait painting established itself in England. In Court circles, in particular, where the *jus et norma loquendi* determined the English literary language, a man tended to be assessed by his looks, manners, clothes, jewels and physical accomplishments (dancing, jousting, duelling, etc.). On the highest levels the competition for the Prince's favour was largely a matter of banquets, pageants and masques, and the degree of a favourite's success was measured by the number and magnificence of his retainers and 'clients'. This world of appearances came to a disastrous end, of course, in the 1640s, and a certain *grotesquerie*, bordering at times on farce, in Marvell's 'Dialogue' can be taken as a half-realization that his medium was on its last legs and could no longer be taken with complete seriousness.

Pope's language, style and mode of thought, on the other hand, are those of a governing class that had learnt the lesson of the Civil War. The conscious reconstruction of almost every aspect of English upper-class life that began in the 1650s – and in which Marvell incidentally took part, though at the cost of writing no more poetry – was directed by 'common sense', i.e. the rational faculty which enables all human beings to communicate on matters of common interest. And 'common sense' inevitably left its rationalist imprint on the language and the literary tradition from which Pope's poetry was created. It is true that by his infusion of the Picturesque (the object of most of his thefts from the Metaphysical poets)

[1] The history of the word *brave*, in the sense of 'well-dressed' or 'admirable' provides linguistic evidence of the duration of this dominance of physical appearances. According to the *O.E.D.* it was first used in this sense in 1568 and it had already become archaic in the eighteenth century.

Pope was able to mitigate to some extent the abstractness of his medium. But by his time the pressure towards social conformity that followed the Restoration had noticeably relaxed. A new upper middle class was in process of formation that was serving as a sort of cushion between the Tory and Whig extremists, and it is in Pope's position as an intermediary between this class and the aristocracy that his personal significance lies.

What general conclusions can be drawn from this analysis of the two passages quoted by Leavis? A point that is worth stressing is the *order* in which the contextual checks operated. Although I cannot hope to demonstrate it here, the four stages in the widening context of meaning can be shown to reappear in every critical reading of a work of literature. The first or verbal stage is the plane of dictionary meanings. The reader at this stage is simply translating the black marks on the page into their mental equivalents. As most words have more than one meaning, the process of translation is necessarily tentative, although some of the individual words' possible meanings will, of course, be immediately excluded by considerations of word-order or grammar. A more drastic weeding out of ambiguities occurs at the second or literary stage, at which the surviving meanings acquire an extra dimension, as it were, as they dovetail into a familiar tradition or genre. At this stage the words begin to come to life and the reader finds himself responding to what is, in spite of the aesthetic distance imposed by the literary conventions, a recognizably human situation. The process continues and develops as the context of meaning widens into the third or intellectual and the fourth or social stages. As a result of the series of limitations imposed upon word meanings and word associations at the various contextual levels, a final meaning begins to emerge. It can be called the correct meaning, the object as in itself it really is, since it is the product of progressive corrections at each stage of the contextual series. And, as the work assumes its original historical setting, the human experience embodied in it begins to be realized and re-enacted by the reader.

The reader who achieves this degree of self-absorption can be called the responsible reader. It is to be noted that the culminating desideratum, the final criterion of correctness, is the awareness of the appropriate social context. By another route we have reached the same terminus – the ultimately social content of critical responsibility.

The discipline of contextual reading, as defined and illustrated in the preceding paragraphs, should result in the reconstruction of a human situation that is demonstrably implicit in the particular literary work under discussion. Within the limits of human fallibility the interpretation will be *right*. But the process provides no guarantee, of course, that the reader's response to the essential drama, however correctly that is reconstructed, will be equally correct. The assumption is that literary critics are not cranks, neurotics or immoralists, though in everyday actuality they often are. In other words, the question of values must not be excluded. In a sense the assertion of value judgments *is* the function of criticism. *Judex damnatur si nocens absolvitur.* But the reservation must be immediately made that the judgment is not separable in criticism – as distinct from ethics and aesthetics —from the particular structure of meanings that is being judged. A poem, for example, is not good or bad in itself but only in terms of the contexts in which it originated. For us to be able to use it, to live ourselves into it, the essential requirement is simply an understanding of those original contexts, and especially the original social context. A social order, as such, is necessarily the affirmation of certain values. In the social context, therefore, the values implied in the poem become explicit, and its relative goodness or badness declares itself. Because of its final dependence on the setting of the poem within its social context the mere process of responsible reading *includes* the necessary value judgments. There is a remarkable passage towards the end of 'The Function of Criticism at the Present Time' in which Arnold makes what is essentially the same point. I quote it because it has not, I think, received the attention it deserves. It runs as follows:

Again, judging is often spoken of as the critic's one business ; and so in some sense it is; but the judgment which almost insensibly forms itself in a fair and clear mind, along with fresh knowledge, is the valuable one; and thus knowledge, and ever fresh knowledge, must be the critic's great concern for himself; and it is by communicating fresh knowledge, and letting his own judgment pass along with it, – but insensibly, and in the second place not the first, as a sort of companion and clue, not as an abstract lawgiver, – that he will generally do most good to his readers. Sometimes, no doubt, for the sake of establishing an author's place in literature, and his relation to a central standard . . . , criticism may have to deal with a subject-matter so familiar that fresh knowledge is out of the question, and then it must be all judgment; an enunciation and detailed application of principles. Here the great safeguard is never to let oneself become abstract, always to retain an intimate and lively consciousness of the truth of what one is saying, and, the moment this fails us, to be sure that something is wrong. Still, under all circumstances, this mere judgment and application of principles is, in itself, not the most satisfactory work to the critic; like mathematics, it is tautological and cannot well give us, like fresh learning, the sense of creative activity.[1]

[1] A somewhat similar position has recently been maintained by Harry Levin (*Perspectives of Criticism*, Cambridge, Mass., 1950, p. xi); 'It may well be that critical discussion has placed too much stress upon evaluation and not enough upon the more objective function of analysis . . . It is salutary to remember that the Greek root for "criticize" meant "to cut, to distinguish" before it meant "to judge".'

III

A usual objection to the sort of position taken up in this essay is that it reduces literature to 'cultural anthropology'. All this emphasis on the social and historical factors makes it almost impossible, it is alleged, to read the poem – the argument is usually conducted in terms of poetry – *as a poem*. We are then invited to consider the awful example of Chaucerian scholarship, or the perhaps even more deplorable case of Greek and Latin literature, and to shudder at the contrast between the intensive study of their verbal meanings and the almost total neglect, except at a Told-to-the-Children level, of any other meanings. As one who has done his time on the treadmill of the classics as well as of *Chaucer-Probleme* I can testify to the general validity of such complaints. But the answer is a simple one: *abusus non tollit usum*. The tediousness of much pure scholar-ship is no excuse for doing without scholarship altogether. The fact must always be faced that critical reading is not *easy*. Its supreme value as mental discipline is that its rewards are strictly proportionate to its difficulties. The more closely you read a work of literature – the more, that is, you learn to respond correctly at all the levels of context – the more you will profit by it. But 'profit' is an inadequate word to describe the contribution to the community – with the status such a contribution inevitably confers – that the trained reader brings to a muddled mass society. If it is true that a work of literature cannot be properly understood or appreciated except in terms of the social context in which it originated, the skilled reader of literature will tend, by the nature of his skill, to understand and appreciate contemporary social processes better than his neighbours. It is important, I think, to emphasize the *utile* as well as the *dulce* of criticism. If we regard literature as life frozen into immobility at its points of highest consciousness and integration, Arnold's prophecy in 'The Study of Poetry' that 'most of what now passes with us for religion and philosophy will be replaced by poetry' will not seem quite as absurd as is sometimes suggested.[1] The values of the modern world seem to the layman to be

---

[1] Eliot's comment is notorious (*The Use of Poetry and the Use of Criticism*, 1933, p. 113); 'nothing in this world or the next is a substitute for anything else: and if you find that you must do without something, such as religious faith or philosophic belief, then you must just do without it'. Arnold's retort would no doubt have been that he was summarizing a historic process. It is a historic fact that for draft purposes the horse has replaced the ox, and the internal combustion engine is now replacing the horse. Similarly, as the anthropomorphic elements have become discredited, the polytheistic religions have been replaced by increasingly abstract forms or monotheism. What is carried over from the earlier phases tends to survive as symbol or ritual. The process can hardly be denied. To say that we must just do without oxen and polytheism seems to beg Arnold's question.

embodied in literature to a far greater degree than they are in modern religion or philosophy. It is even possible – the suggestion is not inherently absurd – that the true contemporary *clericus* is precisely the critical reader.

'But if we conceive thus highly of the destinies of poetry' – the words are again Arnold's; they follow closely upon his prediction of the replacement of religion and philosophy – the exclusion of historical and social factors by some modern critics begins to assume a more sinister aspect. Perhaps without realizing the implications of their critical philosophies, these critics are in fact inviting us to neglect a large part of the human relevance of literature. Their irresponsibility seems to be in process of betraying them into an isolation from the real world that looks very like the Ivory Tower of *l'art pour l'art*.

Let me be specific. Cleanth Brooks is an American critic whom we all like and respect. The practice of 'explication' – which has recently been defined as 'the examination of a work of literature for a knowledge of each part, for the relation of these parts to each other, and for their relation to the whole'[1] – is now a standard pedagogic discipline in America owing very largely to his precepts and examples. A *chef d'œuvre* both of Brooks and of explication is *The Well Wrought Urn* (1947). It has already been referred to more than once in these pages. Although this is in many ways an excellent book, the critical moral that it seems to point is, as far as I can see, sheer escapism. The phrase 'cultural anthropology' that I quoted at the beginning of this section comes in Brooks's preface, and it sufficiently indicates his point of view. What he provides us with are detailed studies of single poems by Donne, Shakespeare, Milton, Herrick, Pope, Gray, Wordworth, Keats, Tennyson and Yeats, from which almost all historical information and absolutely all biographical information have been rigorously excluded.[2] There is much that is acute in the explications, but their total effect, instead of taking us closer to the human situations and the statements on the human condition that the poems contain – in other words, to whatever gives them their value to other human beings – is to bemuse the reader with the structural patterns Brooks professes to detect in these poems. Juggling with terms like 'ambiguity', 'paradox'

---

[1] George Arms and Joseph M. Kuntz, *Poetry Explication* (New York, 1950), p. 18. This book lists all the explications of individual English and American poems that have been published since 1925. There is also an excellent introduction, which gives the history of explication. Mr Arms is one of the editors of *The Explicator*, a most useful little journal that he helped to found in 1943, which is entirely devoted to the printing of brief explications of English and American poems and prose.

[2] Brooks's antipathy to literary history is only skin-deep. *English Institute Essays 1946* (New York, 1947) contains an excellent discussion of Marvell's 'Horatian Ode' by him, in which most effective use is made of historical and biographical evidence.

and 'irony' replaces any serious attempt to analyse the profounder meanings of the poems. It is typical, for example, that both 'L'Allegro' and
'Il Penseroso' and 'Intimations of Immortality' are reduced by Brooks to
patterns of light symbolism. The fact is that his critical terms have too
much to do. By the time 'paradox' and 'irony' have torn the heart out
of poems as different as 'The Canonization', Gray's *Elegy* and 'Tears,
Idle Tears', they have become abstract critical formulas with no more
human significance or use than a triangle or the symbol $\pi$. This, indeed,
is the trouble with many of the technical terms coined or popularized
by other 'New Critics' besides Brooks. So far from bringing the reader
nearer the concrete actualities of what this or that stanza, scene or chapter
really means in human terms, words like 'tension' and 'texture' (there are
many others)[1] tend to divert him from them by concentrating his attention
on abstract relationships that may have a certain logical interest but that,
in most cases, have little or no immediate human relevance.[2] To use the
old dilemma, if this is what these critics think literature amounts to, why
do they think it is worth our while reading it?

I now approach my conclusion. It is not, as might perhaps have been
anticipated, a simple recommendation to extend the function of criticism
to the exploration of literature's social roots. Although I respect and
admire such sociological critics as Wyndham Lewis, Christopher Caud-
well, Edmund Wilson, George Orwell, Kenneth Burke and Lionel
Trilling, it is impossible not to be aware of the severe limitations of their
brand of criticism. The irresponsibility is at least as reckless as in the wildest
of the explicators. It is true that the sociologists are more in touch with

> the very world, which is the world
> Of all of us, – the place where in the end
> We find our happiness, or not at all!

But their contact with literature is proportionately precarious. Owing to
their incompetence or lack of interest in verbal and stylistic analysis their
literary judgements tend to be superficial and secondhand. And this
weakness in the literary substructure renders their generalizations on the
social context of the novel, for example, – the form on which they are

---

[1] They have been collected and defined in a workmanlike way in William Elton's *A Guide
to the New Criticism* (Chicago, 1950).

[2] In spite of its thoroughness, its usefulness and its general good sense *Theory of Literature*
(New York, 1949), by René Wellek and Austin Warren, does not altogether escape this charge.
The central defect is the failure to realize the crucial rôle played by language in the literary
object. In its absence the authors have left themselves no firm connection between literature
and life. The result is an over-emphasis of the formal elements in literature (rhythm, style,
symbolism, genres, etc.), which are considered 'intrinsic', and the disparagement of such
'extrinsic' constituents as ideas and social attitudes.

happiest – incomplete and exaggerated. Even Trilling, who seems to me the ablest of the group, does not altogether escape this charge. Skilful and plausible though he is at mapping 'currents of ideas', his expertness is almost restricted to what I have called the third and fourth levels of interpretation. As an *intellectual* critic and a *social* critic he is admirable, but he is not altogether reliable on the *verbal* and *literary* levels. It is odd, for instance, that he should have thought it worth while writing a whole book on E. M. Forster. It is odder that he should think *Howard's End* Forster's masterpiece. Oddest of all to me is that the longest passage he quotes in his book – Helen Schlegel's reverie during the performance of Beethoven's Fifth Symphony – is the one that I use in my seminars to demonstrate Forster's second-rateness. Although the passage in question is a nice example in places of Forster's comedy the shoddiness and pretentiousness of the symbolism are, I should have thought, painfully evident. The temptation to take the word for the deed, what is meant for what is said, is one that the Marxist or semi-Marxist critic has always found it difficult to resist. In the mad rush towards the all-embracing generalization the literary object as in itself it really is has an unhappy way of disappearing from sight.

It is clear, I think, that we cannot trust either the explicators (the exponents, that is, of what I. A. Richards has called Practical Criticism) or the sociologists. Stimulating, ingenious, provocative and original though their criticism may be, it is too often *wrong* – demonstrably wrong. It fails in that objectivity and sense of fact that Arnold and Eliot have united in naming the critical *sine qua non*. If the analysis of section II above can be accepted, it fails because it *had* to fail, because of a fundamental technical fallacy. Instead of pursuing the meaning of literature to its underlying and essential intellectual and social contexts the school of criticism stemming from Eliot has persisted in criticizing the poem as a poem and the novel as a novel, as though the language in which they were written and on which their existence depends had no immediate connection with everyday human reality. The sociological school fails because of an even more disastrous error in the opposite direction. It is in such a hurry to get to the implicit ideas and social attitudes that it *skims* literature instead of reading it. The conclusion to be drawn about it all will now be obvious. It is simply that if we are to see the object as it really is we must use both methods – a balance, in other words, of literary and sociological criticism, in which one mode may serve as the complement and the corrective of the other. Let us go to school with both Empson and Trilling.

Of this critical balance, this equilibrium between literary meaning in the ordinary sense and the social context in which meaning alone acquires value, 'The Function of Criticism at the Present Time' remains to me the supreme model. There are two phrases in that essay, each only four words long, that everyone who has read the first series of *Essays in Criticism* cannot help remembering. They are the four words in which Arnold summed up the case against the English Romantic poets (they 'did not know enough') and the four words he quoted from a newspaper report of a particularly sordid child murder ('Wragg is in custody'). No two phrases could well be more unconnected and apparently irrelevant to each other. Arnold's essay derives its peculiar distinction from its success in persuading us that the two worlds of reference which the phrases symbollize, the literary world and the social world, are in reality closely interrelated. Yes, in the last analysis Wragg was in custody *because* the Romantic poets did not know enough.

# 15

# Towards a Poetry-reading Élite

THE function of criticism outlined in Chapter XIV has its educational implication too. Who should be the teachers of English poetry? Are such teachers born or made – or born *and* made?

Auden has pointed out that 'There is no biological or mathematical law which would lead us to suppose that the quantity of innate artistic talent varies very greatly from generation to generation. The major genius may be a rare phenomenon, but no art is the creation solely of geniuses, rising in sudden isolation, like craters from a level plain; least of all literature, whose medium is language – the medium of ordinary social intercourse.'[1] And, as far as the English poets are concerned, this *a priori* probability can now be confirmed statistically. *The Cambridge Bibliography of English Literature* (1940), a standard work of reference, has listed 196 poets who flourished during the seventeenth century, 275 poets who flourished in the eighteenth century, and 489 poets who flourished in the nineteenth century. In terms of the country's total population and allowing for the slight increase in the average length of life, this works out as follows:

1600–1700: one poet in every 61,200 souls.
1700–1800: one poet in every 58,900 souls.
1800–1900: one poet in every 63,800 souls.

The virtual identity of these ratios cannot be a coincidence. It is reasonable to conclude that under modern conditions there will be on the average one poet that posterity will be prepared to read in every 60,000 persons. On this basis some 800 poets will have flourished during the twentieth century in Great Britain.

The most interesting implication of these figures is that a predisposition to write poetry is apparently a regularly recurrent natural abnormality, like the tendency to have twins. Although the kind of poetry that the poet writes must be determined by the social environment, the capacity to write it, i.e. an unusual facility in verbal syntheses, is apparently inborn and therefore hereditary. The Wesley, Coleridge and Tennyson families are English examples of the fact that the poet has to be born as well as made. As the hereditary factors are outside its control a study of poetry must be

[1] *The Oxford Book of Light Verse* (1938), Introduction.

primarily concerned with the environmental factors, which will determine whether the potential poets are to be relatively good, as in the early
seventeenth century, or relatively bad, as in the later nineteenth century.
But the part played by heredity, the complicated combination of genes of
which the precise formula is likely to remain unknown, must not be
overlooked. Something more is required in the poet besides a capacity for
taking pains.

Similar considerations presumably apply to the readers of poetry. If
poetry only exists in the poet-reader relationship and the mental processes
of the reader are, as they seem to be, complementary to the poet's, it is
likely that the natural poetry reader will also be a regularly recurrent
abnormality. This is not to deny that every sane human being should be
able to get something out of poetry. But, as there is a dividing line between
the mere versifier and the very minor poet, so there is an important
difference between the good reader of poetry and the reader to whom
poetry doesn't come naturally. I imagine no teacher of literature would
deny these differences of natural aptitude.

In this book I have been primarily concerned with the minority who are
born potentially good readers of poetry.[1] The objective that university
lecturers on English literature like myself must have continually before our
eyes is to ensure, as far as we can, that the potentialities are realized. A
natural reader of poetry who is also a trained reader of poetry will
normally be a social asset outside the world of literature. This is because
poetry reading is not a full-time occupation. (Poetry writing shouldn't be
either; the professional poet is in constant danger of degenerating into a
mere verbal conjurer.) If poetry is, as I have argued, the particular social
order at its point of maximum consciousness, both the poet and the readers
he is addressing must be functional members of society for them to be
able to cooperate in expressing its *idea*. Poetry writing and poetry reading

---

[1] Illiteracy or semi-literacy has restricted the numbers of even the casual readers of poetry.
Until the middle of the nineteenth century more than half the population of this country
lived and worked in the country. But the English countryman has never been a reader. Miss
M. L. Campbell, who has made an exhaustive search into the wills and correspondence of
English farmers *c.* 1590-1650, has found very few references to any books at all and only one
case of a farmer who we can be certain owned a book of poetry (it was the *Canterbury Tales;*
see *The English Yeoman* [New Haven, 1942]). Clare's poem 'The Cottager' shows that there
had been little change by his time: 'prime old Tusser' (i.e. *Five Hundred Points of Good Hus-
bandry*) is the 'only Poet which his leisure knows'. And Taine, whose *Notes on England* (translated by W. F. Rae, 1862) provides an excellent summary of the mid-Victorian scene, found a
Bible in all the cottages he visited, and sometimes religious books, novels or treatises on the
art of rearing rabbits, etc., but no poetry (p. 155). Of course, the ballads and folk-songs
persisted: Clare's cottager could recite 'many a moving tale in antique rhymes', including
'Chevy Chase'.

should not be considered ways of life in themselves so much as the over-spill of successful communal living in *any* profession. They are at once the result of successful social living and the preparation for further successes. The habits of synthetic thinking that poetry encourages are particularly desirable in those professions that are directly concerned with human beings. Hence presumably the number of teachers, clergymen, doctors, lawyers, soldiers and sailors who have always written and read poetry. But these professions have in addition extra-human interests. The profession that is concerned *par excellence* with human nature in its communal aspects is politics, and it is the politicians, in the wider sense of the word, who have made some of the best English poets as well as some of the best readers of English poetry. I include among the politicians such men as Johnson, Goldsmith, Byron, Newman, Carlyle, Arnold, Bagehot, Belloc and Aldous Huxley, but even among the professionals the proportion of serious poetry readers has always been higher than in other walks of life. Of the nineteen Prime Ministers of the nineteenth century, for example, at least eight belonged to the poetry-reading *élite* of their times. Gladstone was almost the ideal reader of Romantic poetry.[1] Lord John Russell was another. And the light verse of Canning, Palmerston and Disraeli, and Lord Derby's translations, were all admirable of their kind.

The poetry, however, that was read with most care and most affection at that time was not English poetry but the poetry of Greece and Rome.[2] Since 1920 or so the number of serious readers of the classics has decreased and there has been a corresponding increase in the number of readers of English poetry.[3] The classical sides at the schools and the classical departments at the universities have been thinning out, partly no doubt because of a slump in the snob values of Latin and Greek, and English literature has been one of the principal beneficiaries. The change is sometimes deplored, not on the ground that English literature is inferior to the classics – poet for poet it is obviously better – but because the reading of English poetry, or so it is asserted, does not provide the intellectual discipline of the classics. It must be admitted that English *as it is often taught* cannot compare with the old classical curriculum as an educational instrument. Struggling with an inflected language so unlike his own did

---

[1] He was one of the first to appreciate the extraordinary merit of Wordsworth's *Peter Bell*. See Morley's *Life*, ch. vii.

[2] '. . . of the eighteen Prime Ministers between 1837 and 1937 ten were good classical scholars and four others had learnt both Latin and Greek' (Sir Richard Livingstone, 'The Classics and National Life', Classical Association, 1941). The four ignoramuses were presumably Lloyd George, Bonar Law, Ramsay MacDonald and Neville Chamberlain.

[3] Until the extinction of the *Westminster Gazette* in 1928 its Saturday supplement ran a weekly competition in Latin verse composition!

teach the Victorian schoolboy to think. The institution of 'prep', by which the following day's translation had to be prepared the night before, compelled him to puzzle out the exact meaning of every sentence by himself. And the next day he was either right or wrong.

Unfortunately it is now possible to get high marks in most school and university examinations in English literature without being either right or wrong. All that is often required in the students is the ability to reproduce a muzzy impression of what they have been reading and to quote indiscriminately. The English Books paper in School Certificate was essentially simply a test of verbal memory. Even today it is possible to get a good Honours Degree in English at almost every university in this country if you are fluent, a rapid writer of fairly grammatical English, and can quote sufficiently freely from the standard works of the standard authors.

But this state of affairs is as unnecessary as it is deplorable. To the modern boy or girl, whose natural English reading is prose, the meaningful reading of poetry will provide at least as intellectually arduous a discipline as the reading of an inflected language. And it will have the additional advantage of introducing the adolescent to situations that will interest him or her as a human being. The old classical treadmill claimed to be *humane*. But in fact until one reached the sixth form one never got beyond the surface sense; all that counted was the struggle to straighten out the grammar. Properly taught English poetry could hardly fail to be the modern *litterae humaniores*. And it is *humanizing* above all that is needed by many members of our new ruling class of the Managers.

The notion that is so prevalent at the older universities that English literature is a 'soft option' that needs to be reinforced by linguistics derives indirectly from Decadent Romanticism. If poetry reading *was* simply a matter of passive 'ecstasy,' and poetry criticism could be reduced to variations upon the theme of 'magic', obviously it would be absurd to give a degree in it. And so the syllabus was extended and extended until you had to read everybody – but so fast that it did you no good at all – and, to add a little honest work to the lotus-eating, the textual criticism of *Beowulf* was made compulsory. The first step, therefore, in a programme of educational reform must be the complete discrediting of Romantic poetic theory. In its humble way I hope this little book of mine may help to do this. The second step will be the elaboration of a new syllabus and a new system of examining based upon the *difficulty* of English poetry, if it is to be properly understood. Some suggestions of the essential reforms at the university level may be worth adding. I shall confine myself to the final examination in the Honours School. The problem of the syllabus has been discussed by F. R. Leavis in *Education and the University* with his usual competence, and I have little to add to his recommendations.

The principal defects in the existing examination system are (i) the emphasis on verbal memory (the ability to quote), (ii) the encouragement of a superficial fluency (the capacity to 'write against the clock'), (iii) the essential similarity of almost all the questions asked (the only aptitude tested is the ability to summarize contemporary critical opinion), (iv) the tendency for the examination to become an endurance test (the student's whole career may depend upon his ability to maintain a consistent level for six hours a day for a week).

As for (i), the premium on quotations, the solution would seem to be for the examining body to provide plain texts of the set books or authors for use during the examination. It should also be permissible for the examinees to make use of their own notes in answering the questions asked. The memorizing of their own notes and essays, to which the term before the examination is now devoted, is a completely artificial procedure. Such a concession would encourage the taking of *good* notes, and a habit would then be formed of enormous intellectual importance in adult life.

(ii), the too fluent pen, might be counterbalanced by the requirement of a short thesis, to be submitted a little before the examination proper, from all candidates for a First or Second Class. The training in logical exposition and the habits of accurate scholarship that thesis writing imposes are of incalculable value. The burden upon the examiners could be reduced by a limit on the number of words allowed and by the setting of certain specified topics each year as the subject matter of the theses.

(iii), the restriction of the questions asked to elementary critical 'appreciation' is a legacy of Romantic criticism. To effect its cure it will be necessary to educate the examiners. More 'practical criticism' *à la* I. A. Richards should certainly be included, and I should like to see questions set on the poet's rejected readings and similar problems of particular poetic 'meanings'. I see no reason why most of the topics dealt with in this book should not be included in university examinations, provided they are presented in *particular* form. The fault with most of the questions now set is that they are too ambitious. Confronted with the request to write on Wordsworth as a poet of nature what on earth can the poor examinee do in an hour except summarize and generalize? But if the question were restricted to Wordsworth's attitude to nature *in one poem*, e.g. in 'A slumber did my spirit seal', there would be an opportunity for the detailed appreciation that can alone be critical.

(iv), the problem of the week's endurance test, would be mitigated by the introduction of one or more theses or dissertations into the examination. It would not be necessary then for anybody to do more than one three-hour paper a day.

A reform of the examination system would go some way to ensuring that the potential poetry reader became a trained poetry reader. And it could no doubt be accompanied by a reform of the textbooks, anthologies and editions of the English poets. But the essential reform is the permeation of our modern managerial society with a 'synthetic' mental outlook.

That is a task that may well seem beyond the capacity of a poetry-reading *élite*, even in conjunction with the many talented poets who are now writing. In his rhetorical exuberance even Shelley never claimed that poets could be the *acknowledged* legislators of mankind. But, though a complete success is unlikely, a partial success is worth fighting for. In favourable circumstances a poem's immediate influence can extend far beyond the limited circle of its original audience. Three classes of readers must always be distinguished. They are (i) the poet's own immediate friends, (ii) the enthusiastic strangers who often tend to turn the poet into a cult, (iii) the general poetry-reading public (Dr Johnson's 'common reader'). The three classes supplement and reinforce each other, and their coexistence is necessary if the contemporary condition of poetry is to be healthy. Romantic poetry suffered, at any rate up to the Polished Craftsman phase (Tennyson and his contemporaries), from the absence of readers of the third class. Their second class of readers – the Wordsworthians, for example, and the Pre-Raphaelite group whose enthusiasms for Keats, Shelley and Blake were equally uncritical – should have acted as intermediaries between the poets (i.e. the first class) and the general public (the third class). In fact, until the 1890s, such advocates and interpreters of Romanticism as Rossetti and Swinburne often did more harm than good.

The pattern of Augustan poetry reading was somewhat different. The inner circle of intimates was almost as small as Wordsworth's or Shelley's. Rochester wrote 'for the private Diversion of those happy Few whom he us'd to charm with his Company and honour with his Friendship'.[1] Their names are to be found in his 'Allusion to the Tenth Satyr of Horace':

> I loath the Rabble, 'tis enough for me
> If Sidley, Shadwell, Shephard, Wicherley,
> Godolphin, Butler, Buckhurst, Buckingham,
> And some few more, whom I omit to name,
> Approve my Sense, I count their Censure Fame.

[1] Robert Wolseley, preface to *Valentinian* (1685): reprinted in *Critical Essays of the Seventeenth Century* (1909), ed. J. E. Spingarn, vol. iii, p. 25.

A similar list is provided by Pope in the 'Epistle to Doctor Arbuthnot'. The second class of Augustan readers is represented by such men as Joseph Spence – whose attitude to Pope was not unlike De Quincey's to Wordsworth – but this class was of much less importance then than during the Romantic period. It merged imperceptibly into the large third class of common readers, who secured Pope's independence by their subscriptions to his *Homer* and who welcomed in turn the unknown Thomson, Johnson, Gray and Cowper.

It is towards the creation and consolidation of a similar class of common readers today that the energies of the friends of English poetry should be directed. The first step, in my opinion, must be the conscious stimulation of a poetry-reading *élite*, who can be the missionaries of poetry in a world of prose. Such an *élite*, if its social assumptions were those of modern poetry, might constitute a new second class of readers, different from and more effective than those of the Augustans and the Romantics. It is likely to be larger and more self-conscious than its eighteenth-century predecessor, and it is certain to be more critical and more coherent than its Victorian counterpart. Its most promising nucleus at the present time, in spite of the occasional arrogance and the deficiencies of scholarship, has, I think, been *Scrutiny*, the very remarkable critical journal that F. R. Leavis edited at Cambridge from 1932 to 1953. In these pages I have more than once criticized this or that pronouncement by Leavis. But Leavis has in an outstanding degree two virtues that have always been rare in the history of literary criticism. One is total incorruptibility. The other is the moral fervour that he brings to the study of English literature. For Leavis the reading of poetry is something that matters enormously. It informs his life, as a philosophy or a religion might do. In a world that is full of his detractors I choose to conclude this 'Conclusion' with a salute to his achievement.

# Index